C000182512

Chasing Rainbows

You may ask why our vehicle was called 'Rabia'….

*"To travel safely among the Duru we needed a **rabia** or companion who could frank us through their territory. He could be either from the Duru or from some other tribe entitled by tribal custom to give his travelling companions protection among the Duru while they were in his company. A **rabia** took an oath: 'You are my companions and your safety, both of your blood and of your possessions, is in my face.' No tribe would be likely to attack a party which was accompanied by a tribesman from a powerful tribe to which they were allied, but a **rabia** could belong to a small and insignificant tribe and still give protection."*
Wilfred Thesiger's
Arabian Sands

Chasing Rainbows

A Journey around the Southern Hemisphere
by Land Rover Discovery

with our best wishes

Peter Crichton and Eileen

Peter and Eileen Crichton

©2005 Peter and Eileen Crichton

This book is copyright. Apart from any fair dealing for the purpose of study, research, criticism, review, or as otherwise permitted under the Copyright Act, no part may be reproduced by any process without written permission. Inquiries should be made to the publisher.

First Edition 2005

Published by Arabian Visions
Website: www.arabianvisions.co.uk
Enquiries: info@arabianvisions.co.uk

Printed and bound in England
By Dar Printing Ltd
Design support by Origin, 01332 864736

Arabian Visions distribute through Barny Books, Hough-on-the-Hill, Grantham, Lincs NG32 2BB
Tel: 01400 250246 Fax: 01400 251737

Crichton, Peter and Eileen
Chasing Rainbows

ISBN: 0-9549481-0-6
CIP Data: A catalogue record of this book is available from the British Library

©Photographs Peter Crichton

Contents

Illustrations

Introduction

The Global Discovery Expedition was to be a single circuit around the world, a voyage of discovery starting and finishing in Saudi Arabia. We would be driving towards the east and our plan meant navigating our way through China and Eastern Russia during our first passage through Asia. We had stuck with this challenging but ground-breaking concept during two years of planning, despite a maze of problems. Obtaining permits and authorizations seemed, at times, to be impossible. Much of the bureaucracy through which we had to work was frozen into intransigence by China's and Russia's break-neck pace in political and economic change. As a result, we developed effective ways to plan overland travel in our Land Rover Discovery that would work in other less challenging regions of the world. Every cloud has a silver lining.

After the journey started we were to find that good planning and some luck made our six month passage through four continents more successful and interesting than we could have imagined. Our own relationship developed positively, transcending that of husband and wife. After twenty years of marriage we discovered, to our surprise, previously untapped strengths in each other.

The voyage had been an adventure for us, to find those special moments that came from travelling quietly and unobtrusively in other cultures and communities. The role of our Land Rover Discovery was central to that plan. Rabia (as we had affectionately come to know her) was our chosen transport and she provided access to those special places. She was our workhorse and we relied implicitly on her for our safety, comfort, security and passage-making, a role she fulfilled flawlessly.

We imagined that our journey would have a clearly defined start, middle and ending. These, we hoped, would fall into place as naturally as the seasons. We returned home to the Middle East, travelling through Europe and Turkey, hoping for that natural feeling of closure - the euphoria of our journey's end. We wished for a graceful conclusion.

We returned to our work in Saudi and enjoyed the material comforts of a stationary life again. We even found the enthusiasm to complete a book about our adventures, but the pull towards more travel with Rabia would not subside; the three continents below the equator had a new appeal for us. Our travel ideas for Australia, South America and Africa began to take shape. We left Saudi Arabia in April 2002 to circle the globe again. Our first circuit had been a plan with a simple objective – to travel in each continent from the most westerly to the most easterly point accessible on our own. That would not be suitable for this journey. We would simply miss too many interesting places. 'Chasing Rainbows' is the story of our journey through the southern hemisphere between April 2002 and April 2004.

Acknowledgements

Our travels would not have been accomplished without the support of other people. During the initial planning for the southern hemisphere journey we were indebted to the staff of NYK Shipping who gave tremendous support to get Rabia to Australia, quite disproportionate to the commercial fee. Also, the staff of Ultramar in Valparaiso helped to clear Rabia into South America with a driven enthusiasm which exceeded the simple terms of our agreement to ship Rabia there.

Travelling three continents over two years in a Saudi registered vehicle presented some particular challenges with the Saudi Arabian authorities and we were grateful to Bandar Al Anzi and his staff for their unyielding support during our moments of need.

Our friends often supported us in astonishing ways and their kindness added greatly to the journey. Vic and Heather Brown in Australia provided home and friendship on three occasions as well as being wonderful company on our trip to the remote tip of Cape York in Australia.

When we travelled in Australia we met with many couples on the road who offered us generous hospitality later in our travels. They showed us the spontaneous kindness that became, for us, a hallmark of that country's people. Jezz and Tracey Bennett, Pat and Keith Goodie, Carmel and Harold Stoll, Ian and Evelyn Clarnette, Neil and Jenny McLennan, Ron and Sue Reynolds, all fellow travellers with their own adventures, welcomed us graciously to their homes.

Ken James of Land Rover gave us some timely support during our southern hemisphere journey, taking time out of his busy schedule to send us information when we needed it. Michelin provided enthusiastic support for our adventure supplying the tyres which carried us round the world. Ahmed Modawi of Ziebart in the Middle East was a terrific follower throughout both circuits and we were indebted to him for extensive help when preparing Rabia for the undertaking. Fuji provided film for our expedition and we are grateful to them for their generous support.

Our friend Linda Samuel once again provided sensitive and well considered guidance during the final drafting of Chasing Rainbows. Her comments added significantly to the final text. Molly Burkett of Barny Books provided support and direction to our work which helped achieve publication.

Finally, Louise Rainbow of the Arts Council England gave us professional advice at a time when publishing our story seemed remote and too challenging. We are grateful to her for her timely encouragement and to the Arts Council for supporting publication of our book.

Rabia- our expedition vehicle

Plate 1 LAND-ROVER sponsored

The Southern Oceon Coastline

Plate 2

The Pinacles Desert

Plate 3

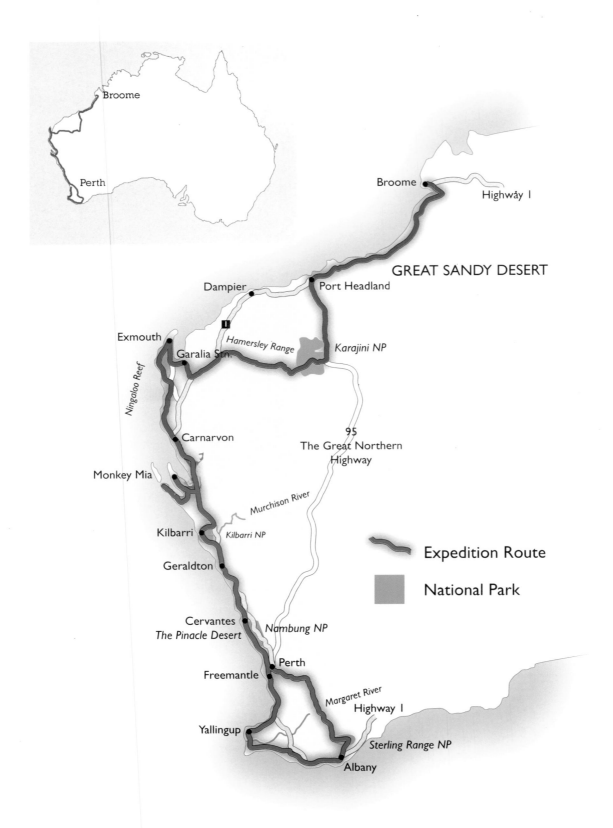

Broome

Perth

Broome

Highway I

GREAT SANDY DESERT

Dampier   Port Headland

Exmouth

1

Garalia Stn.   Hamersley Range   Karajini NP

Ningaloo Reef

Carnarvon

95
The Great Northern
Highway

Monkey Mia

Murchison River

Kilbarri

Kilbarri NP

Geraldton

Cervantes   Nambung NP
The Pinacle Desert

Perth

Freemantle

Margaret River

Highway I

Yallingup

Sterling Range NP

Albany

Expedition Route

National Park

Chapter 1. The West Coast of Australia

Chapter One:
The West Coast of Australia

The hot tarmac of Pier 5 shimmered in the blistering heat of Dammam Port. The air was still and a clear blue sky vaulted the Gulf. Summer in Saudi Arabia was, as usual, materialising with unseemly haste. The bustle of cranes and people had given way to stillness in the oppressive heat and an afternoon calm had descended. Men and machines rested and not even the sea birds showed the usual enthusiasm for raucous activity in the huge port. The steely grey bulk of the container ship Hyundi Advance towered overhead, her massive structure lying at anchor on the adjoining wharf. No doubt her crew anticipated a prompt departure for Singapore and Australia the following day. She was fully loaded and her manifest complete, except for Rabia, our Land Rover Discovery, cocooned in the black interior of a cramped 20 foot container on the dockside. Her isolation was strangely conspicuous in the surrounding emptiness. The presence of the container, profiled like the obelisk from a Kubrick film, flagged a problem. All was not well.

Our planned departure for Australia at the very outset of our travels in the southern hemisphere was unravelling before our eyes. We looked on with a strange feeling of detachment as this last-minute drama unfolded. Customs regulations to export a vehicle by sea had been carefully researched and all requirements met during the preceding weeks. Misfar, our Customs Broker, had processed all these with patience and diplomacy, through a Saudi Arabian port bureaucracy not well known for its customer sensitivity. But a last minute problem had arisen. "We are now missing a special export certificate from the police," announced Misfar, standing beside us. "Customs won't allow the container aboard without it." But the police, it seemed, had made that document redundant two years earlier.

Back in Misfar's office, we found that Rabia's export certificate could be issued quickly, if her departure was on a permanent basis. This would mean she would lose her Saudi plates and, in consequence, her Carnet de Passage would lapse. Her Carnet was essential to our travels in Australia and South America. We left Misfar, unusually animated in his flowing robes, struggling to identify the right person through whom the problem could be resolved. The evening hours in Saudi Arabia are often the best time for quiet business diplomacy. That night, Misfar worked through friends and contacts seeking a solution. We never discovered the exact mechanism, or what business favours he called in, but the following morning Rabia was craned aboard Hyundi Advance to start her long journey over the Indian Ocean. We would catch up with her in Fremantle Port. A few days later, when paying Misfar's bill, we found out how the problem had been solved. Through a friend of a brother who worked in the police department, Misfar had found a way to regenerate the document which had been redundant for several years. We had resigned ourselves to fate, knowing that a solution would only come from Arab-to-Arab diplomacy and we had not been disappointed.

The following weeks were emotionally difficult for us. Our lives were evolving from settled expatriates to nomadic travellers. Leaving Saudi Arabia would mark the end of a rewarding and pleasant phase of our lives. We had worked there for twelve years, enjoying the challenge of expatriate life and we had made many good friends. A routine was to be dismantled, and was to be replaced by new places, people and challenges. Only Rabia would remain to be a solid and unchanging part of that new lifestyle. There was no going back now.

Diary Note, 2 April   (written at 2.30am on the flight to Fremantle)

I don't really know who Australia is.
I can't guess what she is preparing to offer us - what she might expect in return.
Her veracity is unknown, her appetites unclear.
Mostly, her compassion remains in question.
Her form of humour may challenge our travels.
She may choose to be friendly or exert some brutal youthful strength in ways we cannot predict
But we may learn to love her.

Then again, she may become a hateful impediment to progress.
We only know of her youth -
her newness to life -
her striving towards maturity.
Perhaps she will welcome those who also seek the reward of discovery.
But in any event she will be a passionate being!

The Hyundi Advance reached Fremantle on 1 April 2002, on schedule. We travelled through Singapore to join her the day after she docked. Past experience had taught us to be present when our vehicle and contents were unloaded on a new continent. Customs and import requirements were not always easy to plan ahead and surprises were not uncommon. If difficulties were to surface this would happen quickly as Rabia passed through clearance formalities. Being there meant being able to deal with these matters during the import process before they became a problem.

Demurrage (storage) costs usually become chargeable after three working days in most ports. We planned to clear her quickly and be on our way.

Our first day in Oz was the predictable scurry between offices to prepare new paperwork to match the country's bureaucratic but fair immigration requirements. We knew Rabia was there, lurking impatiently somewhere in the forest of containers, still in quarantine, but she was not our immediate concern that day. Our challenge was to clear the bulk of documents and to secure temporary vehicle insurance for our time in the country. That's always best tackled after arrival. Finally, we confirmed an appointment the following day (at high noon!) with the port's Quarantine Officer, when Rabia would be allowed to emerge from her container for inspection.

Quick progress the next day was to be crucial. We hoped to clear formalities and to escape from port bondage. If not, we would cross that time limit when port storage charges would be levied on us. We were relieved to find that genuine friendliness underpinned the formal bureaucratic maze within the port, and we now had all the required paperwork. Rabia emerged from her container, bursting into life on the first turn of the ignition. We worked cautiously through immigration and customs matters towards our high noon appointment with quarantine. We had good reason for our mounting concern.

When we arrived at Fremantle airport we had discovered that Australia was a land passionate about nuts, seeds and beans. More precisely, Australian Customs work hard to exclude them. The outcome from earlier uncontrolled plant and animal introductions had not gone well for Australia. Our first encounter with customs rules was unexpected. The X-ray machine at the airport's arrival hall clicked into red mode and our baggage was laid aside. It seemed that the suspect item was my camera case. Our signed declaration, confirming that we carried no prohibited materials, was read back to us. "Do you want to reconsider your declaration?" asked the officer, probing with beady eyes for a guilty response. The camera bag was opened and our humble bean bag, so carefully made by Eileen many years earlier, to steady our camera on any available hard surface, was immediately lifted before us; a token of guilt displayed to the world at large. The customs officer groaned, guessing that the little red bag contained lentils or rice seeds. Our account of the bag's six year age was immaterial - the ancient lentils had to go. After negotiation, we were allowed to keep the red outer bag and the customs officer offered his pen knife to open the offending package. I made the cut carelessly and the contents spilled all over the customs hall, prompting the thought that we had inadvertently contaminated Australia!

We now realised that Rabia's store of dried food products contained all sorts of contraband. Importing banned materials was a criminal offence - a full confession was called for. Our Tang powdered beverage, our coffee and most spices were subsequently cleared but we lost our powdered soup products and our Oxo cubes. The Quarantine Officer, now in full flight, asked "Do your tea bags contain fruit?"

We declared no taste for fancy tea bags. Eileen finally confessed to importing packets of airline creamer in her handbag. After a stern admonishment we lost these along with the rest of Rabia's contraband. There was, however, one positive aspect to our meeting. "Not for a long time have I seen a car come through here with such a clean underside," announced the officer, now disposed to letting us loose into her country. We were pleased that the scrupulous cleaning of Rabia's bottom had this reward, but we had anticipated this point. Importing the Middle East's mud and sand, we knew, would cause a failed inspection. Thanks to earlier Ziebart under body treatment, a high pressure water jet had brought her underside back to pristine condition.

Only a vehicle inspection by Australia's Highway Authority now stood between us and unbridled freedom. We said our farewells to those in the port who had assisted us and drove to a local weigh station, confirming Rabia's 2320kg all-up weight. The scale operator, thinking we were heading for Sydney directly, shared his current gem of advice. "Watch the 'roos before Adelaide mate, they're all over the bloody road after dark." At that moment we felt a real sense arrival in Australia!

With some hours of daylight left we drove to the Fremantle Vehicle Inspection Centre, where our roadworthiness was confirmed. By sunset we were clear and legally able to travel freely. We had booked into the Trade Winds Motel, on the better side of Fremantle, and Rabia was parked beside our room, ostensibly guarded by the Motel's security patrol. That night we chose not to engage the vehicles security system on which we had relied in cities. Her batteries had not been fully recharged after her long sea voyage, and the system might deplete the remaining power. That decision was one of poor judgement - breaking our own rules - and would be an oversight that we would regret.

There was to be no easy way to come to terms with the major theft that occurred that night. Rabia's door lock was skilfully and silently opened. Brute force had not been used and as if to proclaim the thief's prowess, he left the car locked again, after removing personal effects and equipment worth US$2500 at replacement value. All of our clothing, the car tools, the tow ropes and other expedition equipment were gone. Even small items, designed and built with detailed care for our travels, were taken and these were of no commercial value. Electrical equipment, lighting and our Polaroid camera were all gone. An internal panel had been ripped off in the belief that a locked compartment lay behind. We heard nothing during the night and we were stunned into a shocked silence that morning. We felt devastated. This was an invasion of private space, an intrusion, a violation. The only theft we had endured in our first global circuit had been in Northern Pakistan and later we had reflected, with some admiration, on the tactics and planning by the elderly man and young boy. They had conducted that robbery at the speed of light.

We heard after the event that the Motel had a history of night thefts and we had not been warned. "They are all drug related," proclaimed the manageress, as if to somehow excuse the incident. We rushed around Fremantle that day, repressing our shock and anger, whilst shopping quickly to replace stolen items. Tools and personal effects were our immediate priorities. That morning, we had only the clothing we stood up in. Fortunately our laptop, GPS, and cameras were in our room. But this theft in Fremantle had been a sinister and professional rape. For many nights after the theft, we woke in a white rage. There was much healing to be done.

Our route for Australia had been set with some care. We planned to circle the continent, remaining as far as possible on or near the coastline. Perhaps with some good off-road driving we could even reach all eight major compass points on land. But first, we would make a short circuit on the coast to the south of Fremantle, partly to reach Australia's most south-west point on land. But our main concern was that we wanted to check that our equipment was in full working order during this passage, before heading into more remote areas. Besides, there was the splendour of the Southern Ocean to see, as well as the giant Karri forests near Albany, and we were in no rush. We had resolved to slow our travel pace, giving more time for places, people and scenery. We had sometimes felt a sense of unseemly haste in the northern hemisphere, travelling more as passive observers than participants in life around us. We had also been quite selective on travel timing, choosing Australia's autumn and winter months. This would correspond to the northern region's dry season. We were starting our journey in early April and although we would benefit from dryer weather later, we would face autumnal conditions in the south-west. We thought this a good trade-off.

The southern circuit was a colourful prelude to our journey. We realised later, as we covered endless miles of often dry and barren landscapes, that the south-west had huge variety in a relatively small geographic area. Also, it gave time to adapt gently into travel mode in a new continent, whilst enjoying some spectacular coastal scenery. We scrambled through the fabulous caves between Yallingup and Augusta, enjoyed the golden surfing beaches at the turbulent meeting of the Indian and Southern Oceans, and gazed in wonder at the giant Karri trees of the southern forests. At Walpole, we climbed the flimsy catwalk constructed through the high forest canopy, hanging precariously like a fragile thread through the treetops. We ignored the unsettling rocking and swaying motion of this engineering feat 50 metres above the ground, as we watched the unique tree-top world around us. We bushwalked, canoed and ate 'bush tucker', gradually building a rhythm and identity to our travels in this green corner of the continent. We were beginning to sense the youthfulness and vitality of Australian life, a prevailing freedom and spirit of adventure that would become the hallmark of the country by the end of our time here. In this open lifestyle we met many people who offered spontaneous friendship - a welcome that we enjoyed. Sometimes just a smile and a word, but often there would be more generous hospitality.

Doddy was a case in point. He was the 'Mr Fixit' of a campsite at the Margaret River Estuary, a rotund dishevelled bachelor with not a little Aboriginal blood. He lived in a ramshackle caravan on the periphery of the site, 'home' for someone making the most of what life had to offer. Doddy was not rich, earning A$12 per hour for his day job, and augmenting income by lobster fishing. Like 'Trapper Ray' and gold miner Wayne, whom we had met in the Yukon, he led a life of carefree and disorganised individuality, but lacked 'a good woman' in his life. His pride and joy, we heard, was a 14 foot boat with a short-shaft 15HP outboard for which he had saved for over 10 years. We set up camp nearby and our trip caught Doddy's interest. "Come and share a barbecue tonight on my site," he announced, "I'll invite some friends as well." The invitation was genuine and we accepted. We did not go empty handed; taking a rather expensive Shiraz we had acquired during an extravagant moment visiting a vineyard that day and a mountain of sausages. Doddy extracted three giant lobsters from his fridge and cooking commenced on his makeshift oil-drum barbecue. His bucket of prize seafood went a long way that evening. The beer flowed freely amongst the other guests and in the darkness Doddy's six species of frog, which he had introduced to his patio border, croaked and called in response to our human cackle. At first light the rumble of breakers close by signalled a rising surf but Doddy had already left to augment his stocks from the turbulent Indian Ocean just offshore.

Australia's south-west corner holds an isolated chain of mountains called the Stirling Range. Although not especially high, they harbour a unique collection of Australian flora and fauna. The 4WD trails which thread through this area were of special interest to us since we wanted to travel on some rugged territory to check Rabia. We were not disappointed. This single chain of peaks, 10km wide and 65km long, is designated as National Park but is none-the-less, a wild place clothed in natural heath and shrub through which summits rise majestically to 1000 metres. We found the park's gravel tracks agreeably rough, testing our suspension and cargo stability through long stretches of harshly corrugated gravel and dust. There had been no scraping or levelling of the park's tracks for some time. But the mountains entertained us that day - changing colour dramatically from grey to red as the landscape was washed with alternate cloud and sunshine. That night we camped early in an open forest setting off a remote track. We used the remaining daylight to deal with potential problems exposed by the day's hard driving. Generally minor, we had come to accept that equipment failure with our mode of travel would mostly concern electrics, where connections, fuses and small wires would tend to suffer from dust and constant vibration. We finished our tasks just as flocks of screeching parrots flew in from the north, invading our calm with noisy banter. Flashes of bright feathers blossomed momentarily in the high tree canopy. By sunset peace reigned throughout the forest and the world around us lapsed into a silent calm.

We returned to Fremantle mentally prepared and ready for our onward travel. We had replaced nearly everything that had been stolen, or made up replacement parts that would suffice but our anger still surfaced. We both knew it would be of no value to fret over something that could not be reversed, no matter how much we wished it. The journey ahead was foremost in our thoughts now and we recognised the healing process was underway. We had no desire to remain in the area; perhaps we would spend some time enjoying Perth when we returned after completing the circle. We visited with friends, Jezz and Tracey and their young son Tully, in the north of the city. From here there would be no reversal of our travels provided we were in good shape and remained problem free. We planned for one continuous passage, selecting, as far as possible, a coastal route round Australia. In many areas there would be picturesque tracks and beach routes which would match our objective but, when these options did not exist or were too dangerous to tackle on our own, we would travel on normal highways. When we had studied regional maps to select a provisional route, we had been pleasantly surprised at the number of occasions in Western Australia that we would be able to enjoy 4WD route options with good camping possibilities on the coast. Later we found that conditions on these tracks were often variable and their current state was best checked beforehand by asking the locals.

From Perth we followed a mainly coastal route for 250km to reach the Numbung National Park and the Pinnacle Desert. Viewed in the soft evening light, the rolling coastal sands and rock pinnacles took on an unworldly appearance. Rugged fingers of jagged rock erupted from the desert, casting long dark shadows over yellow sand. Winds had profiled the sand fields with delicate ripples, now brought into sharp focus by the low evening light. Through these sands the rock columns rose abruptly to four metres like a silent ghostly army or some macabre set of giant chess pieces. We drove through this unique landscape and saw the sun set over Hangover Beach. A few families loitered quietly here, in the last glow of evening sunshine. The sky had cleared leaving some high cumulus frothing in the sun's fiery descent. We were to see many beautiful evening landscapes elsewhere in Australia, washed by beautiful sunsets into pure art, but this was our first and would remain especially memorable. That night we set up camp nearby, in the dark. We had found a natural rhythm to our respective tasks and soon we enjoyed a candlelit dinner under a starry sky.

The following morning we caught up with mail at the nearby Cervantes Backpackers. An email report arrived from the agency in England who handled our home rental. Their account of a broken fence, a damaged garden pool and storm damage to our greenhouse seemed remote to our lives now. We felt detached from these dramas occurring at the other side of the world.

More than 300km of wild coastline stretched north from Cervantes. Known as the 'Batavia Coast', it could more accurately be described as the Shipwreck Coast.

We were to hear that at least seven of the East India Company's ships perished here in the 17th Century; a sad ending for many lives on an otherwise beautiful coastline. This concentration of nautical disasters was no coincidence. To reach Indonesia, sailing vessels would sail directly east from the Cape of Good Hope until they reached this stretch of Australia's coastline. With good navigation and prudent timing, the boat would then turn north to reach Batavia (now Jakarta). The vessel 'Batavia' was the first to miss her turn and was shipwrecked in 1629. Her surviving crew, awaiting rescue on land, probably built the first European structures in Australia. Their crude shelters still partially remain.

We followed this coastline on a bright blustery day, seeing first hand the strong forces at play offshore. Powerful waves thrashed the high cliffs and from sheltered beaches a few brave surfers rode the high rollers on a knife edge. We could only guess at the dramas played out here nearly 400 years ago, when tiny vessels crashed on coastal reefs, leaving a few brave survivors to hold on to life in a new land, hoping for rescue.

We took the coastal route to reach Kalbarri National Park where we would rest before our onward travels north. The Murchison River meanders through scenic gorges here, chiselled deeply into an otherwise flat and barren landscape. Bushwalks descend through brightly banded sandstone cliffs to reach the river's inviting pools. White-barked gum trees cling precariously to the valley ledges, providing cool shade on narrow terraces for spiny lizards and other wildlife. We joined a group of backpackers, led by Dave, a local bush guide, and hiked for one hour to reach the valley floor. In autumn the river lies dormant, just hinting at its vigour when in full flow after the rains. Long stretches of deep green pools snaked between narrow red walls, linked by shallow rapids. Flocks of birds gathered in the cool sanctuary of the valley floor and we enjoyed canoeing quietly through this tranquil silent landscape. The noon sun briefly reached the deep interior, lighting a string of bright diamonds down the river from our sandy beach.

In a relaxed mood after lunch, conversation drifted easily through the group. Our young travelling companions were mostly Australian and talked with pride of their country's outstanding sports successes over recent decades and this conversation led to a moment of deeper insight. "But it won't last," announced Dave, introducing a new line of thought which had a hint of controversy. Dave claimed that Australia's past successes could be attributed uniquely to the support provided to young people through the massive framework of sports clubs and the voluntary help provided by adults out of school hours. The system had worked well to help youngsters with talent, he claimed, but was now breaking down under the threat of widespread litigation, and through outrageous club insurance premiums. It seemed to Dave that Australia was moving quickly to become the most litigious society in the world and his country's impending loss of sporting prowess would be just one symptom. "Where does personal responsibility for our actions start?" asked Dave with a hint of deep feelings coming through. We had moved into something wider now, which seemed to hold greater significance for him, and was perhaps out of place with this idle moment on hot sand in the Murchison Gorge. We didn't have to wait long to hear the details of Dave's frustration.

We had wondered about the massive rucksack carried by our guide that day, seeming out of scale with our simple trek in the bush for a few hours. He explained that he had to carry every advanced technical device available which might play a role in the event of injury to a client. This was to comply with his expensive personal liability insurance to lead groups. His heavy satellite phone was essential to summon help, otherwise he could be sued for negligence and his insurance policy would lapse. Even then, he could still be sued for causing the accident. "Frankly, I can't keep the business going financially now, faced with this bloody bureaucratic nightmare," he pleaded. How could he be responsible for every single action of his clients whilst enjoying a countryside walk? A small red light flashed in our subconscious - we had detected this bureaucratic problem infusing everyday life here since our arrival and it seemed curious in this young and self-sufficient country. We wondered where it would end and how a proper balance could be reached.

Someone suggested a canoe race. The serious mood was broken; the moment of deeper insight was gone. Through the youthful babble, outrageous rules were proposed for the impending fun race; personal assaults between canoes would be permitted. Dave said no. After all, he had his personal liability to think about. But we still had fun!

The following morning we joined the North West Coastal Highway, Australia's Route One round the continent. Some 400km north, we would reach Shark Bay, a coastal area now designated a World Heritage Site. Not that the landscape offered huge appeal - the attractions here were all water based. The region is best known for the daily public interaction with dolphins at Monkey Mia, but other fascinating aspects of the region draw thousands annually. Spotting dugongs and whale sharks offshore had a strong seasonal appeal. The guidebooks also mention the massive meadows of sea grass in the bay's shallow waters, suggesting these to be the largest in the world.

Stromatolites on the beach at low water are a major crowd puller. We found it was difficult to raise our excitement at these apparently lifeless mats of sediment, moulded into bread-like humps over the sandy shore at Hamelin Pools. These small mounds of black crusty rock would have reminded us more of dead coral heads had we not known of their formation by miniscule organisms called cyanobacteria. These were the first life form to appear on earth 3.5 billion years ago in primordial seas and we should have been impressed by this, the largest remaining colony, as we viewed the carefully protected area from the raised boardwalk. We studied our distant ancestors with feigned enthusiasm.

Bottlenose dolphins have visited Monkey Mia for over 30 years. The informal encounters that originally occurred here developed into times of fun for dolphins and humans alike, frolicking in the shallow waters by the beach. Perhaps the take-over of this happy process by the Department of Conservation and Land Management (CALM) was inevitable as its popularity increased, but we were saddened during our visit. We paid our fee and both felt a growing sense of unease as we joined other visitors on the beach. This was to be an encounter tightly monitored by the CALM officers in attendance. Herded into groups, we were allowed to step into the water to a depth a few inches above our ankles. We were to wait here for the arrival of the dolphins. The resulting interaction was a disappointing sterile affair. We had enjoyed natural encounters with pods of dolphins elsewhere, one memorable event occurring beside our yacht off the west coast of Scotland. On that occasion, the shared moment was a robust affair, full of exuberance by dolphins and humans alike, and without the expectation of reward by the dolphins. It had been an experience of just plain old fashioned fun, with each party's pleasure evident to the other. Here, in the sterile controlled conditions imposed by CALM, a couple of adult dolphins edged listlessly towards the line of people and made a few quiet swim-bys beyond the arc of feet. Immediately after this performance they presented themselves on cue to the warden for their anticipated reward. We were sad that no physical contact was now allowed - previously visitors were permitted to stroke the passing dolphins with the backs of their hands. Maybe, we thought, the dolphins actually wanted that contact. There was no spontaneity and no scope for an un-orchestrated meeting between man and dolphin. Maybe Monkey Mia's dolphins need more fun! We wondered why so many people travelled here for this sterile event and suspected that commercialisation had gone a step too far in this CALM managed eco-experience.

Shark Bay is enclosed by two long spits of shrubby and dry land which lie north-west into the Indian Ocean. We had travelled the length of the more in-shore spit to reach Denham and Monkey Mia. The second spit was of greater potential interest – travelling there would take us to Australia's most westerly point and we would be taking another step towards our objective, to attempt to reach all eight major compass point limits on the continent. We would travel on narrow unsurfaced and dusty tracks to reach there. Our maps suggested that there was a track marked as a vague dotted line and with typical Australian pragmatism it also had a name - The Useless Loop Road. We thought the use of 'road' an overstatement of the reality. Plumes of red dust erupted behind us as we drove the route, leaving behind a comet tail visible for several miles in the afternoon's still air. The scenery was barren and shrubby, devoid of much interest.

We stopped at the historic, but still operating, Tamara Homestead to confirm our intention to camp that night on their land further along the peninsula. The small home and ramshackle collection of outbuildings needed maintenance badly but still supported sheep farming in a very marginal form. Antique farming equipment lay rusting around the homestead, both graveyard and monument to an earlier success. The tough couple in residence were glad to welcome us, but we sensed a struggle for existence that may not endure much longer. Later, we reached our objective and camped overlooking a strangely calm and silvery sea. The flies vanished as the evening coolness descended on our site and soon after sunset the moon, now just a thin crescent, materialised above the eastern skyline. That night, relaxing in this isolated silence, the southern stars blazed with stunning clarity overhead and the Milky Way spanned the velvet sky like an incandescent carpet. We felt, perhaps for the first time here, that unique sense of 'aloneness' in the Australian outback.

Diary Note 19 April

We have travelled for two weeks and the quality of the terrain in the tropics is beginning to reveal itself. This is a barren expansive place! Hours of driving over unvarying terrain has a numbing effect on the senses. The road today rolled on endlessly in a straight line to every new horizon. The landscape bordering our track beyond the verge's red sand was filled with low bush. There is a constant westerly wind and the poor sandy soil cannot support a meaningful root system. Consequently, nature seems unable to make any height and, with no shade, there must have been unremitting stress for earlier explorers here.

Our route today was from Carnarvon to Coral Bay, the first real point of contact with the Ningaloo Coral Reef, which runs for 1000km up the west coast of Australia. We had built up high expectations, knowing of the relative beauty of this unspoilt marine wilderness. This passage was no less severe than the preceding few days. There is desolation here, not dissimilar to Saudi Arabia. The shrubs and bushes become less dense, exposing more unbroken red or brown sand. Wildlife thrives on the carrion that lies on the roadside after the nightly kangaroo kill. We crossed the Tropic of Capricorn this morning and almost immediately the landscape deteriorated even further.

The Useless Loop Road had served us wonderfully and we pressed on through Carnarvon to reach our next shoreline objective - the Ningaloo Marine Park and Western Australia's beautiful and unspoilt Coral Coast. We had over 500km of driving ahead to reach there and, as we crossed the Tropic of Capricorn, we realised our travel plan was about to engage in a scenic trade-off. Whilst we would soon spend leisure time on an exotic coast and enjoy swimming over an unspoilt coral reef, our daily driving time to reach there was becoming more challenging.

Eileen suggested counting the kangaroo corpses - a sort of daily body count of the previous night's carnage. Although a macabre pastime a DDKBC (daily dead kangaroo body count) would help break the monotony. Today the DDKBC was well over 20 - last night must have been mayhem on the North West Coastal Highway. At least it added meaning and significance to the high number of vehicles sporting robust 'roo bars' (bull bars in western language). Without this protection to the vehicle, a collision would be fairly terminal to both the kangaroo and vehicle. When we first arrived in Oz we had noted that a large number of 4WD vehicles were adorned by extravagant bull bars, often chrome plated for better effect. We had wondered then if this was just car decoration, perhaps a masculinity symbol in the Australian male. As we travelled Australian roads we soon found there was a high collision risk with animals after dark. Despite our own careful driving, we were to collide with a small kangaroo in the Gulf of Carpentaria during the early hours of daylight. The hapless animal appeared from nowhere, with little warning and despite its small size, bent Rabia's steering rod between the front wheels, before its untimely demise at the side of the road.

The North West Cape lies at a defining point on Australia's coast. This finger of land, just above the Tropic of Capricorn, marks the spot where the shoreline turns north-east towards the Great Sandy Desert. The Ningaloo Reef runs the length of the Cape mirroring the larger Barrier Reef extending up Australia's east coast. But there the comparison ends. Although both are fringe reefs, Ningaloo lies closer to the shore, often just 100 metres from the beach. More than 250 species of coral have been recorded here and the diversity of marine life is, in many ways, better than the Barrier Reef. Access is certainly easier for the visitor, since coastal trails lead to quiet beaches from where the reef's colour and diversity are just a short swim offshore.

We were relieved to leave Route 1 to reach Coral Bay at the southern end of the park. Although the settlement remains quite small, there was controversy brewing. A massive holiday complex and marina had been sanctioned by central government planning. Protestors claimed, perhaps with good reason, that development on this scale would ultimately threaten the fragile balance within the marine park. We were pleased we would make our quiet passage up the coast whilst the beaches and reefs were still unspoilt, and before the onset of commercialisation on a Queensland scale. We found a good 4WD trail from Coral Bay that followed the remote coast to Ningaloo Homestead and then on to reach the formal Cape Range National Park on the peninsula's west coast. That day, we meandered through 115km of coastal wilderness, meeting no-one except the homestead owner - to whom we made a donation for our remote camp site, planned for Sandy Point that night.

But the passage was not without moments of excitement. A male Emu, chaperoning twelve youngsters, ambled by our route and displayed ferociously at any attempt to approach his brood. Our presence on his patch was challenged with much stamping of feet, aggressive hissing and exuberant wing flapping. To our embarrassment and discomfort, Rabia bogged down on the soft coastal sand dunes. We had to reduce tyre pressure and work hard in the hot temperatures to free her from her bondage. We camped early that day, the onshore wind subsided and gentle waves lapped onto chalk white sands. The inshore shallows settled to a brilliant turquoise, shading to deep blue offshore where two turtles tumbled playfully. Behind our camp site huge brick red termite mounds stood, adding form and texture to the otherwise barren hinterland. That night the Milky Way arched over the sky like a band of dazzling mist. We felt pleased with our progress but wondered if we might drop our guard with our travels progressing so smoothly.

We entered the formal National Park the next day, crossing the dry creek bed of Yardie Gorge from the south. By good luck the tide was out in the creek and we avoided wading through salt water. We drove north into the Cape to reach Turquoise Bay; probably the best location to enjoy Ningaloo Reef as it sweeps close inshore. The colourful coral heads were only 50 metres from the beach, protected by the main reef wall further out to sea. There was a unique aspect to the bay which added a special dimension to snorkelling here. Waves, surging over the outer reef, flooded the bay and created a constant tidal stream close inshore. These currents flowed parallel to the long beach to reach a break in the outer reef further north, where they surged back into open ocean waters. We swam into that warm current from a point well down the shoreline, and drifted with the prevailing flow for 2km, watching the changing display of colourful gardens on the seabed. This was a very lazy way to snorkel over the coral reef and in the clear waters some exotic marine life entered the bright stage set below us. Some turtles came briefly into vision, drifting gracefully in a slow marine flight. Then three small sharks made a fleeting appearance, grouped we thought in a loose pack. A mother dolphin with her baby lurked tantalisingly on the threshold of vision as she shepherded her offspring into deeper water. Exotic reef fish fussed around coral stacks, darting for shelter in the tree-like branches of coral when we floated too close. The sun was high and in deeper waters, shafts of sunlight breached the apparent infinity of blue to mottle the white sands below. The streamlined profile of a much larger white tipped reef shark lurked there weaving a sensuous but sinister track on the seabed. We broached the increasingly strong flow, swimming back to the beach before the tidal current swept out to sea through the reef's open fissure.

Before moving on we rested on this beautiful coastline for two days, enjoying peaceful camping in tranquil surroundings. We left the area through Exmouth - a pleasant town which serves as the commercial centre for tourism in the North West Cape. One seasonal aspect of that industry, of growing importance, was whale shark spotting. This gentle giant passes the peninsula's coastline from April to July. Eight companies offered day trips to make fleeting encounters, all claiming professional supremacy over the others. With luck each client would see, or even swim with, these monsters out in open water. Odds were improved by a spotter plane, circling over the area to pinpoint a sighting for the fleet of boats. It seemed to us that the expense of A$280 for one day was an amazing cost since there was no guarantee of the promised 'experience of a lifetime' with the world's largest fish!

We drove east from Exmouth, crossing 125km of wilderness to reach Giralia Sheep Station, where we hoped to gain an insight into life there. Our 'station stay' would be brief but would give us a glimpse into the workings of these large and often historic farms. During our long passage from the main highway we saw no other vehicles, and the narrow road seemed to intrude on the vast landscape. The homestead had been marked on our map as an historic landmark, its relative isolation and longevity emphasised by the absence of other noteworthy map points in a wide radius. After transferring the co-ordinates to our GPS we had navigated there easily.

We ate breakfast in the calm tranquillity of early morning on the homestead's patio. Our journey that day was to be a gruelling 500km to reach the Hamersley Range where we would enter the Karijini National Park. We were breaking our coastal route briefly to include this inland highlight, driving due east through the arid Pilbara region. We knew Karijini contained some of the most spectacular and colourful gorges in Australia, deep chasms holding unique eco-systems in their cool interior, high cliffs glowing a fiery red.

Maintaining a coastal route seemed an unnecessary plan to us - we were not slaves to a tight expedition schedule during these travels. We had enjoyed our days by coastal beaches and the adrenalin had flowed driving Rabia over some challenging coastal tracks but we wanted something different now. We would hook back north to rejoin the coast at Port Headland after our short detour.

There was a new quality to our journey to Karijini. We felt the hugeness of the outback. Driving across these long open landscapes of red sand, there was a feeling of endlessness - our destination remaining somehow unreachable. We felt an unworldly isolation here. We were a mere speck progressing through an infinity of hot emptiness. Through the aridity, bright bushes of spinifex mushroomed from the sands. Here and there, some bold outcrop of weathered rock broke through the desert's barrenness. Apart from a few drifts of high cloud above the rocks the great sweep of cerulean sky was clear. If there was to be an experience on land comparable with sailing the ocean during our world travels, we felt this was it.

400km into our journey to Karijini, we came across a battered Holden stranded at the side of the road. Both car and owner had seen better days! The Aboriginal family were in distress; four children and their mother sheltered from the sun in a small patch of shade beside their car. The husband flagged us down. He had a wild appearance; a straggly grey beard hung below a deeply lined dark face. His dusty unkempt clothing was darkly stained with sweat and, although his body language confirmed personal distress, we still had some security concerns as the roadside drama unfolded. We had heard of mock roadside breakdowns forming a stage set for robbery.

We slowed, cracked open the side window and kept Rabia's engine running. "I need water," pleaded the hapless driver and with the family in trouble we would

Denver's Story – The Giralia Homestead

Denver and his wife Rae had run the sheep station for 50 years. He had worked initially as a 'jackaroo' apprentice from 1953. Where possible, the homestead's ownership had continued through the eldest male since 1916 up to the present day. Two generations remained in the wings ready for future service - Denver junior and baby Denver. Mail was confusing.

The station occupied a massive 228,000 hectares and until Cyclone Vance struck (destroying their aircraft) most musters before shearing were completed by plane. Now motorcycles, supported by chartered helicopter services, were sufficient. The station supported a herd of 25,000 animals. Denver spoke with some deep insight about the main business decisions to run the operation well. The timing of shearing: releasing the wool before the main market secured a premium. The proportion of stock sold for live meat export required care to maintain long term viability. Many stations had gone broke selling too much stock to generate income. "Selling wool in Perth means entering a buyers market," said Denver, preferring the buyer to be on his home ground. Stockmen were employed only on a casual basis when needed. At the employment peak, eight shearing lines would deal with the homestead's complete stock in three weeks, after which staff would be released. "Sheep quality is crucial," claimed Denver, who injected 150 new superior stock rams every five years. But despite all the strategic planning, hard work seemed the main ingredient for success.

The family spoke with pride over dinner about their bitter struggle for two years to recover from the effects of Cyclone Vance in 1999. Winds of 267kph had hit the station on the 25 March and 6,000 head of sheep were lost. The homestead was wrecked. Their green brocade curtains from the dining room windows were found hanging from a power line one kilometre away. But their home was not the priority during recovery. Unless the windmills were rebuilt quickly to provide water, the remaining sheep would perish. The stock loss was not covered by insurance and although the property was, new bureaucratic farm building standards in Australia required a much higher investment in new buildings than could be recovered.

In common with many historic stations, innovative projects to generate income now played an important part in life on the station. Home stays formed part of that development and recently the SAS, US Navy Seals and British Marines had used remote corners of the station for training. It seemed the desolate sand dunes near the coast had much to offer.

not bypass this emergency. His car had lost coolant and the engine had boiled. We both knew that topping up would not resolve the underlying problem but we decanted some litres of our water reserves without hesitation.

Behind us, in the distance, we saw a huge plume of red cloud rising into the sky and soon the profile of a massive road train began to take form. The driver's cab hauled four separate tanks of Shell petrol and normally the huge assembly would not stop, especially in isolated locations of the outback. But the driver throttled back and drew his road train to a dusty halt, staying cautiously some way back. He climbed down from the high cab and strolled over. Dressed in short shorts with a wide hat, he could have stepped out of an Australian movie. He was not entirely at ease but was also not able to drive by if someone was in genuine need of help. There was a code of conduct at play here, in line with similar principles applying on the high seas. He took stock quickly and said he would assist with any additional water requirements by the family and suggested we move on our way. We were grateful for his intervention but wondered if he though we were naïve for stopping in the first place.

We have found that interesting destinations should have some mystery, leaving their charm to unfold as a real-time experience, rather than be laid bare in advance from books and brochures. Karijini was a case in point. After the arduous journey to reach the park, we were not prepared for the wild beauty of the place. Narrow canyons tracked through the landscape, weaving and intersecting to form a network of deep serpentine valleys. In the cool interior, streams and pools were bordered with lush ferns. Some tamarisk trees gave shade and added delicate form to their depths. We enjoyed a great feeling of personal 'discovery' during our two days here. It was a place to descend on mysterious narrow trails to reach green creek beds, to swim in clear pools by waterfalls, to wade through dark chasms, to see the mystery of the place.

Early morning walks along the precipitous rims held their own charm. Viewed from here, high cliffs dropped a near vertical 100 metres; in sharply defined bands of iron rich sediments shaded rust red. Bright yellow grasses and some white barked gum trees ringed the gorge lips, imparting softness above the stark descent into deep unseen places. One memorable walk along the very core of Dales Gorge threaded between narrow walls for 2km on a green but rough valley floor. We heard the rumble of the waterfall ahead before we saw its descent into Fern Pool. We swam here, in the refreshing cool water at the base of the cascade. Fish swarmed in the shallows, but there could not be total comfort knowing that we shared the water hole with a python, reputedly lurking in the rocks by the waterfall. Some primeval dread surfaced to our consciousness, unsettling the otherwise restful moment.

The Aboriginal community had known of Karijini for 20,000 years and our time there ended with a visit to the park's cultural centre. The professional displays were managed by members of the Bangima people.

Broome beach at sunset

Plate 4

On an outback road

You **will** learn to swim....!

Plate 5

Emu

Goanna

Echidna

Weat Coast wildlife

Plate 6

Gorge in Karajini National Park

Plate 7

Sunrise at Windjana Gorge

Plate 8

Bell Gorge, The Kimberley

Plate 9

Purnululu National Park (The Bungle Bungle)

Plate 10

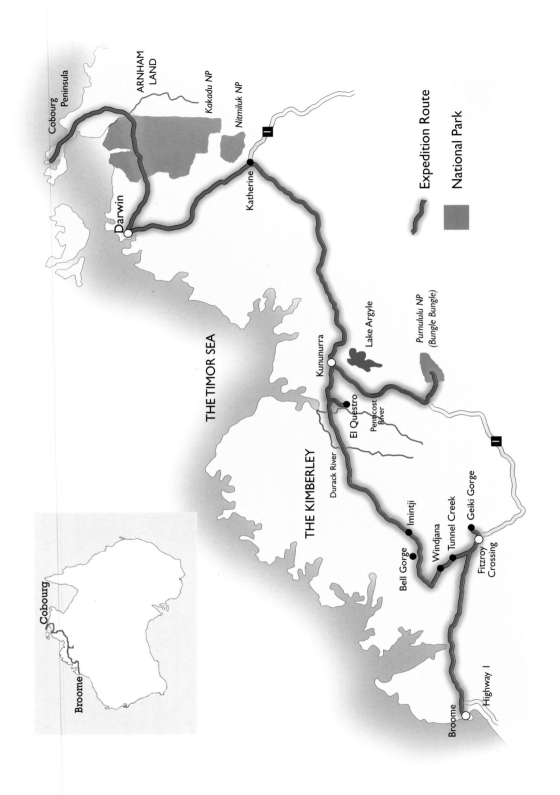

ARNHAM
LAND

Cobourg
Peninsula

Kakadu NP

Nitmiluk NP

Darwin

Katherine

Expedition Route

National Park

THE TIMOR SEA

Kununurra

Lake Argyle

Purnululu NP
(Bungle Bungle)

El Questro

Pentecost
River

THE KIMBERLEY

Durack River

Imintji

Windjana

Tunnel Creek

Geiki Gorge

Bell Gorge

Fitzroy
Crossing

Highway I

Broome

Cobourg

Broome

Chapter 2 The North West

We headed north, driving the surfaced Great North Highway to reach Port Headland and to rejoin our coastal route. The town's stark presence became obvious some distance from the coast. Salt is mined here, or more correctly harvested, from the huge coastal salt pans and the monumental pyramid of stock product gleamed in the evening light. The town's huge skeletal structures built for dockside ore handling also took form in the distance, in silhouette against the fiery late afternoon sky over the ocean. Entering the place late on a Saturday was not a joyous occasion. Most shops were closed. There was no sign of human activity and Port Headland seemed a charmless ghost town.

We had camped each night since leaving Giralia Homestead and needed to refresh both ourselves and our equipment and perhaps enjoy some human contact. We settled for the Dingoes Oasis Backpackers as our base. There was some urgency to clean Rabia of the thick coating of red iron oxide, which had also infiltrated her interior. The corrosive dust would need quick removal. We worked hard the next day, cleaning, washing and catching up with routine matters, but also enjoying the company of fellow travellers. Young people, we had found, recount their successes and failures with candid spontaneity. We were beginning to realise that many backpackers would plan carefully for their basic travel finances but would quickly discover in Oz that accessing the main tourist sights, usually remote, often stretched them to a point of frustration. There were plenty of local group travel options, frequently innovative trips in 4WD vehicles, but these were not cheap for budget travellers. Sally, a young English girl, was in transit from Darwin to Perth but the side trips (such as Karijini) were just an expense too great, out of reach financially, and limiting her trip to a series of bus hops between backpacker accommodation in major towns. It was a problem we were to encounter time and again.

The coastal route to Broome from Port Headland borders the Great Sandy Desert; a place of infinite emptiness - 600km of semi-arid savannah stretched before us. There was little variety to relieve the monotony over these flat expanses. The open landscape was broken by occasional rocky outcrops and the only living matter was spinifex and occasional gum trees sucking a fragile existence from dried stream beds. During this passage the coastline was tantalisingly close but remained mostly out of sight. We were reminded of sections of hard travel elsewhere - one over the desolate wilderness of central Oman, bordering the Rub-al-Khali and the other over the Bad Lands of central USA on a grey miserable day. After seven hours we were bored.

We could have easily missed the turn-off to Barn Hill Station on the coast. We rushed the last 10km, guided only by a pair of wheel tracks, and seemed to float on the thick dust, sensing the quick onset of darkness. With unseemly haste we parked Rabia on a campsite under a coastal acacia, grabbed glasses and beverage and just reached the nearby cliff top in time for sunset. The ocean horizon was briefly washed with a crimson glow from the dying sun. The massive seven metre tide was out, leaving a stark patchwork of pools and streams snaking through dark sand. The sky's vermillion glow was reflected with mirror-like sharpness on these glassy pools. The bright sky, the blue ocean and glowing textured beach added a calming moment, a climax to an otherwise demanding day.

We reached Broome the following morning to find a place of exotic qualities, still retaining a hint of frontier contrasts. Exuberant tropical plants bordered the streets. 'Exuberant and exotic' also described our accommodation, where we were to make preparations for the 4WD Gibb River Road and other more demanding off-road stretches of Northern Australia. The Last Resort Backpackers came recommended by the Lonely Planet Guide, and was YHA affiliated. The good news for us was that the hostel had one double room left. We booked it, perhaps too spontaneously. The bad news, we soon discovered, was that the residents, exclusively young, were dedicated to a 26 hour good-time day. By early afternoon, heavy metal music resonated through the wooden building from the juke box. A boisterous group huddled round the pool table, bottles of the latest designer alcoholic mixer drinks in hand. Elsewhere, young exhibitionists lazed on outside balconies dressed in minimalist but classy beachwear, just avoiding indecency by the narrowest of margins. The place was definitely alive! Parents back home, we thought, would not be amused by this liberal interpretation of a useful gap year.

By 11.00pm a curfew should have locked in to offer the prospect of sleep. It didn't. The clattering pool balls and noisy high spirits continued unchecked. At 3.00am, with a fading sense of humour, our mild complaint briefly calmed the boisterous common room, but mayhem soon returned and continued into the early hours. We wondered what part responsibility and discipline played in the lives of these adults-in-training!

We complained, of course, and over breakfast the owner, Peter, came to talk to us. After apologies he related to us his account of serial problems over recent weeks. He was at his limit, he protested, unable to control events after dark. "Last week we threw out a young lady for fornicating in public," he said as if to excuse his complicity in operating a backpacker's hostel out of control. We thought later that it took two to tango and wondered what happened to the young man.

Broome had a more positive and colourful aspect to show us. Camels, originally imported from the Middle East with Afghanistan handlers for early outback travel, still provided a service here, carrying visitors on evocative sunset rides. On Broome's beautiful northern beaches a convoy ambled along the shoreline under vivid skies in fading light. Later, we saw the full moon rise over dark sand flats interspersed with silver pools forming the once-a-month spectacle; the illusory 'Staircase to the Moon'. This was a fitting end to our first 5500km in Australia - another defining moment in our travels.

Chapter Two:
The North West

There was something different ahead. We could sense an impending change. We would cross the Kimberley, greater in size than the UK or Japan, not on the Great Northern Highway, but on the Gibb River Road (GRR) - a 710km rough track originally developed to drive cattle to the coastal abattoirs and ports from the isolated homesteads on the plateau. The route still provides an arterial life line to remote stations and Aboriginal communities, but in recent times has also become a favourite recreational route for 4WD vehicles. The track is closed in the wet season from November to April but, during the dry winter months, it offers access to one of the remaining wilderness areas in Australia.

We wanted advice about conditions ahead at the beginning of the dry season and wondered who we could approach locally. Perhaps the route would be in poor shape just after the last rains. "See Phil at the tyre shop down the road," was one suggestion. We introduced ourselves and Phil silently eyed up our rig with a knowing eye, probing for weaknesses. This was not a man who would pull punches. His first words of encouragement were to the point. "Parts of the road are not scraped yet. If last season's corrugations don't get you, the shards of new quarry waste bloody well will." Then, as if to drive home his point, "It's the worst road in Australia. Where is your second spare?" We confessed to owning only one spare tyre and felt Phil's disapproval. But he said the road was open and, in a more benevolent tone, assured us that petrol would be available at an Aboriginal community half way through the route - a crucial point.

We planned for a passage through the Kimberley which would last six or seven days, leaving time to enjoy the exquisite scenery along the way. We would need the same cautious travel philosophy that had got us through other remote places in Pakistan, China and Siberia as it was becoming clear that this was not a route to be taken lightly. We had listened to others and we detected that both man and machines would frequently self-destruct when travelling the GRR in bad conditions or at excessive speed.

On 2 May we drove to Fitzroy Crossing and briefly visited the Geiki Gorge. Although we were not on the GRR here, we would drive from Fitzroy to join up, using a rough connection called the Leopold Downs Road. On that route we would see two additional Kimberley landmarks - Tunnel Creek and Windjana Gorge, both of which lie someway east of the main GRR track. On that first day out of Broome we saw that we were now in an area populated mainly by Aboriginal people. We had found that most Australians were open-minded but, on one point, views seemed to be unusually polarised. The standing of the Aboriginal community in modern day Australia generated more extreme opinions than we had expected and this had perplexed us. It seemed too simplistic to classify these indigenous people as either drunken thieves living off the State, or deprived people who had got a bad deal over the years. One aspect which was not in dispute was that alcohol created major personality changes for this social group and, here in Fitzroy Crossing, we saw that effect at first hand amongst the strongly Aboriginal people. We arrived on Social Security payment day - cheques were collected late morning and by early afternoon 'slabs' of beer were disappearing from the Off-Licence faster than candy at a children's party. A noisy brawl developed nearby between five or six men and women and we resolved to try for a deeper personal understanding of the underlying issues which were in play. Thirty percent of the Kimberley is Aboriginal

Fate was kind to us. Our entry to The Kimberley was gentle, perhaps leading us into a false sense of security. The Leopold Downs Road had been freshly scraped after The Wet. Mountainous corrugations had gone and with a new coating of quarry waste this section of the route would have been passable by a normal vehicle with good clearance. The hidden risk was to assume that the new surface was benign and to forget that the material contained shards of rock with dagger-like properties. We remembered Phil's comments; "They can cut your side-walls to ribbons and knife through steel belts as if they were cotton threads." By late morning, after 70km, we thought the trade-off between corrugations and dangerous gravel was working well for us.

We stopped early to explore the dark cavernous interior of Tunnel Creek. The tunnel carves a deep passage through the Napier Range for 750 metres; pools of still water remained in the black interior after the rains. We were the only visitors at that time and the walk through the tunnel was a wet and eerie affair. There were no concessions made to ease our passage, no lights or handrails and no route guidance. This was an adventurous 'hands-on' experience! We made the best of interior sand bars on the cave floor, but otherwise waded or swam through the dark pools. Small fish and shrimps thrived in the tunnel's dark waters brushing against our legs as we passed through. "Just as well these are not piranha," we thought. At mid-point, the roof had collapsed and daylight filtered down to the cave floor which blossomed into a lush garden of green moss, ferns and a few small trees. Continuing through the blackness of the second tunnel, we saw the far end of the cave. A cold light filtered through from the exit, casting the cavern's craggy interior into unworldly profiles and massive stalactites hung from the ceiling like organ pipes in a ruined cathedral.

We moved on to camp that night at Windjana Gorge, some way along the track, planning to walk through the valley at sunrise the following morning. It was still dark when we rose. The gorge entrance by our campsite was deathly quiet. Nothing stirred. Even the soft chirping of an early songbird seemed oddly intrusive in the pre-dawn silence. Our crunching footsteps on the gravel flats beside the inky river echoed noisily along the valley. We had come here to watch the rising sun fan over the spectacular west wall, a sombre assembly of weathered rock in the pre-dawn light. We hoped for some dramatic interplay between first light and the coloured cliff face stretching far up the valley and we were not disappointed - the sun swept down the cliff quickly, adding texture and colour to the red and grey wall. (Plate 8). Daylight reached the dark river bank where soft green grasses and vines took on a tropical appearance. But others were waiting for the warmth of a new day to reach here. Large numbers of fresh water crocodiles live peacefully and unchallenged throughout the gorge, holding a sacred importance to the local Aboriginal community. We watched the sullen crocs lumber from the cool waters, crawling wearily onto the sandbars in search of new warmth on the gravel banks. Overhead, the high cliffs were infused with vivid highlights. We both felt that brief moment of magic as the low morning glow washed the landscape. The day was underway in earnest and this was Windjana at its best!

We left Windjana, driving the last 20km of the Leopold Downs Road, to join the GRR. Turning north-east we soon discovered the importance of care in the Kimberley. The track surface could change abruptly, alternating between gut-wrenching stretches of corrugations and loosely laid rough quarry waste. Track maintenance had been scrappy and intermittent during these early weeks into the new driving season and only the very worst stretches had been selected for scraping and recoating. Driving from one surface to the other required an adjustment in speed and the boundary was not easily seen. We had found that Rabia's resonant frequency on corrugations (the speed when she would vibrate in synchronisation with the bumps and hollows) was between 40 and 60kph. In that range she would amplify the irregularities of the road surface below. We could cruise on gravel at 60kph with care, but if we hit an old set of road corrugations without warning, Rabia would tango an alarming synchronised dance with the track. There was one other more radical option and that was to accelerate, rather than brake. Above 70kph, an uneasy stability occurred as shocks and dampers failed to respond to the wash-board surface. This was a risky business - by any standards the GRR was not a 70kph road and this option had no appeal for us. We would have to decelerate at some point, which would trigger a dreadful twenty seconds. The Shuttle's re-entry could be no worse!

Speed was not a prime concern as we had come here to enjoy the scenery. There was a stark grandeur to our new surroundings, made more impressive through our increasing isolation and the road's fragility. The King Leopold Range stretched across our route - a ridge of austere sandstone weathered into rugged beauty. Some massive geological forces had uplifted and distorted the landscape here. The GRR made its crossing at Ingles Gap, passing through folded beds of bright sandstone on steep cliffs. We had earned an early stop by mid afternoon and followed a small side track for 30km to Bell Gorge, probably the jewel in the crown of the Kimberley's landmarks. We swam in clear waters under a hot sun, washing ourselves free from the day's dust. Pandanus palms and tamarisk offered some cool shade beside the gorge's upper pool. From here, white water thundered over a staircase of black basalt rock ledges to a deep pool in the core of the lower reaches. (Plate 9). Thick ribs of contrasting ochre rock banded the cliff beside the falls. We were alone and felt the thrill that must have overwhelmed those first western explorers to stumble on this place and see its unspoilt beauty.

Before sunset we found a clearing close by to camp for the night. Palms and coolabah trees circled our site, arching over us in an extravagance of tropical textures. From the tall grasses nearby, a rare species of bilby scurried beside us, foraging at dusk, quite fearless of our presence. That evening, dinner was a stir-fry with a difference; we had found some kangaroo meat for sale in Broome. At least here we knew the species from the label - in Asia we had often bought meat in local markets not knowing the animal from which the flesh had been crudely hacked. Perhaps that had been an aspect of our earlier travels that added some element of fun. Meat bought that way had never been inedible and we had avoided gastro upsets. Later, in South America, meats bought in local village markets were to be even more exotic but the kangaroo that night had a surprisingly delicate flavour.

By 9.00pm the greenery overhead was barely silhouetted against the sky. The body of the forest beside us was lost in an inky darkness and we played the beautiful haunting music from Out of Africa which seemed to match the mood of the place perfectly. One track hit a discordant note with the roosting parrot colony nearby and their screeching response added a brief moment of disharmony to our peaceful site. Not sure if their raucous calls were of approval or dissent, we moved to another track and danced a slightly cumbersome waltz on our earthy dance floor. What a night it was - black velvet sky, a sickle moon, the wink and glitter of stars. In our splendid isolation the moment was one of pure magic.

Next morning, our surroundings came to life abruptly as the grey light of pre-dawn infused the eastern sky. In one tumultuous outburst, hundreds of white parrots and cockatoos took to the air from the surrounding coolabahs, shrieking a dawn chorus which lacked both style and grace. By 7.00am the first rays of low daylight spread over the upper canopy. Here and there a pendulous cluster of waxy acacia leaves caught the early sun and sparkled like pearls. Soon the undergrowth caught the heat of the new day, flies started their irritating invasion of our private paradise and the day's routine rolled forward.

The Kimberley changed now, to become a surprisingly flat landscape, devoid of rocky escarpments or high mountain profiles. A rolling savannah bordered the track. We reached the Imintji Aboriginal community where a small store provided some essential supplies. Outside, an ancient petrol pump stood in conspicuous isolation on the dusty forecourt. Petrol was available but at exorbitant cost. "Beggars can't be choosers," we thought, knowing that the GRR's 700km could not be crossed without refuelling somewhere. It was hot now and a group of locals loitered on the store's veranda, passing the day in idle chatter. We were welcomed into the conversation and soon found that one person was an Elder of the community, someone of special standing. We heard about their efforts to deal with alcohol abuse. "This is an alcohol-free community. Young people who abuse our rules have to leave here and will not be allowed back unless they change. But we try to help them," added the Elder, in a more conciliatory tone. An effort was being made to address at least one underlying problem. Here, at least, they were not in denial. Old tribal disciplines were in place.

We drove north and began to see that the underlying appeal of the GRR was not the driving experience, nor the open landscapes adjoining our passage. The Kimberley was majestic and remote, but wide colourful panoramas along the way were not the primary appeal. The 4WD experience, challenging as it was, might attract some just for the thrill and excitement. But the route offered something else much more fundamental - it gave access to unspoilt wilderness, outstanding places, full of wild charm and interest. Bell Gorge had been one but we were now planning our travels to give sufficient time to explore these places and enjoy their remote beauty. Finding the entry points was not always easy. We learnt to rely on our GPS implicitly to pick up access tracks or footpaths to reach them. (The coordinates were lifted from a survey map). Galvin Gorge was a good case in point. There was no vehicle access here but a footpath led to its hidden setting. The split-level fall within the gorge was still vigorous after The Wet, thundering into the deep pool below. Swimming here was a delight. Water lilies blossomed in full flower and, in the afternoon light, cast a purple hue over the lower stream. Unusual palms and ferns, new to us, added an exotic appeal to this small but spectacular place.

We had forgotten the Fremantle theft but occasionally we would find something missing from our equipment, jarring us back sharply to our distress and anguish at that time. During our travels on the GRR we had passed a few oncoming vehicles, driving through a hail of stone chips and gravel. We had prepared for this during work in Saudi Arabia, carefully building a windscreen shield for Rabia. When we came to fit this screen we discovered that a small bag of components had been stolen along with our other possessions - a mindless act with no benefit to the thief. The screen guards were unusable without the fixings and the impact on our mood was surprisingly strong - the depression was not rational and seems quite out of place now. The healing process was not yet over. How long would this take, we wondered.

Over the next few days we continued north, easing the harder driving conditions with restful interludes at increasingly tropical landmarks. We were certain now that we were seeing the place at its best. The rivers were not a muddy torrent and the landscape was green and lush. Perhaps we did not fully appreciate the turmoil and destruction that erupts in the Kimberley during the tropical wet season, when the GRR would be closed. If we needed a better insight, one of our travel destinations down the road was to leave us in no doubt. At farming stations and homesteads further south there had been some damage visible after the rains and these had not yet been repaired. Jack's Watering Hole was to add a new dimension to our understanding. Jack's homestead, near the Durack River, had offered food, camping and bunk accommodation as well as a friendly welcome over the years. We knew the location and as we reached the crest overlooking the homestead's land we pondered the imminent pleasure of a cool beer. But only grazing land stretched to the Durack. Jack and his homestead were gone - the buildings swept cleanly off the land by a raging flood. Not a trace remained. Jack had moved on and the beer would have to wait.

Our progress into higher latitudes brought us closer to the track's crossing with the Durack River and, more importantly, the Pentecost River where we would face the challenge of wading deep water. Rabia had not had to wade through rivers during her first global circuit and this would be the first of many obligatory encounters in Australia. Our concern on the GRR was our timing. We would be compelled to drive through the Pentecost still flowing strongly after the recent Wet. We felt increasingly uneasy about this challenge. Stalling Rabia in one metre of water would quickly flood her cargo area, despite meticulous care over door seals.

We were pleased to find the first crossing, the Durack, flowing to a maximum of 500cm and we edged our way over the submerged gravel causeway smoothly. If the Pentecost was equally benign we would easily pass the last serious barrier on the GRR. We reached there and stopped on the south bank to take stock. Ahead was 100 metres of fast-flowing river. The narrow red track emerging from the water on the north bank had all the appeal of the Holy Grail. Between these two banks the best line to cross was not clear and one of us would have to wade through the flowing waters before Rabia to check for boulders and holes, and to search out a good route. Eileen drew the short straw!

Eileen edged gamefully beyond the mid point, so far confirming a good direct route through the river. Another 4WD vehicle drove up behind us. "What about the Salties?" proclaimed the new arrival over my shoulder, cutting straight to the point on his mind without embellishment. It took a moment of thought then the reality dawned. We were now firmly in the tropics and the Pentecost flowed straight into the Cambridge Gulf a few miles from here. Salt water crocodiles were a life-threatening risk in these waters and we had failed to pick this up. Eileen's steady progress to the far bank took on a new dimension. Had we been setting the scene to appropriate music, the theme tune from Jaws would have been throbbing in the background but fortunately we saw no crocodiles lurking in the river or on the banks. The waterline reached Eileen's thighs and confirmed a satisfactory but challenging 700cm of wading depth. It was Rabia's turn to make the crossing but we would think twice in future before walking across North Australia's rivers.

Back in the dry environment of Saudi Arabia, preparing Rabia for wading had been an intriguing challenge. We made a canvas blind to unfold over the radiator grill and the lower bonnet; a common precaution. But more innovatively we designed a canvas and plywood wrap to surround and isolate the fan, pulleys and belts behind the radiator. This could be fitted quickly and prevent spray from reaching our batteries, distributor and air intake. (Described in Appendix 1). The drive belt system, we argued, would catch water in relatively shallow depths and the distributor was especially exposed to any resulting spray inside the engine compartment of our Discovery. The Pentecost was to be our first proving ground. By bad luck, Eileen had missed spotting a deep hole just 50 feet before the far bank and, near the end of Rabia's crossing, she dropped frighteningly into that, her bow wave momentarily sweeping over the bonnet. She survived her perilous descent and we were pleased to escape without stalling.

Our next camp was at El Questro Station, some 50km before rejoining the Great Northern Highway. This was where we would leave The Kimberley. As we approached the heart of the station's complex, we passed a long and perfectly manicured runway and sensed that this was no ordinary homestead. The estate's one million acres was still grazed by cattle but here was a homestead where the owners had embraced tourism in a big way. From our travel book, we read that El Questro had become a major travel destination, promoted widely as a wilderness park. Professionally run on a commercial footing, we soon detected a segmented business strategy for each market, serving the rich separately from those less well off. We were to find out how far that extended the following day. It felt strange to have these lines of demarcation forming here in the outback, like the ubiquitous aircraft curtain drawn between passenger classes. But this was a place where the folks on the hill, flying in by helicopter and living in refined luxury paid A$1000 per day for the wilderness experience, whilst we camped in a clearing by the Pentecost for A$25. Between these extremes, other options eased the burden of desperately, seriously, roughing it in the outback. Tented cabins provided 240v power and cooling fans. For those not fully at ease with the wilderness experience, or who suffered from urban withdrawal symptoms too great to bear, there was the swimming pool, the restaurant and the bar. This was not a place without life's little luxuries!

We had to stop ourselves becoming unduly cynical, since there was little to criticise beyond the strangeness of economic discrimination. There were some wonderful sights here with good access. The waterfall at Emma Gorge cascaded 50m into a beautiful tropical pool, which was also fed naturally by a hot thermal spring. Swimming was good here! The Chamberlain River flowed through a magnificent gorge nearby, where Barramundi fishing offered great sport. We chose to explore Zebedee Springs early in the morning. A stream of hot subterranean water emerged from a fissure in the nearby sandstone wall to chuckle quietly through a forest of exotic Livistona Palms. In that cool interior a series of deep pools descended in a staircase of black rock through the steep stream bed. Lush ferns thrived in the mineral rich dampness. There was a timelessness in this shady retreat, a unique restful beauty. We never found out who Zebedee was. No-one could say how the name had become linked with these mysterious pools but we felt sure there was some fitting romantic story.

We had asked at the Reception about visiting Zebedee Springs. "But you must leave by 12 noon," said the young girl sternly, adding "We don't want to stress the place," to offer a justification for the rule. The reason, we knew, was different. During the afternoon the pool was dedicated for the exclusive use of the rich and famous who wished to enjoy a hot soak and sip complimentary champagne in evocative but contrived isolation. It just would not do for the folks from the hill to have this wilderness experience disturbed by others. Perhaps to salve our mild sense of social inequality, we argued that we would feel the same, if we had paid such a high price for the experience.

We emerged from the GRR on 8 May. We were pleased by our good condition with few scars to show. Others had suffered badly - one fellow traveller sustained two torn tyres in one day and his 4WD had been badly grounded. We felt mildly smug that our Michelin tyres had not suffered at all from the gruelling ordeal and we had only to replace Rabia's rear silencer box, shaken loose somewhere down the track, to get back to normal order. Beyond Rabia's physical condition, the journey had reaffirmed for us the underlying *raison d'etre* for 4WD vehicles and their application to overland travel. Put simply, our Discovery had provided secure and reliable travel across inhospitable terrain, giving access to the places where our real understanding of the country had taken shape and form. We had seen again that with Rabia's differential lock engaged and driving in low ratio, she could be coaxed across almost anything without complaint. We didn't need to reaffirm that just for the fun of doing so. Her amazing ability was there, in reserve, not to be abused just for the thrill. She was a resource, not a toy.

With our first real challenge behind us we reflected on our own relationship. This had blossomed from simple man and wife to that of team members in partnership, in tune with each others requirements. As with all expeditions, stressful moments had sometimes created conflict. We would sometimes generate opposing solutions to a challenge and strong emotional views had sometimes surfaced. But mutual respect had never broken down and good compromises had been selected to move the journey forward constructively. Damaging outright battles had never occurred - we had somehow made the journey into one of good moments, sharing a common sense of purpose. Despite living together on a 24/7 basis we managed to avoid invading each others private space. We thought this to be an important aspect for success in any extended expedition.

After rejoining Highway 1, we camped at Kununurra Lakeside Park. Dusk was now at 5.00pm and with sundowner in hand we joined a couple at a lakeside clearing. The attraction was a large freshwater crocodile, lurking on the gravel slope a few yards away, waiting expectantly for food. "You can feed Charlie here," proclaimed our fellow traveller, hinting at some developing tourist attraction in the making. We noticed the park's swimming jetty and pontoon was a stone's throw away. We thought 'swimming with crocs' had not quite the same appeal as CALM's close encounter experience with dolphins at Monkey Mia - Charlie just didn't have the same cute appeal!

Our natural progression would have been to press on to the north-east, towards Darwin, but by driving the GRR we had bypassed one of Australia's scenic wonders, buried deep in the mountains to the east of the Great Northern Highway. The Bungle Bungle (now designated as Purnulula National Park) had only been discovered by the outside world in 1982. Before that, it had been known only to the local Aboriginal people and a few drovers. This was a place of outstanding grandeur so we decided to backtrack for several hours to visit it. Whilst the massive beehive shaped rock domes of the Bungle Bungle are now more widely known, of a stature equivalent to Ayres Rock, access to the park remains as challenging as ever. Most visitors take the easy option - to fly over the mountains by light aircraft or helicopter, avoiding the 55km track through rough terrain. Rabia made good progress and completed the crossing from the main road in three hours, fording several deep streams in the process. We could see why the track was limited to 4WD vehicles.

By 4.00pm we reached the western perimeter of Purnulula but we needed to find a camp site quickly. Rather than using a designated camping area outside the rocks, we headed for the core of the range where we elected to stay for the night. The park's gravel tracks were deserted and we reached the trail head at Cathedral Gorge shortly before sunset. The domed rocks stood out with a crimson uniformity, glowing in the weakening light. Banded layers of grey and pink ascended in regimented order to the 100m pinnacle summits. The display seemed unreal, somehow unnatural and unworldly. To the west the domed profiles were already in darkness, rolling in massive jet black corrugations against a yellow horizon. Soon, dusk invaded our wilderness, sunlight remained only on the very crests of the nearby domes and giant beehives towering high above our camp site.

This was our most isolated camp in Australia so far. In the encroaching darkness these mysterious rocks cocooned us in silence. Nothing stirred and overhead the sky burst into life. Familiar star clusters appeared in intensity quite new to us. To the north, there was the Plough in its familiar profile but now set very low on the horizon. Orion, our most familiar constellation, hung overhead to the west, moving out of sight with unseemly haste. Scorpio, a friend with new structure and brightness in the southern hemisphere, ascended to be a dominant part of the sky overhead whilst Sirius, with its special brightness, shone like a beacon forming a spectacular reference point. We sat spellbound for an hour; speech was unnecessary.

Binoculars were passed periodically between us as we both succumbed to the spell cast by one of nature's best panoramas.

Occasionally in our travels something really special happens. We know beforehand, with a growing feeling, that we are passing through a door into something quite new, an experience with an added dimension. At dawn the next day we felt we were crossing such a threshold; we would be assured of a 'diamond' day in our journey. In a rush, daylight flooded our giant amphitheatre, drenching the Neolithic structures in a riot of colour and we saw again the unusual symmetry of the landscape. The domes' outlines seemed to follow some uniform geometric equation, profiles set with disciplined order but bundled into some three dimensional sculpture to the far horizon, a conception of nature beyond understanding. Of course, this giant work of art was simply the outcome of erosive forces. Wind, water and the inherent softness of banded limestone had all contributed to different degrees. But the mechanical forces at play could not detract from the sheer majesty of this place. The array of brightly coloured domes dominated the landscape from skyline to skyline rising to 200 metres to the north of our site.

That day we were to explore the very core of the area. Deep gorges led through the eroded mountains, narrowing to shoulder width in places. Here, looking up, the narrow slit would weave its way skyward through the red sandstone. The strong light of midday reflected down the twisting walls with a fiery orange glow. Cathedral Gorge and Echidna Chasm were highlights, each concluding in a vast open cavern where the walls rose to a ragged overhang some 200 metres overhead.

Palm trees grew in odd corners. Deep crevasses down rock faces held green ribbons of vegetation, nurtured by some isolated water course and protected from periodic bush fires by their isolation. Where the gorge widened sufficiently for regular daylight to penetrate, minor tropical forests had created a local habitat for birds and wild life. In these strange corners, unfamiliar bird calls rang out overhead whilst throughout the bush, frogs jumped, snakes crawled and small fish swam around in clear pools. We were good park visitors that night. We resisted our preference for bush camping and registered into a formal camping area!

There was a small helicopter based in the park and we decided to indulge in one of our infrequent extravagances. Never prone to impulsive spending, we had thought this through and concluded that we really wanted to see this stunning landscape from the sky. We had persuaded Brent, the pilot, to depart from normal hours and take us over the area just after dawn. He was fascinated by what had prompted our request. When we took off, the morning light was catching the Bungle Bungle domes almost horizontally. Black shadows emphasised the eroded contours and brought out the colours in banded sandstone that only morning light can provide. The air was now crystal clear after the chilly night. The daytime heat haze had not yet descended and we hoped for some spectacular photos through the open sides of the helicopter. We were not disappointed.

Brent's Story

Brent had started his working life as a slaughter man by trade. At 25 he felt something was missing from his life, perhaps the prospect of exciting unpredictability in an otherwise bland routine. Despatching animals somehow lacked scope to develop a passionate fulfilling career. In need of a clean break, he paid $32,000, all his savings, to learn to fly. Successful fixed-wing training led quickly to helicopters and with a good performance record he had been taken on for seasonal work throughout Australia - a sort of high-class itinerant worker with a difference.

This season was his third in the Bungle Bungle, ferrying visitors over the rugged scenery. He would move on, perhaps in spring, to try for seasonal work at the Twelve Apostles on the south coast. "The pay is good there," he said, preferring this to the option of stock herding by helicopter in the bush. It seemed that retrained stockmen made better heli-herding pilots than others. Although trading a horse for a helicopter, they perhaps understood better the psychology of stampeding beasts.

We retraced our route out of Purnulula, leaving with a new awareness of the cultural significance that these remote places had for the Aboriginal people. Later, when we reached Kununurra again, it was Social Security pay-day. The bottle shops had opened at noon and by late afternoon groups of Aboriginal people staggered round the town centre in an alcoholic haze, poor shadows of a past proud people. What damage had befallen this race, we wondered, by their ancestors' headlong migration from the wild seclusion of Purnulula? Their traditions had thrived for 20,000 years and were rooted in a strong relationship with the land. What part had Europeans played in that downfall by their arrogant and ruthless imposition of standards quite foreign to these people? The questions were complex but we were beginning to sense more of the real underlying issues.

We camped once more at Kununurra's lakeside. The glow of twilight reflected off Kona Lake and we sat peacefully on the swimming raft. The mirror flat surface broke, with barely a ripple, seven metres away. First, two large eyes appeared, staring with a cold intensity, then the black spiny length of the croc's back surfaced like a submarine. The observers were being observed! Charlie had come back for evening snacks. Although we were certain the lake contained only the freshwater variety, returning to shore from the raft held a subliminal fear at that moment. 'Swimming with crocs', was definitely not a commercially attractive concept! The panorama was quickly enveloped in darkness and the westerly glow faded to a purple haze on the woody horizon beyond the lake.

We moved on the next day to Lake Argyle - Australia's largest stretch of inland water, formed by a massive damming project on the Ord River. The region's extensive new agriculture now depends on retention of the wet season rains. We joined the late afternoon cruise to find out more. Our fellow travellers were mostly older retired folk, conservative in dress and manner. First the cruise covered the orthodox aspects of the lake - fish farming, feeding the island rock wallabies, looking at cat fish and, more interestingly, seeing the archer fish spitting water ferociously at their target, a hand-held morsel of bread, one metre above the water. All this was good entertainment but what we had really come to enjoy was the complimentary champagne and swim in the middle of the lake at sunset. A rather good vintage of Australian sparkling wine flowed freely and the transition in our 45 fellow passengers was breathtaking. Soon, garments were changed for bathing costumes and dozens of near geriatrics threw themselves off the boat with abandon into deep water. Happy whoops echoed over the lake, more sparkling wine was served and the scene in the very middle of Lake Argyle was extraordinary. The boat returned to the dock in near darkness with its passengers in high spirits.

Nearby we bought fish and chips for supper. The fish was Silver Cobbler - catfish by any other name - and it tasted good. The background story made an interesting study in good marketing. When the lake had first been formed, an entrepreneur had decided to invest in Barramundi - that favourite of Oz fish. Massive numbers of young fry had been released at great cost but were quickly consumed by the dominant species that had successfully invaded the new lake, the wild catfish. Each successive attempt to introduce Barramundi failed and financial disaster loomed. In a brilliant shift of marketing strategy, the entrepreneur realised there was little point in swimming against the tide (so to speak), tested the three types of marauding catfish that were destroying his venture and found that one had culinary potential. That species was harvested and through good advertising was sold successfully throughout Australia with a new name, Silver Cobbler. This, of course, was sold as fillet without the give-away catfish head. Overnight, the price rose from 60 cents to $18 per kilo and the business thrived.

The next few days were a time of elegant simplicity. Back on Highway 1 we cruised north, often sharing driving to cover distance. We reached Katherine, 500km down the road in one continuous passage, crossing a time zone in the process which required a curious adjustment of 1.5 hours. We could recall many time zone changes in our global travels but these only worked in complete hours and we wondered about the origins of this anomaly. The change was good though, since we benefited from longer daylight in the evenings.

We camped outside Katherine that evening. The gorge close to the town was known as Nitmiluk National Park. Politics and land ownership issues were intertwined with the site's tourism development in complex ways that we could not understand. The Aboriginal people had won a court case to regain ownership of the gorge which had then been leased back to Australia's Land Agency for development. There was no doubt that the area had a strong Aboriginal heritage, transcending a European presence here. Seventy percent of the park's management board were now Aboriginal people and, in balance, we thought the character of the gorge was well preserved through good management. But our interest in gorges was beginning to wane; Nitmiluk's 15km waterway and dramatic cliffs were spectacular; no doubt about it, but this was our eighth gorge since leaving Broome, all different and beautiful places. We were suffering from a surfeit of awesome places, like children eating too much ice cream. The extraordinary was becoming the ordinary and we resolved to keep gorges off our itinerary for the foreseeable future.

To reach Darwin we travelled north on the Stuart Highway, diverting at Pine Creek into back country. There had been a gold rush here in the 1880s. Prospectors had rushed here from Asia and Europe, and the remnants of mining hardware still litter the landscape. We had enjoyed our time in the Klondike and wondered what we might see in the Northern Territory that could stir our imagination. The local tourist office had suggested we take the historic Northern Goldfields Loop Road out of town. We followed the gravel track through the wilderness but there was a curious lack of signs to old mining sites. The information boards on the route, promised in Pine Creek, were just not there. We heard later over a beer in the Grove Hill pub, half way through the loop (a remnant of the gold rush), that the present landowners regard their currently dormant mines as potentially valuable assets. "When gold goes to $600 they come back into service," said Stan the bar owner. It seemed there was a difference here. After the Klondike gold rush the Yukon had been repeatedly re-mined to absolute extinction with increasingly sophisticated gear. Mining here had simply stopped, as gold prices dropped and water ran out. It would not do to attract public interest to dormant mines with potential, so signs had been discreetly removed.

We camped at the back of the pub overnight. This was a unique place! Its old structure of steel and corrugated tin sheet placed its origins back in the mining days. Its location, so far off the beaten track, made the hotel a destination rather than just a place to stop. The next morning dew sparkled in the first light. Stan's collection of rusty antique car bodies took on a soft quality, their brown hulks glistening with dampness. Cobwebs glowed in their dusty interior. Left to decay, their utility spent, the old bodies were beyond redemption. Other memorabilia of the gold rush littered the surrounding fields. Old pumps lay in weedy grass rusting to oblivion. Other machinery took on that special quality of man-made hardware left to decay, the original function lost in a rich patina of mature oxide, their pitted surface deprived of meaning. Here and there, a tenacious patch of old paint added a glow of industrial green within the general scheme of ochre and brown. They became monuments to some past age, hinting at the passions, hopes and dreams to which they were silent witness.

Darwin beckoned, but without undue haste. On 17 May we reached the city; a place made uniformly attractive by enforced urban renewal. Cyclone Tracey had exercised her might here on Christmas Eve 1974, flattening the existing city. Although a disaster at the time, the effect now was good. The city fairly sparkled with clean modern buildings. This was a thriving vibrant community. We had camped each night since leaving Broome seventeen days earlier, sleeping on top of Rabia. It was time for conventional accommodation for a few nights and we settled for the Globetrotters Backpackers where we found friendly and congenial company. We rested here enjoying the sights and facilities of Darwin and even temporarily joining the sailing club for the weekend.

We had decided when planning our route that Darwin would be our final destination in Australia's North West. From here we would drive east, round the Gulf of Carpentaria, where Highway 1 became the Gulf Track. But then we felt uneasy with that plan as we would bypass a large part of Australia's coastline, perhaps missing something significant. We checked the possibility of travelling further to the north-east from Darwin and found an intriguing but challenging option. To the east of the Gulf of Carpentaria, a horn of land juts north to form Cape York, Australia's most northerly point. We would explore that later, but to the west of the Gulf, near Darwin, an equally desolate area called Arnhem Land, offered a challenging opportunity to reach into a remote coast. During that early research in Saudi Arabia, we found that Arnhem Land was an area not often visited. It was entirely under Aboriginal ownership and control and was a restricted area. There was a worthwhile destination, the Cobourg Peninsula, to which a track of sorts gave access. But there was a catch. Because this was a sensitive area it seemed that only fifteen tourist vehicles per week were allowed through. The entry permit could take up to six months to obtain and, strangest of all, the passage to the peninsula must be completed in one day, after fording the East Alligator River on the border with Aboriginal territory. We had pondered if all this planning was worthwhile but we finally made a successful application for a permit. We were then committed to an entry date, 27 May, six months away.

We were now ahead of schedule and had some days in reserve before that date. The official entry point was at a dramatic ford called Cahills Crossing on the East Alligator River. Between Darwin and that crossing we had time to explore Kakadu's tropical wetlands and to learn more about Aboriginal rock art at Ubirr - probably the best place in Australia to study this at first hand. We planned to camp here but mosquitoes were a challenge in Kakadu, thriving in expansive seasonal lakes and hot days. "We have laid on sufficient at each bush camp," said the friendly park warden, his words laced with heavy sarcasm. "If you need more we have reserve stocks." We were not amused. We had found that mosquitoes could make an otherwise idyllic camping spot into a nightmare at dusk. Our style of travel made this a serious matter.

Aboriginal Corroboree

Plate 11

Australian Road Train

Plate 12

Waterfall in the Atherton Tableland, Queensland

Plate 13

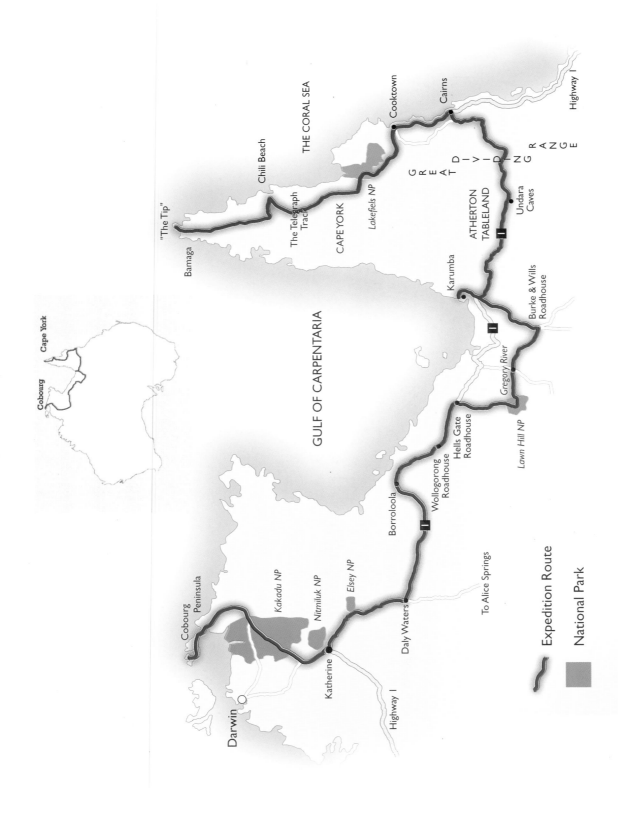

Darwin

Highway 1

Cobourg
Peninsula

Katherine

Kakadu NP

Nitmiluk NP

Elsey NP

Daly Waters

To Alice Springs

Borroloola

Wollogorong
Roadhouse

Hells Gate
Roadhouse

Lawn Hill NP

Gregory River

Burke & Wills
Roadhouse

ATHERTON
TABLELAND

Undara
Caves

Karumba

GULF OF CARPENTARIA

Bamaga

"The Tip"

The Telegraph
Track

Chili Beach

CAPE YORK

Lakefiels NP

THE CORAL SEA

Cooktown

Cairns

Highway 1

GREAT DIVIDING RANGE

Cobourg

Cape York

Expedition Route

National Park

Chapter 3. Crossing the Top End

The wetlands were a bright colourful place during the day. Carpets of yellow and white flowers floated on silent ponds in flooded plains. Trees rose through lakes to form a verdant canopy overhead. Wildlife thrived above a watery landscape. Vivid parrots screeched in mock battle, all sound and no action. In contrast, flocks of white egrets, those most elegant of birds, silently stalked their prey amongst vivid water lilies in shallow billabongs. Giant fruit bats hung silently in daytime sleep, often nursing youngsters tenderly in folded wings. At sunset all manner of nocturnal creatures would stir into life around us in the warm glow over Kakadu's plains. For a while all would be peaceful, but shortly before darkness the mosquito invasion would start and despite all our creams and pungent smoke, the relentless attack would force us to an early retreat into the safe confines of our bedroom on top of Rabia. Later in the evening dingo packs howled noisily, sounding like the hounds from hell. We heard a family of black boars, foraging aggressively near the car. This was no fun during our evening hours and we felt quite challenged.

It was not difficult to understand why a strong Aboriginal culture developed here. The flood plains were rich in resources and had sustained human life for over 20,000 years. Without a written language though, story telling was an important vehicle for the flow of knowledge between generations. Aboriginal rock art seemed to have provided additional back-up to that process; a sort of cultural text book. Throughout Kakadu, but in Ubirr in particular, these images came alive with clarity and form not often accessible in the rest of Australia. We saw the graphic imagery of spirits, people and animals and in most cases these held a huge significance in Aboriginal culture. We could imagine generations of fathers bringing children here to these rock ledges to explain their meaning, to learn how the spirits would influence their lives, and what would offend or please them. This was indeed an historical archive, a reference from generation to generation.

But one aspect left us with concern. It was clear that the paintings were retaining colour and form over many years - sometimes thousands - well beyond their natural 'expiry' date. Given their position on exposed rocks and the raw materials used, perhaps they shouldn't be there. We heard that renovation of these sacred sights was permitted. Managing and caring for the heritage was one way to interpret the process. With the huge commercial importance of these sights to the current generation of Aboriginal people, we wondered what pressures may be forming to add artificial clarity and colour to these images. Were the images still 'original art' after many generations of over painting? There was no doubt though that nothing could detract from the significance of the outlines. After all, these may have been one of man's first attempts at self expression. At least the original outlines remain, if not their complete integrity.

We crossed to Arnhem Land, wading the tricky ford over the East Alligator River. This was a place of strange tidal flows - some wizardry of nature was at play here. During a rising tide, the river would flow backwards up the valley, flooding the causeway to 0.9m. Within the span of a heartbeat, the upward surge would halt, and then reverse. After ten minutes the river, now flowing in a conventional way towards the sea, would be a noisy torrent. Danger lurked in other forms too. The previous year a fisherman, casting from the causeway at high tide, had been taken by a crocodile. Cars had been swept over the high weir adjacent to the causeway during untimely attempts at crossing. We chose the safe window at low water, but watched with apprehension as two crocodiles rested on the far bank.

We reached Cobourg in 4.5 hours, driving the rough and dusty 288km track in one passage. We crossed through open bush savannah and briefly entered a stretch of tropical rain forest at mid point. We saw little sign of life and the small Aboriginal settlements along the way were sleepy, almost dormant places. We registered our arrival in Cobourg with the local ranger station and drove to Smith Point, overlooking the Timor Sea. A small cairn had been built here several centuries ago to mark the most northerly point on land in Western Australia. At this latitude we were just a few seconds of arc short of the tip of Cape York on the other side of the Gulf of Carpentaria.

What a place Cobourg was! She enchanted us with her raw beauty. We had our own Garden of Eden for a few days, a kind of tropical paradise. She enticed us to travel her narrow trails which threaded through a mosaic of dense forest, mangroves and coastal grassland. We explored deserted beaches on the Arafura Sea where it was not difficult to imagine ourselves as castaways. Colourful birds flocked by the billabong beside our campsite. Huge Banteng buffalo stampeded through the undergrowth making a noisy intrusion into our solitude. They had been imported from Indonesia many years ago and they now live wild in Cobourg. We never saw the crocodile that crawled by our site before dawn each morning to make his daily passage from billabong to sea but we were glad we were sleeping off the ground! His claw prints remained, deeply imprinted on the sand and his one metre step was a witness to his giant size. Despite the blue waters, swimming here had marginal appeal. The sea was to be admired but not enjoyed; we left it to the crocs, sharks and deadly box jellyfish that thrived here.

We would soon start the long trek across Northern Australia and then on to the 4WD track through Cape York. This was a fitting end to our time in Western Australia. We had completed 9500km and this isolated semi-tropical wilderness seemed to impart a kind of full stop on our travels, a transition from one section to another.

"Yurluya ganklarda ngaliguru-tharndugu marnu,
Murnajirla yurlul gankalarda ngaligurugu marnu."
" Look after the country and the country will look after you."
Aboriginal saying

Chapter Three:
Crossing the Top End

During the early days of foreign exploration the British Government had tried to build a settlement in the Cobourg Peninsula, the remains of which we explored before leaving. Dutch and French expansion in the East Indies led to a hasty British attempt to create a strong presence in Northern Australia. Victoria Settlement was formed in 1834. Port Essington Bay was, for sure, a great anchorage but the prospective site had first been surveyed just after the wet season, falsely suggesting that there was plenty of water available. The settlement failed to create a trading bridgehead between the new continent and Indonesia as intended and attracted only a few pearl fishermen and trepang traders. After 11 years of oppressive conditions, lack of sweet water, malaria and a hurricane, the settlement was abandoned. All that remained during our visit to the site was a few walls and an evocative, sad graveyard, now overgrown by forest. The inscriptions hinted at the deprivation and hardship. We wondered what personal triumphs and disasters were played out in this forgotten settlement over those short 11 years.

May, by tradition, is a time for bush fires in the Northern Territory. During our exit from Cobourg, we had our first close encounter. At one point we saw thick grey plumes of smoke billowing into the clear sky some 5km ahead. We drew closer and the drama began to unfold. The raging inferno had reached the road from the west and was trying hard to bridge the track in front of us. Soon, the track was obliterated in dense smoke, through which a wall of flame danced skywards. We were quite close now and felt the powerful air currents feeding the up-draught in the core of the fire. In that smoky commotion, dozens of black winged kites rolled and dived in a feeding frenzy - all manner of insects and beetles were falling like rain, drawn from the upper canopy by the strong turbulence. It was a curious business and we noticed to our surprise that the upper canopy remained undamaged after the fire had moved on.

We waded back through the East Alligator River from Arnhem Land, turned south through the lower regions of Kakadu National Park and rejoined the Stuart Highway on its way to Alice Springs. Some 400km on, at Daly Waters, we would turn east and cross the Top End on the Gulf Track. Back on the open road again, there was little appeal in the dry savannah landscape, few landmarks to stimulate our minds. When we were less enthralled by our surroundings, we often pondered some obscure point to help pass time. That morning the naming of creek crossings in Australia was our subject. Even an insignificant dry creek bed would be announced with a banner sized road sign, imparting an importance to the scrubby valley which was out of all proportion to its geophysical significance.

Just out of Kakadu we crossed Big Nellie Creek - no more than a narrow indentation threading through barren savannah. What a thought-provoking name! Had the creek been physically bigger in earlier times and named after Nellie? Or was the creek named after a mysterious Nellie who was disposed to larger proportions? If the latter was correct, we pondered how the original Nellie felt about her scale living on for posterity, embellishing the small bridge over the creek forever.

Then, to add a new dimension to our idle thoughts, we reached a second crossing; the imposing road sign here proclaiming this to be Little Nellie Creek. In terms of depth and width, it was definitely bigger than Big Nellie Creek. We concluded with increasing curiosity that there must have been two people, a big Nellie and a little Nellie in someone's life. Perhaps some drover or gold miner who first stumbled into the area and on whom two Nellies had made some lasting impact. To pass the time away, we built a mythical story around the Nellies while driving the 80km to reach Pine Creek where, incidentally, we saw not a single pine! Later that day we crossed Big Dinner and Little Dinner Creeks, taking our travel weary minds into the realms of pure fantasy.

We camped again outside Katherine. By now, we had seen many aspects of the Aboriginal peoples attempt to adjust to the 21st Century in Australia, not always successfully. There had been some moments of real insight, fleeting glimpses of their past culture and of their beliefs and traditions. We had seen frustrations spill over to become anti-social behaviour. Sometimes their failure to come to terms with change and alternative legal precepts had vented as anger and rage. That night we were to spend time with a group of people who had apparently transcended these threats and who shared their dance and music with the outside world with real pride. The Corroboree that evening was captivating. The troupe of colourful half-naked dancers stomped and sang their way through a lively programme accompanied by much puffing on didgeridoos that were well worn through use. (Plate 11). The lack of orchestration and structure added to the overall effect. Their graphic performance put to dance hunting expeditions, stories of wild animals, white cockatoos and even a fishing expedition. It was easy to understand how these traditional patterns of movement had formed. The tribes had acquired a deep understanding of their land and its animals over thousands of years. Perhaps, after all, expressive dance and rock painting could convey information between generations with insight equal to the written word. Both the oldest and the youngest participants (aged 75 and 4) took pride in their heritage and their sense of fun that evening spilled over to us. We were captivated! We felt like participants - as if we were there, in the troupe's village 130km to the south. We had been swept into the mood and it was stimulating and insightful. This was no band of screaming natives - there was tenderness, sensitivity and expressiveness in their performance. We were glad to share the moment.

Den's Road Train

The profile of Den's massive road train sat centre stage in Rabia's rear view mirror. His dust plume billowed behind the vehicle showing the huge machine in stark outline. Den was travelling at 110kph and had a schedule to meet. The 82 tyres which supported his rig were rolling nicely and he would not voluntarily slow down the 150tons assembly for anyone. Rabia was making her stately progress down the Stuart Highway at 80kph. "You don't mess with this sort of rig," we thought and pulled over to let the cab and four trailers thunder past. We were mesmerised by this unique Australian experience. It took time for the massive road train to roll by before we were engulfed in the comet tail of dust behind the last trailer. Some 30km down the road we caught up with Den who was delivering petrol at a roadhouse. He had driven through the forecourt onto the road again, leaving the tail-end to thread through the roadhouse and onto the highway. We stopped, took some photos, and chatted with Den about his exceptional vehicle.

Den had been driving with Shell for 10 years. I asked about reversing the train. "You can reverse about 30 feet before you lose control," he responded, adding "...but you just don't get into that sort of position." He was perhaps stating the obvious. Den's regular route was from Darwin to Alice Springs. He would make the return trip in four or five days then have three days off. His daily limit of combined driving and delivery time was 16 hours. New routes required careful research, checking that the rig could make all the turns along the way. "I have a satellite phone and GPS in the cab," he said, confirming that he had permanent communication with the outside world in an emergency. (We had that much in common!).

The cab looked quite small and the act of driving seemed straight forward. The Mack power, all 700 horse power, worked through 18 gears and was no problem for Den. A sleeping area off the main cabin made this home from home. He could not stop for animals on the road. "Cows and horses make the worst mess," said Den. Most animal collisions were not a problem generally. He said that 'roos were hardly noticeable and the only problem was blood and mess over the windscreen. Den finished unloading. We said goodbye and his massive 120 feet of vehicle drew out quickly onto the highway to Alice and was gone in an instant.

The next morning we drove south to Elsey National Park and what a gem we found! This was a place of clear thermal springs, tropical forests and meandering rivers. Elsey is small. Its close proximity to the massive lands of Kakadu means that it is often bypassed. Elsey was to give us our last moments of tranquillity for several days. From here, we would cross the arid miles through the top of Oz to reach Queensland.

Turning off the Alice Springs road at the Hi-way Inn, we both felt the change. We knew 1600km of isolated track lay ahead to reach Karumba at the east end of the Gulf of Carpentaria. This would be something new for us - a challenge to mind, body and equipment. Highway 1 made a good job of circling Oz but through the wastes of the northern savannah beside the Gulf, it would become an apology for a road - a mere dotted line on the map. We had no delusions and our expectations were not high. It would be a single carriageway, unpaved and corrugated. Our crossing would be challenging and perhaps even hostile. This would be like a long farm track with attitude!

After Borroloola, there would be a scattering of roadhouses and a few scrappy Aboriginal communities but that would be all. The track's low standing reflected its historic origins. The eccentric explorer Ludwig Leichhardt had followed the line of this route in 1845 to make the first attempt to reach the ill-fated Victoria Settlement overland. Later, the trail blazed by Leichhardt became a stock route, simply linking the massive cattle stations and pastoralist homesteads developing during the early 19th Century. After the epic cattle drives declined, there was no reason to upgrade, and the track remained a meagre grit road.

We almost reached Cape Crawford that day. We had crossed miles of supreme emptiness, with huge blue skies between unbroken horizons. We were hot, dusty and tired and settled for a modest bush camp in a stand of weeping eucalypts. That night, in the austere silence of the outback, a rare bleak mood descended. Not yet one-third round Australia after two months; we pondered our motives and grappled with self doubt. What had really driven us to this? Could we actually complete the plan? Rabia's performance was just too good to last - perhaps she was storing up some cataclysmic failure when she would drop our travel plan into chaos. How could 22,000 pieces of contrived metal, plastic, rubber and glass sustain this punishment day after day? The engineer in me rumbled with disquiet. Were we after all just two naïve Brits abroad attempting the ridiculous, living on borrowed time? We could not shift our disturbed mood that night. We were restless and edgy about our motives and prospects. Even the magnificent skyscape after dark failed to calm our fractious thoughts. It was to be a low point during our time in Australia.

We had 500km of tough terrain ahead the next day, a demanding drive with no room for personal doubts. Introspective thoughts vanished in the morning's airless heat and by late afternoon we had made good progress to reach Wollogorang Homestead, an isolated cattle station with a great history. By now we had a raging thirst. There was no ice left in our cool box and our tinnies were all warm. Shaking ourselves free of the day's accumulated dust we headed for the small bar in the main building. Even now the air held oppressive warmth and a cold beer was never more welcome. The chilled liquor tasted like pure nectar. We shared the moment with Brian and Cathy, a couple who worked on the station. The conversation flowed easily. We had all had a hard day one way or another and we were winding down. Brian was a mature stockman and his deeply weathered face and robust ruggedness were his hallmarks of a hard outback life. He had been working with Brahmin cattle that day. "They are all exported to India and Indonesia," he said and added that the Middle East market was strong but difficult to service. The cost of shipping live animals all that way had become too expensive. "We tried selling frozen carcasses from here to cheapen the meat, with halal slaughtering and all, but it failed." There was a hint of regret in his voice. It seemed the Unions and animal rights groups brought the plan down. "Too inhumane," said Brian, adding graphically, "knives and blood all over the place." We wondered which of the rough diamonds who worked here had said the obligatory Islamic prayer as the hapless beasts were dispatched. The conversation moved on to a softer topic - Barramundi fishing - a huge sport in Northern Australia.

Three days into this route and we were travelling the Gulf Track's worst section. A bad Wet had left the gravel surface damaged; deep potholes lurked under loose bull dust to catch the careless or unwary. The landscape was bland and the clutter of spinifex grasses, now dry and yellow in early summer, added some brightness and texture on the red terrain. Progress remained good under a hot fiery sun.

Disaster! A half grown 'roo jumped from the undergrowth, big ears and black terrified eyes appearing momentarily over the bonnet. No warning - just a heavy thunk as flesh and metal made grisly contact. Rabia shuddered momentarily. The poor animal had sprung in front of us, kamikaze style. "Kangaroos need a better escape strategy," we thought. It seemed that natural selection was doing little for *Macropus Rufus*. Of course, we stopped - what had become of the 'roo and, of more practical importance, had we damaged the car? The 'roo had been thoroughly dispatched to animal heaven. It had been a mercifully swift passage. Rabia, however, had acquired a bent steering rod - not terminal damage to the part but showing sufficient distortion to be of concern. We were fussy about tyre wear, hoping our current set of Michelin tyres would see us round the world and we knew the rod needed straightening to reset wheel geometry correctly. A tree provided anchorage for the delicate straightening operation. We lashed the rod to the immovable trunk and carefully nudged Rabia in reverse until the rod was straight. We had found that self-sufficiency in all things mechanical could be fun!

We needed fuel and were pleased to reach Hell's Gate Roadhouse, despite its austere setting. The building sat amongst hillocks of grey rocky conglomerate rising in curious contrast with the surrounding savannah. In earlier times drovers were escorted here on their journey west but once beyond the rocks they were on their own, left to handle marauding Aborigines in Western Australia as best they could. Over time it became known as Hell's Gate, capturing neatly the quintessential meaning of the place. Now, things were different and the roadhouse was a pleasant oasis. We refuelled and moved on.

We had endured the Gulf Track's corrugations for long enough. Shaken into submission, we wanted to divert into genuine 4x4 territory to reach our next destination - Lawn Hill National Park. We could take an excellent short cut over the land of Bowthorn cattle station, saving 200km but we needed permission and so called at the homestead. Kerry McGinnis, the owner (and author of two books on the outback) welcomed us warmly. We would spend the rest of that day on her property and she readily gave us permission to cross. Over tea, she told us about her 35 years on this land from childhood, helping her father create the business. Here was a woman of amazing qualities with a commanding character, moulded by her remote and hard upbringing. The station was at the top end of small comprising of 900 square miles and she was managing 2500 head of cattle - small by most standards, but she sold stock young. Rain was Kerry,s overriding concern. In any year less than 25 inches or more than 45 inches would be a disaster. For the last three years they had had only 12 inches annually. "Nature seems to want us to fail," said Kerry ruefully. As we left we heard, with no real surprise, that she and her sister had made the bricks for the current homestead when they were youngsters. What a lady!

During the remainder of the day we crossed a huge expanse of flat savannah with an occasional forest and a scattering of gum trees. We were on our own. No-one passed us and the tracks were often indistinct and difficult. "Thank God for GPS navigation," we thought. After 150km we arrived at our destination. We had felt strangely at home during that passage and we were pleased with the journey. Perhaps the terrain had been closer to that of desert driving and, without surface corrugations, it had been comfortable. We had crossed quite a span of wilderness since Hell's Gate; probably the equivalent of driving from London to York.

Lawn Hill gave us sanctuary, peace and beauty. This was another gem buried in the otherwise harsh northern outback. The gorge was silent at 8.00am the next morning. It was a special moment of quietness as life paused in restful contemplation of a new day. Our hired canoe was the perfect way to enjoy this. Paddling silently along the narrow river, we saw first light reach the high valley walls. The new brightness reflected down to the pandanus and cabbage palms lining the narrow banks beside us. We passed ribbons of tropical rain forest, backed by majestic red cliffs and watched the world around us come to life. Out of nowhere a thousand budgerigars made a supersonic fly-by, a body of green, blue and red whirling and diving in perfect synchronization between the cliffs in the morning light. This seemed to us to be an expression of sheer enjoyment at that moment, and we both thought how appropriate this was compared with a life in a cage. We drifted quietly into the next pool.

Later that day we shared our dinner with Joey, a friendly kangaroo that patrolled the camp site (perhaps because we felt guilty about dispatching his relative that morning.) Joey had developed a few tricks - bad table manners by any standard. He would scrabble for food, deftly lifting tasty morsels from plates and forks without an invitation. We heard the following morning that poor Joey was to be netted and would be removed to an alternative site located 150km away. He was just too big now for this conduct. It seemed that kangaroos with a friendly disposition had a dim future in National Parks.

We left Lawn Hill on a modest but unsurfaced track heading east. The countryside was no less barren than during previous days - a landscape of repetitive brutality, sweeps of dry savannah to be endured rather than savoured. We stopped early that day, finding a bush camp on a sandy spit by Gregory River. There was permanent water here and we had stumbled on to a good spot. Ancient paper bark trees overhung the water like willows over an English stream but the many exotic palms reminded us that this was the tropics. During the night a fresh wind whined in the tree canopy and the old watermill nearby groaned and scraped in its dilapidation, sounding at times like a pack of howling dingoes.

Karumba had been a fitting target on the Gulf Track. The town's location at the bottom right-hand corner of the Gulf of Carpentaria somehow provided a full stop in our minds - a destination of comfort and reassurance. Beyond here, there would be the promise of variety through the Great Dividing Range. After all, we would be in Queensland and Karumba was only 1100km from Cairns.

We had 340km ahead to reach there, just one day away. In the scheme of things this proved to be Rabia's moment of complaint, her first hint of mutiny. She squealed her protest shortly into the day's drive over the bleak Queensland plain, announcing the onset of some malady of substance. After our time of self doubt a few days back, was this to be our moment of supreme failure? It was already hot and the road to Burke & Wills Roadhouse 100km away would become a fiery cauldron and not a place for vehicle surgery. An examination revealed a screeching metal-to-metal contact somewhere in the front end of her engine, perhaps a bearing failure on the AC compressor or water pump, perhaps the alternator or worse, the power steering unit. We improvised a stethoscope from a piece of tubing to locate the source of the noise but failed. Curiously, no component seemed to be overheating, and the cooling circuit was functioning normally. We were baffled by the obvious but untraced complaint from her mechanical parts. There was nothing for it - we would drive on with care, knowing that we might invite terminal failure. By Burke & Wills, the hideous noise had eased. Nothing seemed wrong so we continued north to Karumba. The complaint softened then vanished. We surmised that it had perhaps been a pebble rubbing in some hidden recess, grinding harmlessly against an external pulley or shaft. Maybe Rabia had worked some auto-magic and had self-healed!

We reached our destination and secured a place for the night wedged between rows of camper vans on the foreshore. The Barramundi season would start soon and it seemed that every fisherman in Oz was here. There was a mood of eager expectation about the battle and slaughter ahead. That evening we dined on Barramundi and chips at Ash's Food Parlour then watched the sunset from the foreshore. The tide was out exposing a desert of sand far into the Gulf where glassy pools reflected a fiery crimson glow. The day had been hot and a distant haze blurred the horizon, merging sea and sky in one unbroken sweep of colour. There was to be no defining moment at the onset of dusk. The sun dissolved gently into a red haze, its final descent masked, its power sapped to become an incandescent glow.

We still fretted about Rabia's malady. Was she in remission? The morning inspection revealed all. There was good news - all her ancillary equipment driven by four belts from the engine was in good order. The water pump, steering pump and alternator were thankfully alright. But there was bad news - a tensioning pulley on the drive belt to the water pump had failed. The bracket and pulley pin were still there but the pulley which tensioned the belt had gone. Rabia's strident squealing had been the wail of the pulley bearing in terminal failure. She had run silently all afternoon but the drive belt had been loose. Somehow, the cooling system had continued to function normally but without an effective drive belt. The solution was not immediately apparent and we could not continue like that. Had no other idea surfaced, a small wheel from a shopping trolley might have been fashioned into temporary service. But there was a good solution. The drive belt for Rabia's air conditioning compressor was also tensioned by an identical pulley. We disconnected that and fitted the tensioning pulley onto the water pump circuit. With this improvisation, we reinstated the essential water pump circuit correctly and were back in service. But without AC it would be uncomfortable. We hoped to find a replacement in Cairns.

We crossed the wide sweep of Queensland's savannah, then on through the Atherton Tablelands and over the Great Dividing Range. We were in equilibrium again and dropped our pace during the journey to reach Cairns. We enjoyed those six days and the time passed quickly. The burden of stress and isolation slipped away and we made a smooth transition to Queensland's Coral Sea coast. The attractions along the way seemed endless; they were there to be enjoyed. We shared moments with the crew of the historic Gulflander and Savannahlander trains as they paused at old stations. We scrabbled in dried river beds looking for garnets and explored a dark world underground. 'Share a tube with a friend', read the roadside billboard, and we found a strange subterranean world, unique to our planet - long dark caves formed into tube-like tunnels when the liquid core of lava vented from solidifying volcanic flows.

There was one moment of excitement along the way. Shortly after Mount Garnet we were purring along, making good progress and thinking good thoughts. The scenery was changing and an altogether softer landscape was developing. We were passing lush green farming land now and soft billowing clouds banked up in the blue sky. We hoped for a refreshing dip up ahead in a hot thermal spring and the Dubliners rattled out their Irish folk music on the cassette player. Our GPS suggested we were well into the Great Dividing Range, although we had to admit we saw no hills that came close to attaining greatness. All was well with the world but then we saw a blue and white police car ahead lurking at the side of our single track road. The message was clear - pull over and stop. For the first time since Siberia we were flagged down by gun-toting police officers. We had done nothing wrong but were innocent victims of a random alcohol check in Oz, in this case in the middle of nowhere! I performed the necessary breath test and verified our authority to be there with Arabic number plates. We moved on, glad to have had only modest liquid refreshment at lunchtime.

There was no doubt we had arrived in tropical Queensland. Hillsides were wet and green. Kangaroos climb trees here! Flowers and shrubs blossomed with an intensity of colour unique to the tropics. Dangling vines draped from trees like ships rigging in disorder. We swam in clear lakes and heard rain trickle through silent rainforests. Water tumbled over ledges under misty slopes to vanish in a muddle of lush wet greenery. We sensed a new dimension to our journey, a new vigour surging back into our travels.

We reached Cairns and transformed ourselves into expedition administrators again, planning our day with boring practical efficiency. A tensioning pulley was scavenged from a Discovery in a wrecker's yard - done! We re-welded Rabia's exhaust tail section - score it off the list! We helped with a press meeting and photo shoot at the Land Rover agency - finished! Our backpacker accommodation in Cairns was fun and came as a welcome break from bush camping. We dined out and found Cairns a lively and colourful place in the evening, filled with laughter and bright lights.

We re-supplied and headed north to Cooktown. It felt good to be on the road again. We crossed the Daintree Rain Forest, passed Cape Tribulation and reached the 4x4 Bloomfield Track, engulfed in heavy greenery all the time. We camped for the first time in a tropical forest and it rained - great floods of it thundering on our home and the forest around us. We needed an inner lining on the roof tent overnight, but the next day things had improved. Early morning in a wet forest had its own appeal. Strange calls echoed through the canopy high overhead. The air was still and the new sun failed to penetrate the forest with any substance. Around us the undergrowth hung listless and dark. Nearby, heavy vines and creepers glistened in glossy shades of green in contrast with the foreboding blackness of dense thickets some way off. Nothing stirred in our confined world.

We were more prudent the next night and took shelter at the Lion's Den pub, buried in the depths of an isolated corner of the rain forest, half way to Cooktown. The corrugated tin shack had been here since 1875 and generations of stockmen and tin miners had left their mark on the place. Local residents flocked in after sunset, a rough bunch of social outcasts mostly squatting in shacks deep in the local jungle. But they were a friendly and hospitable crowd. John, a fellow customer, had lost himself in some doubtful existence in the forest, a feral by any standards. "I retired at 26 and came here from Townsville," he said. We wondered what else was sold here apart from the beer!

We arrived in Cooktown during the town's annual horse-racing weekend. It was Ladies Day and exotic hats and colourful clothing brightened the stands by the track. Horses thundered through their races. Bookies made a lively trade and the beer tent attracted a noisy bunch of customers. The atmosphere was relaxed - perhaps Cooktown Races lacked the sheer intensity of horse racing elsewhere but the mood was good. Neither of us were gamblers by nature but we were swept into the mood. Eileen was in charge of our accounts and confirmed we were 50 cents down on the day's entertainment.

We found Cooktown a cheery place with a comfortable and relaxed atmosphere. Tourism had reached here but there was not the frantic pace of Cairns or Port Douglas. We felt at ease. This was a place in which we could happily live. We had come here to rendezvous with friends of long standing, Vic and Heather Brown, who were travelling from their home in Sydney to meet us. We would drive north together, through Cape York to the very tip of Australia. Vic and Heather were old hands at outback travel and we had shared good times driving the sands of Arabia together. We had not seen each other for several years and we wondered how time had changed our friendship. How would we adapt to team travel after so long on our own? Vic and Heather were warm outgoing people and we felt assured of a great journey together. Cape York almost demanded the security of team travel. We shared similar ideas about off-road travel, balancing enjoyment and risks against safety and without this common view we would not have teamed up. But with two vehicles we could perhaps take more adventurous travel options and maybe afford to loosen our normally tight grip on off-road risk taking. There was no doubt Cape York had some challenging options.

Cape York remains one of Australia's last frontiers. The track to this northern tip of the country is difficult and the 1000km journey has become a favourite 4x4 challenge. The peninsula also has an important history. James Cook mapped the eastern coastline after making urgent repairs to *Resolution* in Cooktown. (A collision with a nearby reef had been close to fatal for the tiny boat.) When he reached the Tip on that great journey before heading home he made a formal claim for the continent on behalf of Britain, planting the British flag on a small island. Perhaps this was the most profound moment in Australia's history. Later, in 1887, when the country needed to find a telegraph route into Asia to help improve communications, a line was completed from Cooktown through the peninsula. The construction route for the telegraph poles had been cut with difficulty, passing through tropical savannah on the eastern slopes of the Great Dividing Range. Many rivers carved deep valleys to the coast and impeded progress. Rain forests often slowed construction and progress during The Wet was impossible. The track which serviced construction at the time was essentially for pack animals and rugged carts but remained to become the basis for the current route through the peninsula. In its northern reaches, some old poles still remain standing beside the Telegraph Track. (TT)

Our first few days together, driving through the lower regions of Cape York, were a pleasant relaxed time. The grit track was dusty and dry and the usual plume of dust erupted behind the lead vehicle. We stayed apart, separated by a kilometre or so whilst driving. Travelling with company was a new experience for us and added a pleasant aspect, sharing our moments of excitement and surprise when we found a place of interest. The weather in late June was perfect - warm days, cool evenings and dry air. We stopped to walk the bush track to the Aboriginal art sites near Laura which were quite different to the works we had seen in Karijini. Although the same 'dreamtime' concept was portrayed in the spiritual figures and ancestral beings, the style and character were altogether different. Later, we detoured into Lakefield National Park where we found a landscape rich in wildlife. The flood plains had dried after the Wet leaving a green savannah and lagoons covered in water lilies. We camped here, in secluded corners by quiet billabongs. Fishing by our camp site did not provide dinner as we had hoped but it was restful recreation at the end of the day.

After three days we reached the Archer River Roadhouse. Driving had been easy - the road had been well graded before the new driving season started and the track had not been the lethal bone shaking horror that we had anticipated. We were making good progress and our time together was evolving with a relaxed even flow. We decided to divert east the next day to reach Chili Beach on the Coral Sea coast. We knew the track would be difficult, a notch or two worse than the Telegraph Track. There would be perhaps four hours of tough terrain but the decision between us just evolved as the right thing to do at that point in our travels.

Halfway through our journey the next day we crossed a saddle called Tozers Gap, and descended into the largest area of lowland tropical rain forest in Australia. We found a wild place of unique flora and fauna and exotic landscapes. But the drive in was tough, climbing over forested hills and down into numerous creek beds. There were hidden dangers on the stream's slopes where the track had been broken and fractured by deep washouts. On higher ground giant corrugations covered the surface of the narrow track and, in a light-hearted moment, we searched for a collective noun to best describe this off-road phenomenon. A 'chattering' of corrugations won, followed closely by a 'cacophony'. Despite these worsening conditions, we were in good spirits and definitely having fun!

We set up camp on Chili Beach overlooking a wide bay and sheltered by a modest patch of jungle. Not many travellers divert here from the TT and we felt wonderfully isolated. We were on a wilderness coastline with a classic tropical feel. Mature coconut palms leaned seawards at gravity defying angles, battling against the prevailing onshore winds. White sands stretched for miles. The wind increased, hissing noisily in the thick palm fronds overhead and the surf crashed onto the nearby beach on the incoming tide. We slept fitfully that night and resolved to move to a more sheltered location back from the shoreline.

We walked the beach at dawn. A fiery light sneaked over the horizon out in the Coral Sea and the yellow glow flooded the nearby landscape. The tide was out and the beach glistened in the morning sun. The wind had eased and shallow waves rolled ponderously up the gently shelving beach. This was a morning to feel the sand through your toes, to rummage in the oceans flotsam above high water and explore mysterious bays hidden round distant headlands. A few hundred yards offshore a small island stood in grim silhouette against the rising daylight. On this island, Captain William Bligh's tiny boat landed after he was cast adrift during the mutiny on the Bounty in 1789. The records show that he and his small band of officers escaped starvation after weeks at sea by dining on boiled mussels harvested from the island's shoreline. It looked mysterious, almost forbidding, in the morning light that day. Cook of course had passed here just 19 years earlier during his epic voyage.

The day evolved into frivolous activity and blissful idleness - one to simply enjoy passing time in the wild beauty around us. We reckoned that a good game of French Boule could be played on the firm sands below our camp and fashioned a set from coconuts scavenged from the beach. During late afternoon, sparkling white wine was served and battle commenced. What enjoyment we had from such a simple improvisation! The ladies won the contest handsomely. During dinner that night a cassowary called into the darkness nearby and some parrots rustled overhead - we were not as alone as we thought.

To rejoin the TT we followed an alternative trail heading north-west. The Frenchman's Road made a good shortcut, saving perhaps 100km, but there was a price - we had to cross the Pascoe River. With some understatement the map showed the point as a 'rough crossing' and we hoped that our fearful anticipation of a problem ahead would prove to be worse than the event. We reached the Pascoe at high noon to find there had been dramas here already that day. As we arrived a group of 4x4 vehicles were leaving to head south after making the crossing. Some cars had floundered, not just wading through the one metre deep river bed but also driving the steep and slippery banks out of the crossing. No-one smiled, and the sullen faces hinted at recent moments of stress and conflict as the party had winched and cajoled their vehicles out of their difficulties. Their bleak demeanour did not reassure us about our own prospects.

We made an initial assessment by walking through the stream. Although not wide we found it was deep. Rabia had not faced such a watery challenge. The river was flowing swiftly and there was a hole to be avoided. Below the surface the bed was rocky and some large boulders lurked unseen to catch the unwary. After a slippery descent down the steep banking to reach the stream, we dressed Rabia for the crossing - our specially made inner spray shield was fitted round her drive belts and fan and the front blanket was unwrapped over her radiator intake. By now the adrenalin was flowing. This was no time for hesitation and we plunged into the fast flowing current decisively. Rabia bounced over some hidden rocks. We were in the fast flowing current now and with water lapping on the upstream door we reached mid point. Something cracked loudly under the vehicle but she kept on rolling. She inched slowly onto the rocky ledge on the north bank and we were out! The second hurdle faced us and we engaged low ratio and locked the differential. In front of us the steep ascent rose out of the valley onto higher ground. Through prior use the track had degenerated into a muddy, rock-strewn assault course and the climb seemed interminable. The track was mostly out of sight because of the gradient - Rabia's bonnet blocked the view. We crawled up trying hard to recall the preferred route over the slope. Finally, we eased onto flat ground to rejoin Vic and Heather, who had crossed first. Rabia was undamaged, except for the broken shaft of our spade, stored under her rear bumper. This had been the cause of the heart stopping crack during the crossing.

Several other small but nasty crossings slowed our progress on the remaining 60km of the Frenchman's Road. We rejoined the TT and headed north again towards the Tip. It had been a technically demanding day which would be typical of other sections ahead. Rabia had proved her effectiveness at the limits of bad terrain and we knew now that she could surmount most obstacles given patience and astute gear selection. We didn't know it at the time, but her climbing ability would be crucial to travels later in South America.

Although progress was good during the next two days the track worsened. River crossings and giant wash-board corrugations on the track slowed our pace. On the worst sections Rabia would progress into wild vibrations, as though possessed by an automotive version of an epileptic fit. But as driving worsened the scenery offered us compensation. We visited some exquisite places and camped in beautiful surroundings. We swam in the clear pools of Fruit Bat Falls and set up base one evening by the Elliot Falls - probably the finest site on the way north. Refreshing pools descended in picturesque steps amongst golden paper bark trees.

Shortly after Elliot Creek we reached Canal Creek. The 600cm of water was not demanding but the far bank rose steeply through 200m and looked like a battle field. Over time, prior traffic had fanned out to the sides probing for new routes through boulders and rock slabs. One enthusiast in a group ahead of us had been defeated. He had chosen a route with doubtful prospects directly up the face and his

Toyota was suspended on its sub-frame and gearbox, front and back wheels turning ineffectively to gain traction. No doubt about it - this vehicle was going nowhere! Amazingly, there was a simple route round this face. By driving down the river bed a little way then ascending through the forest we found a good bypass, but that had not been a sufficient challenge for the vehicle ahead. We recognised we were in the company of a cut-and-thruster who saw the slope as a testing ground for man and machine. The hapless driver and vehicle were released from bondage by two vehicles winching together from the top of the slope. The screeching of metal on granite was an appalling sound and after giving assistance we left the group at the top of the slope to assess their fate.

Near the end of the journey we crossed the Jardine River by ferry to reach Bamaga. That night we camped at Punsand Bay very close to our final destination in Cape York. We drove as far as possible to the Tip the next day and walked the remainder of our journey to reach the famous post and sign at the end of a craggy outcrop. What a wonderful conclusion to our trek! This was our third of eight major compass points at the limit of mainland Australia we hoped to visit and we shared a moment of celebration, happy about our successful trip. At this point we were quite close to the equator - just 10 degrees of latitude - and we knew there could be no further progress north in Oz, no more tracks to follow, no more crossings to negotiate. It had been an exciting time but our thoughts moved to our return journey.

We chose an easy means of return south from here, back to Cairns. Retracing our steps through Cape York was not an appealing idea. We could only cover old ground and face the same challenges but in the opposite direction. Our option was to catch the supply ferry from Bamaga to Cairns. Trinity Bay made the journey twice a week and our passage would take two days. She was a majestic conversion from a vessel built in 1911. Our vehicles were loaded into 20 foot containers and craned aboard. Although this was a small cargo vessel, we found our accommodation to be almost of cruise ship quality. The majority of our fellow passengers were also returning from journeys to the Tip, some travelling by motor bike. We left the port at sunset, a fitting end to our travels through Northern Australia. It was a calm evening when Trinity Bay cast off. A warm glow infused the sky over the small harbour. The sun would soon set and Aboriginal children waved from the pier breaking briefly from their evening's fishing. We glided by a familiar coastline to the gentle throb of the ship's engine, watching the white beaches and tropical forest slip away from us. As the vessel moved further into the Torres Strait they became faint lines of white and dark green over an oily blue sea. From the deck we watched Cape York dissolve into blackness.

The Coloured Rocks, near Cooktown

Plate 14

The descent into Palm Creek

The Telegraph Track

Crossing the Pascoe River

Plate 15

Chili Beach, Cape York

Plate 16

Driving 75 Mile Beach, Frazer Island

The wreck of *Maheno*, Fraser Island

Plate 17 Ziebart sponsored

The wreck of the *Cherry Venture*, Cooloola NP

Plate 18

Coast line near Coffs Harbour

Plate 19

Under a sky darkened by bush fires

Plate 20

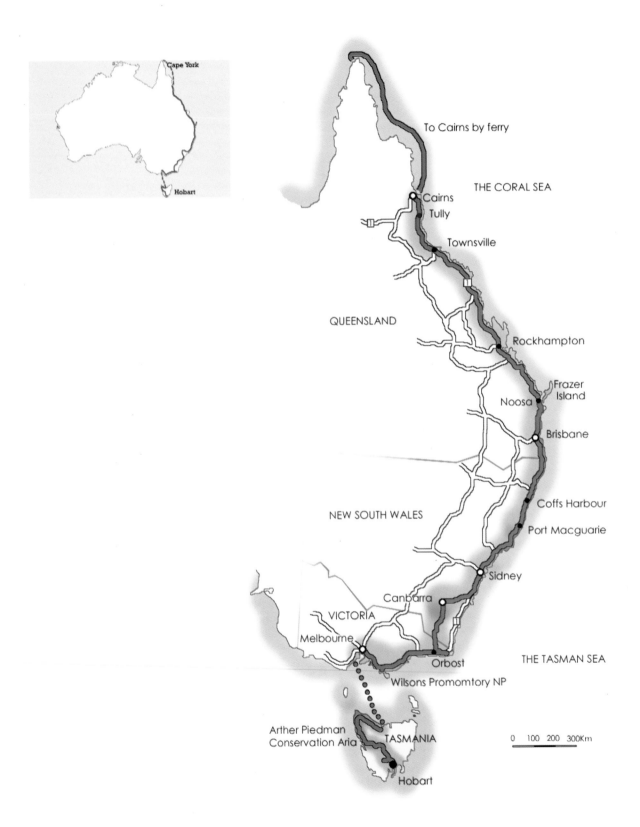

Cape York

Hobart

To Cairns by ferry

THE CORAL SEA

Cairns
Tully

Townsville

QUEENSLAND

Rockhampton

Frazer
Island

Noosa

Brisbane

Coffs Harbour

Port Macguarie

NEW SOUTH WALES

Sidney

Canbarra

VICTORIA

Melbourne

Orbost

THE TASMAN SEA

Wilsons Promomtory NP

Arther Piedman
Conservation Aria

TASMANIA

0   100 200 300Km

Hobart

Chapter 4. Australia's East Coast

Chapter Four:
Australia's East Coast

Cape York was a significant moment in our journey. We had driven over 14,000km during the last three months since reaching Australia. Our relationship with the country had matured during that time and her raw beauty had often reduced us to a state of speechless wonder. But she had also induced a kind of mind-numbing boredom crossing her open spaces. We had got to know her well, learning that she demanded a healthy respect and that she would not be taken for granted. We had crossed the immensity of her savannah grasslands and her rust red deserts and she had been neither harsh nor unkind to us.

The route ahead would be a different experience, following the coast to Sydney and on to Tasmania. We would be on metalled roads if we remained on Highway 1, travelling down a progressively urbanized coastline. There would be less isolation, fewer remote camp sites and perhaps more controls to deflect us from rough camping. We had no wish to lose our sense of adventure by shopping in supermarkets and staying in urban camp sites. Australia had shown us her wilder youthful aspects and we wondered how she could match that, travelling through the sophistication of her east coast. Perhaps we would find new insights to Australia through more contact with her people.

After we disembarked at Cairns, Vic and Heather drove straight back to Sydney. We would travel south at our own pace. Our maps revealed that the coast was divided into sections, the outcome of tourism and regional marketing. From Cairns, the Great Green Way led to Townsville where it became the Capricorn Coast and then the Sunshine Coast to Brisbane. Then there was the Gold Coast, followed by the Holiday Coast from Coffs Harbour to Macquarie. We concluded there would be fewer opportunities for wilderness travel but, with careful planning, we could divert off the main road to more isolated coastal routes.

Highway 1 was becoming a well constructed tarmac road and would rise to urban greatness again beyond Brisbane, finally developing to be of a motorway standard. We thought back to our time circling the Gulf of Carpentaria and to the gritty single track of Highway 1, seeing it improve in Queensland to be a well maintained and plausible highway again on the approach to Cairns. During earlier travels, only one other national highway, through central China, equated to this enormous transformation, evolving from muddy rural track through Ningxia Province to a chaotic motorway in Beijing's urban sprawl, 2000km down the road.

On 12 July we scurried around Cairns, tidying up loose ends before heading south out of town. It had been a warm autumn and the cane crop was ready for harvest through the rolling folds of the Great Dividing Range. Acres of tall fronds swayed in the light breeze, the feathery heads a subtle shade of purple in the afternoon's watery light. No doubt about it – this was a territory driven by the sugar cane industry. The processing plant at Tully was in full swing, and would digest two million tons before the season was over. Harvested cane arrived by the train load with a disciplined order. Heavy equipment in the factory ground the stems into pulp and giant vats performed some unseen wizardry to extract and refine the raw sugar, disgorging a fibrous dry waste at the end of the process.

We diverted inland to visit Paronella Park, a unique and slightly bizarre Spanish style castle and garden complex, built by one amazing individual. José Paronella arrived in Australia from Spain in 1913. For the next 13 years he worked cutting cane, then purchasing, improving and re-selling cane farms. In 1924 he returned to Spain, married and brought his new wife back to Australia. José first saw the 13 acres of virgin scrub along the Mena Creek in 1914. After he returned with his bride he purchased the land for £120 and started to build his pleasure garden and recreational centre for the enjoyment of the public. He toiled continually to 1948 to build the castle, plant the garden and develop the creek into a very unique place. Unfortunately he died of cancer shortly after completion but Paronella Park continued as a pleasure garden just as José intended. The park is a work of art and has gained National Trust listing.

We were acutely aware of the Great Dividing Range as we drove south through the Great Green Way. It was just there, all the time, often crowned with frothy clouds hovering over the summits. By now we were tiring of the repetitive vistas of sugar cane beside Highway 1 and yearned for some coastline scenery again for a few hours or, even better, a night on the beach. Before Townsville we took a small back road, a tiny artery of a track, heading west for 5km. Just as we were on the point of turning back, the coastline appeared through the bushes and Bolgan Beach unfolded before us. Not that there was much here – just a slipway and a small formal campsite set back in the trees. The bad news was that we could not rough camp on the beach, but one spot remained in the campsite, beside Al's caravan.

Al's was not the most modern rig. He was probably in his 70s and for him and his wife this was more home-from-home than holiday caravan. A bowl of fruit graced their outside table and pot plants gave an air of permanence to their patch. Two small dogs yapped their claim to ownership of the small patch of turf by the van. Al was a willing talker and as camping neighbours go, he was congenial company. As he set the small fire to boil water for their evening shower, he talked about his circumstances. "We have been round Oz four times," he said proudly. In that time, he had been through three rigs during 15 years of travel. He needed a willing listener to get into full flight about the family wanderings but he was a kind soul and we warmed to him. He shared his knowledge and advice about Oz that could be useful to us. It seemed that there was a sizable sub-culture dedicated to

Paronella Park

serious retirement travel. The trick was to build up a private catalogue of camping spots which were free and not in any guide book. This knowledge gave a kind of honour and respect amongst the mature travelling fraternity - a kind of traded equity.

Al had real pride in his knowledge, which he shared with us in hushed tones over his camp fire. "The first garage out of Sarina has a great site round the back," he revealed. "Fred will let you stay there if you fill up", and added, "I shouldn't tell you this because the locals keep this place to themselves, but just before Tiaro …" and went on to describe how to reach some heavenly spot on the Mary River.

We reached Townsville at the end of the Great Green Way. The Sunday Market on Flanders Street Mall was in full swing. There was a holiday atmosphere about the place and the colourful centre was noisy with the hustle and bustle of a popular market. Over coffee we decided on an easy option for that night. We would move into the city campsite. After all, we had enjoyed Al's company the night before and there was no telling who we might meet or what new aspect of Australia might be revealed to us in this high density urban site. Besides, Townsville had a pleasant feel about it. After booking in, we watched the sunset from the nearby beach. Later, back on our grassy patch under a huge fig tree, our neighbour strolled over to visit. "G'day folks," announced Mick. "G'day," we replied and invited our lonesome neighbour to join us for coffee.

Mick had spent two weeks with his sons exploring Magnetic Island. But now his bonding time was over and he was returning to work. He was in his 40s, bearded and with the appearance of someone who worked in rough conditions but Mick was one of life's unique people who did something quite special. For many years he had been responsible for developing new schools in remote Aboriginal communities in the far north of Australia. He spoke calmly of the challenges and problems investing the huge sums of government money provided for education in remote areas. His willingness to continue seemed to come more from hope rather than past fulfilment.

"I usually have a staff of 10 to start a new school," Mick explained. Once set up he would move on to a new project. There had been a recent success from Mick's work, opening a Seniors programme at one settlement where the historic skills to make boomerangs and other traditional artefacts were nearly lost. That knowledge had been saved and passed on through formal tuition to the next generation. The products had sold well and the commercial success had helped the village regain some pride in the old tribal talents. The mood was relaxed now and we had moved on from coffee to a pleasant Australian sparkling wine from Rabia's cool box. Mick was unloading some inner concerns. "Sometimes we lose a pupil for an hour – just falls asleep on us – nothing we can do." Attendance was often down to 60% of the qualifying youngsters in a community and aggression was a problem for his staff. Even in the confines of their tribal territory, their own homeland, conflict could erupt between the Aboriginals on a massive scale. "Sometimes there are fifty women, maybe a hundred and fifty men, all battling it out," he said. Life was not easy.

Sometimes, when a school has been running well, it would be transferred to Aboriginal ownership and that was when problems could start. Aboriginal customs on shared assets dictated that perhaps 5000 'seals of ownership' would be needed on the sale document. No-one then took control and within a year the school would be trashed, an investment lost and no-one really cared.

We had heard that individual wealth was assumed to be a common resource within the tribe. In one more extreme interpretation this concept had formed an apology for the high incidence of Aboriginal theft, but here was someone describing the real impact in the rural Aboriginal communities. There was no incentive for his educated Aboriginal staff to do well since there would be dozens of non-working family members lined up to share the income. "What's the point for them to work," Mick said despondently. He hinted at other problems. As Elders retired the status of their younger replacements was falling because of lower respect. Worse still, without a written language the stories and traditions were dying away and the structure of the clans was weakening. We were saddened to hear that the Government's generous but ill-planned efforts seemed to hold so little hope for the future.

Two noisy intrusions broke the calm at dawn. Egrets were feasting around us on an early breakfast of fallen figs, their frog-like croaks adding a discordant note to the morning. Nearby, a camper without much talent was spluttering his way through a tutorial on a didgeridoo. Mick had left for the outback before first light. He had 15 hours of driving ahead of him to reach Mt Isa. Then he would drive for 3 hours over the desolate wastes of the North Simpson Desert to reach the community with which he was currently working. He would be there for some time, struggling to make progress on his current project. We admired him for his optimism, his hope for a break-through in these remote and lonely corners of outback Australia.

Travelling south on the Bruce Highway was easy. We had reached the Capricorn Coast but there had been no obvious transition from the Great Green Way, no change in the landscape to flag our steady southward movement. It was strange though, that we rarely saw the coast, lost to us on the other side of deep greenery or just over a crest of the low coastal range. Our detours eastwards revealed some hidden shoreline but a continuous coastal route on tracks or beaches was rarely possible. Sugar cane still dominated the landscape, a carpet of unbroken olive green between horizons. Our GPS gave us our best clue to our solid progress. The reading crept up the latitude scale, each additional degree offering reason for minor celebration. At Rockhampton we reached 23° south, crossed the Tropic of Capricorn, and headed for the small coastal settlement called The Town of 1770 (its real name) for the night. This was probably the most tranquil place in South Queensland and a beautiful shoreline destination with just one pub and a few shops. We felt pleased; without much ado we had slipped out of the tropical north. We were meeting more people and there was little that seemed to threaten our journey. However, we still had one concern burning away in our subconscious. Where was the adventure to come from now? How would we capture the excitement of something new in our travels? Australia had provided a steady flow of unplanned and unexpected wonders. She had been generous, bestowing frequent thrills and we had become addicted to her surprises.

In a curious twist of fate, our arrival on Frazer Island the next day was to dispel that concern, at least for the time being. The island delighted us for four days and was a profoundly different experience, not just from Queensland's east coast but from anything in Australia. A few words of explanation will help put this World Heritage site into context and underline its uniqueness. Frazer is the largest sand island in the world. Nestled close to the Queensland coast, 190km north of Brisbane, it is still a wilderness. It stretches for 120km, rises in places to 300m and the structure of the island is a testimony to the powerful forces of nature. For a million years wind and sea have carried sand up Australia's east coast to be halted here, forming colossal dunes. But this is no barren heap of lifeless desert. On the island's newer east coast, pioneer forests thrive as nutrients begin to accumulate and the roots help bind the shoreline into steep slopes. Further inland, where the sands have perhaps six thousand years of maturity, the trees grow taller and become more complex, forming dense patches of woodland. On the western slopes of the island, opposite the mainland, nutrients are too deep for roots to reach and heathers and mangroves thrive. But the island's gem, the real wonder of the place, is the lush sub-tropical rain forest that grows in the very core, sheltered in the mature Satinay trees which rise 70m above the dunes.

Numerous fresh water lakes add a beautiful counterpoint. The majority are 'perched lakes' which lie in depressions between sand dunes well above the sea. One of these, Lake Bloomagin, is the largest perched lake in the world and, backed by forest and fringed with radiant white sands, it must also be one of the most beautiful. The island is not dormant and massive sand movements are still continuing. New sand, accumulating on the ocean-side beaches, flows inland forming localised deserts, known as sand blows. The advance is sufficiently speedy and fluid to prevent colonisation by plants and the dynamic forces are not dissimilar to those of a wave crashing up a beach. The advancing sands, travelling at one metre per year, engulf forests and lakes in their path. But as the dune advances, so also does the trailing edge a kilometre behind, to reveal the dry skeletal trees originally engulfed 1000 years earlier. It's a curious experience to see a lifeless forest emerge into daylight again.

After disembarking from the tiny ferry to Frazer Island, we dropped tyre pressure and climbed steep slopes through eucalypt trees beyond the mangroves. There were no surfaced roads. Instead, narrow tracks snaked through the forests on soft sand. Only 4x4 vehicles are permitted. This is sand driving at its best. We were heading for the camp site in the core of the island, a grassy clearing set deep in mature rain forest. In the small hours, our sleep was shattered by the hellish howl of a dingo. After a brief pause, responding calls echoed through the silent forest. There was a full moon that night and from our bedroom window above Rabia we saw the large wolf-like silhouette amble through the open camp site into the darkness of the undergrowth. We heard later about the purity of this strain of dingoes. Regrettably, their behaviour had become unacceptable in recent years through contact with humans. They had killed a 9 year old boy in 2001 so the animals were now culled, especially those who showed aggression near the island's camp sites.

Our travels over the next few days alternated between sandy trails inland through mysterious forests and on white sands and beautiful beaches. There was a profound difference between the two areas. One moment we would be edging round the fringe of a beautiful fresh water lake beside thick forest and soft white sand. The next, we would be driving effortlessly down a flat beach, huge waves crashing on one side of Rabia and coloured sandbanks towering overhead on the other. Beach driving had some unsettling aspects though. In the distance, the flat expanse would dissolve in the haze of sea spray and we shared the flat sands with landing aircraft - a very strange experience. The beach ride was so smooth it felt like floating on air.

It seemed that something new would reveal itself to us in every corner of the island. We walked under a full moon over beautiful sand fields and along knife-edged slip faces. The light contoured the wind blown dunes into exquisite profiles. Some patchy clouds rolled over the moon and the cold whiteness of the sand became alive with flowing patterns of light and shade. By daylight the older sand, exposed on the shoreline, glowed with fiery red, yellow and brown colours. There were wrecks to visit! The sandy shores of Frazer Island have become a graveyard for many ships over the centuries. The most famous, the Maheno, was driven ashore in a cyclone during 1935. Now, her remains lie stranded on the beach, her rusty patina glowing in the sunshine.

The day we left Frazer Island was one of sublime pleasure, a day in paradise for any keen off-road driver. We had camped the previous night behind some low dunes beside the beach. In the grey light of dawn some gentle bird song brought the day to life, not the aggressive banter of noisy parrots to which we were accustomed. Low banks of delicate cloud streamed over the horizon. It was going to be a spectacular sunrise. We felt the life-giving dampness in the early onshore breeze and fine droplets sparkled on the fragile grasses which were invading the dunes between beach and forest. Soon, the sun edged over the horizon and other visitors used the new light to search for breakfast. A sea eagle hovered, still and silent in the up-draught, looking for morsels brought ashore by the night's high tide. He would have to look hard. Others had used the half light to patrol the waterline. A distinct set of dingo tracks were cast in the soft sand, adjacent to the flotsam line on the beach. The paw marks broke into a scatter as perhaps a slow beach crab had failed to make a timely retreat into its burrow. Life was hard on the beach!

There was a brief moment of crimson splendour as the sun cleared into open sky. The crashing waves caught the low light from the east bringing the crests into crisp focus. Spray danced like diamonds in the backlight and then was lost in the foaming surf. Up the beach, to the north, a moving dot signalled the approach of the first beach traffic of the day. It soon passed us, rushing perhaps to catch the first ferry. By 9.00am the tide was falling to leave a flat and even way that no formal road could match. We broke camp and headed south for the ferry in beautiful conditions – clear blue skies, a freshly washed beach and mile-after-mile of pristine shoreline. Heavy surf thundered onto the beach beside Rabia. There was no other traffic and the sense of isolation was profound, almost as if we were the first here. Sea birds gave some sign of life, gliding in the morning's breeze.

We drove to Noosa, following the length of 75 Mile Beach on the island (actually 90 miles long), then crossed by ferry to the top end of the Cooloola National Park. (Plate 17). The beach drive then continued for a further 40 miles along the mainland coast to reach Noosa, giving a complete day on hard flat sand. The tides were favourable - low water was at 1.00pm leaving the harder sand surface below high water mark exposed for much of the day. On the beach track down the coast the cliffs beside us towered skywards, colossal banks of sand washed with vivid colour. The waves still thrashed onto our sandy highway and we saw some whales making their seasonal passage offshore. We reached another huge wreck, the Cherry Venture, half submerged on the open beach, locked forever in sand up to her old water line. (Plate 18). The beach shelved more steeply as we approached Noosa and we drove near to the water, avoiding the soft sand above high water. The tide was rising quickly and if we had a breakdown now, Rabia would be stranded to face the tide like King Canute. But we were cruising effortlessly at a steady 80kph, on one of the best possible surfaces and felt secure. We reached the end and crossed the Noosa River by ferry. We were on tarmac for the first time that day. No doubt about it, it had been a glorious experience.

The next day we cleaned Rabia of salt with a pressure washer then headed south through the Sunshine Coast and found Brisbane an unwelcoming city. The people were certainly friendly and the place was beautiful but the city's strategy was to deter vehicles from visiting. Parking turned into a nightmare and we activated plan B. We drove out of town circling to the south, to find somewhere to stay near a commuter rail station. We would visit Brisbane the next day by train. "There is a hotel up the road about 2km," said a friendly pedestrian near our chosen station, adding helpfully "beside the McDonalds." That set the tone for us but the Salisbury Motel was not somewhere you could easily miss in any case. Large neon signs pronounced its presence, great glaring red and green stripes, but the place looked modern and clean so we booked a room.

Pokies and other Australian Sports

It was quite obvious to us that we had stumbled into that unique Australian phenomenon, the Gaming Hotel. The main building had been designed to offer easy gambling to the local population. Around the bar were massive screens, displaying live coverage of different Oz sporting venues that evening but the bar menu was attractive and we were hungry. Over dinner we watched greyhound racing and the curious sport of 'trotting', best described as a horse and cart with speed. The current odds for the next race were displayed on separate monitors. Liquid refreshment was available. This was a gaming lounge at its best.

In an adjoining area, a video connection to some larger casino elsewhere displayed the odds for the current game of national 'Totto'. '7 from 7' won $9000 whilst '10 from 10' provided $2 million to the winner. The decor was lush but gaudy, a contrived luxury of deep red carpets, imitation chandeliers and heavy curtains. Neon signs lit each service counter. The casino, the bank, snack bar and the pub all got the bright light treatment. Lucy came in with her long blond hair and her high tech cordless microphone, all smiles and boundless enthusiasm. She announced that the client with that evening's winning bar ticket could make two free spins of the roulette wheel. His prize would be $1000 if his number came up. There were 100 numbers on the wheel and the odds seemed poor. He failed, predictably, but Lucy's promotional banter was impressive.

The second greyhound race at Richmond was starting. Bets were being placed and the excitement was mounting. A lady at the bar was getting drunk quite quickly, probably drowning her sorrows. An adjacent hall housed the casino's 40 'pokies' under dimmed lights. These were simply modern versions of one arm bandits but without the arms! Lucy was in action here, visiting each customer to offer encouragement, to announce winners throughout the casino and generally support the steady flow of more gambling cash. The games were intriguing - Gold Strike, Red Chili, The Quest. The flashing lights and strange bells seemed to cast a hypnotic spell on the clientele.

On the wall by the bank several notices detailed the hotels policies to encourage responsible gambling. One read, 'If gambling becomes a problem the financial transaction policy is available to you'. Wonderful! We took this to mean that you could state your limit, after which the hotel would throw you out. As a final gesture of support to help the fallen, the hotel displayed contact details for Gamblers Anonymous, The Salvation Army, The Christian Outreach Centre and Life Line.

Lucy's enthusiasm and encouragement never waned. She patrolled the gaming lounges, broadcasting successes and offering only a friendly smile to a losing client.

Plan B worked well. The early commuter train the next morning whisked us into town and we saw the centre from its best angle – cruising the Brisbane River. We returned to Salisbury and drove south to Paradise Point to stay with friends. The Gold Coast stretched to the south glittering with high rise showy wealth but lacking the beauty and charm that had driven its rise to popularity. We felt sure Surfers Paradise would do little to persuade most keen surfers that this was indeed paradise. But this was the region in eastern Australia where winters were not cold and summers were not unbearably wet, and that appeal had driven the property market to astonishing heights. This was a great place in which to retire or just invest! The next day we continued south to Byron Bay to reach Australia's most easterly point. The headland and lighthouse were a popular tourist attraction and was almost too easy to qualify as one of our expedition's destinations.

We had a growing feeling of finality about our travels as we approached Sydney. There was no doubt about our steady progress into lower latitudes. Days were still pleasantly warm but the air was becoming cold at night. We would be driving the final miles to the city on a superb motorway but we tried, perhaps too hard, to delay that inevitable moment. After passing Coffs Harbour we diverted off Highway 1 to find a coastal route through Port Macquarie to Seal Rocks. The sun shone brightly and surfers drifted in coastal bays catching the odd high roller from adjacent headlands. From the higher vantage points on our route we saw the coastline roll away in a series of wide arcing bays, each under attack from a powerful sea. We camped at Seal Rocks, realising the significance of the moment. This was our last camp before Sydney. By nightfall, we had prepared a fire but not as a luxury. We needed the heat now, to add some warmth to the cooling air. Our frugal supplies of firewood soon ran out. The air was still, almost stagnant and a penetrating cold invaded our dark clearing that night. After all, it was winter. Perhaps it was time to head for Sydney.

The next day we resigned ourselves to the confining grasp of the motorway. Highway 1 had acquired some sophistication in New South Wales. We had been close to its route round Australia many times and sometimes had travelled on it between stages of more remote coastal travel. It seemed fitting that we should drive into Sydney on one of its most developed sections.

In Sydney we again met up with Vic & Heather, enjoying hospitality at their home. Their kindness and guidance added greatly to our time in the city and without their help many of the nicer parts would perhaps have eluded us. The quiet morning walks to hidden corners and dining off the beaten track all added a special dimension.

We had discovered that good timing meant everything when planning travels in Rabia. Australia's north in The Wet would have been impossible and we had correctly selected the best months. Closing the Australian loop during the winter months, would not be pleasant – it would be just too cold in the south. Besides, we had been on the road for four months, driving 19,000km and we needed a break. We were reaching that point when places with an extraordinary quality would become the ordinary. Land Rover Australia agreed to help by storing Rabia and we left for the UK, booking our return for five months time. It would then be mid summer down under – an ideal time to start the journey again. Camping would be more pleasant and there would be longer hours of daylight.

Late summer and autumn in England passed quickly and our time there never felt more than an interlude, a pause to catch our breath, regroup and plan some essential details to handle Rabia's impending shipment to South America after closing the Australian circle. On 20 January, just as the English winter set in, we flew back to Sydney where we were once again guests of Heather and Vic.

One of our first tasks was to deal with a looming Carnet problem. Australia is a signatory to the international convention which governs the Carnet de Passage system. This was drawn up through the UN to facilitate the passage of vehicles over international borders for short periods without incurring local import taxes. For vehicle-based expeditions like ours, a Carnet is essential. It becomes a document as valuable to the car as our passports were to ourselves. For a Carnet to apply correctly, each country must have a process to match entry and exit data and this can be complex. In Australia the country's Customs Department had embraced the challenge with a professional zeal that only a driven bureaucracy can reach. If we overran Rabia's permitted entry period there would be trouble. We needed to extend her Carnet in case she was not shipped to South America before it expired. Perhaps we should not have been surprised that, after all, the system worked smoothly once we tracked down the correct office and completed the multitude of forms. We had anticipated much worse.

Rabia came out of storage in good condition, starting on the first turn of her ignition key. She roared into life signalling, we thought, her own enthusiasm for more travel. Our plan was to continue down the coast, diverting briefly to Canberra and through the Snowy Mountains, before crossing to Tasmania from Melbourne.

However, we had a new problem – South West Australia was alight during January that year. The drought had continued into the summer and walls of fire were rampaging through the region doing terrible damage. Whole communities had been evacuated and 400 homes had already burnt like matchwood in the fires since December. We saw no hint of this before Canberra, ambling down the coast then following a great little track inland through the Badawany Wilderness Area. It felt good to be on the road again but we heard on the radio of the developments ahead. It was a strange experience. We saw no hazy sky, no hint of smoke – just clear blue skies and a lazy landscape languishing in the summer's heat. But when we reached Canberra we sensed a change. We had planned a swift programme here, to visit a selection of the capital's sights that appealed to us – Parliament Building, the National Art Gallery and a few others, concluding with an especially moving Last

Post ceremony at the Australian War Memorial. (It was Australia Day weekend). Throughout that day the blue haze over the city deepened and a smoky odour hung in the air. There was trouble ahead and, with the worsening reports from the nearby National Parks office, we were unsure of our best route to travel south.

We broke camp at Canberra early the next morning and drove to Cooma, the gateway to the Snowy Mountains. We had planned to drive from here to Jinderabyne, to join a great unsealed route, the Bonny Way. This track would take us to Orbost and Australia's most south-west point. We knew we could not proceed from Cooma without information. It would be reckless and irresponsible to put ourselves at risk so we checked at the information centre. Our expectations were low. That morning's fire map showed huge areas alight around our planned route. "All the parks are currently closed," confirmed the helpful assistant. But it was worse than that. "Jinderabyne is about to be evacuated and the fire is burning strongly in a westerly wind over a 300km front," she added, with sadness in her voice. We had an optional route to Orbost. We could drive south to Bombala then divert onto the 170km Bonang Way through the southern regions of the Snowy River National Park. "It's open," said the assistant, not knowing at that moment that the route from the south had just been closed that morning.

During travels in the north, we had seen rampant bush fires, felt their power and heard the crackle of exploding bark and the roar of hot wind. They had impressed us with their destructive speed and the immediacy with which life ceases in the advancing wave. We had no wish to place ourselves in that danger and drove on to Bombala. By early afternoon we were on the Bonang Way finding a track that snaked through eucalypt forests and open farmland. The sky turned silver, deepening quickly to a strange yellow hue and a fresh breeze whispered through the tree canopy. The fire would be raging into new life in the mountains to the west. The dragon was on the move!

We continued driving south through darkening forests. The sky deepened to a shade of dark crimson. We stopped Rabia – something unusual was happening. The wind died to leave a strange silence. The only sound was a mechanical hum from a tractor in a distant field, doggedly ploughing in early afternoon by powerful headlights. The forest's interior was black and nature was retreating quickly, confused by the growing darkness. Two lyre birds, their long feathers streaming like kite tails, flopped over the track in clumsy disoriented flight. Night flying insects clouded into our headlights at 2.00pm, stimulated by the untimely dusk. (Plate 20). We drove on through the eclipse-like darkness and saw no other vehicles that afternoon. It was a strange journey - the fires were well to the west but their immense clouds of fire smoke were streaming high above us and would only dissipate over the Tasman Sea, well to the east. The air was clear, almost fresh and we could not smell the smoke, nor could we see the waves of fire or hear the roar of its advance. Sometimes the shadow of some unseen threat can be more evocative than the thing it depicts. The huge crocodile in Cobourg had impressed us, not by its sighting, but through its ghostly giant foot print. Now in Victoria, the smoky shadow had left the fire's power to our imagination in much the same way. We had seen the dragon's breath.

Victoria remained under tight fire control over the next few days. We drove the coastal route to Melbourne, passing through bleached fields. Higher ground looked like giant sand dunes, temperatures were high and we could not imagine ourselves to be in a more arid place anywhere in the world. Only the odd tree kept Victoria in geographical context. This was not normally a State with such a dry climate. We reached Wilsons Promontory, a tastefully preserved wilderness, and walked the short trail to Australia's most southerly point on the mainland. There was a hot sultry feel to the day but a modest breeze swept cooling air over the cliffs from the Tasman Sea. Although we were still many miles short of closing our circle, this was a profoundly satisfying moment. There were no more compass points to reach in Australia, no more promontories to struggle to. The attempt to reach all eight points during our journey had added a sense of completeness to our plan and it had been fun. Some points had been easy to reach, such as this one, but others had been much more difficult. One had defeated us. The most north-west point had been out of reach on a distant Kimberley beachhead but we still felt a sense of pride having finally been to the other seven. Each destination had overlooked its own exotic sea round Australia's shore and had been a worthy objective, if only for the view.

The next day we drove out of the reserve heading west. Just after Inverlath, we found a small side road that would stay with the coast. We parked at a small lookout for lunch and, as we prepared to leave, a convoy parked beside us and quickly unloaded shovels and large power tools. This was a busy team of people. There was a meaningful, no-nonsense order about the group preparing to descend to the beach. We said our 'g'days' to each other. "Is this a meeting of the Oz professional sand castle builders?" we asked cheekily. They took our facetious question well and we heard that their task was much more exotic – they were dinosaur hunters. Some of the team were professional palaeontologists and they were in a rush, with only three hours either side of low tide to work on their selected site. Their current enthusiasm was fired by an earlier find at this location.

We were looking forward to Tasmania and passed through Melbourne to reach the ferry terminal. At St Kilda, to the south of the city, a long and noisy parade was halting traffic but everyone was in good spirits. The Pride Carnival procession was a happy band of Melbourne citizens with alternative sexual orientations, and what a gay band they were! Lesbian Pride, Gay Pride and other indeterminate groups were here with their most extravagant displays and flamboyant manner. Cheering families lined the road. Cafes and pubs were crowded and balconies were overflowing. St Kilda was clearly the place to be on that Sunday afternoon.

We were in carnival mood ourselves when we reached our ferry that afternoon. We tried, with failing success, to maintain our happy mood through a bureaucratic minefield to get Rabia aboard. We had booked our place on the internet and had not received the listing of terms and conditions. Conflict soon developed during our security inspection. "You can take your vegetables aboard but you must consume them before landing." The thought of munching through 2lbs of carrots was not appealing. Soon, more serious problems began to surface about our spare fuel containers and our troubles worsened. With no prospect of ending the futile impasse, the security staff huddled around our solitary vehicle on the pier. Finally, an officer from the vessel authorised our loading and, released from responsibility, the shore staff relaxed and walked away. Someone else had used common sense and absolved them from accountability.

Tasmania delighted us from the moment we disembarked. She captured our imagination and overwhelmed us with her landscapes. We were planning to drive to Hobart in the south to make a fitting end to our east coast journey. We searched for a good route through Tasmania's wilderness areas, perhaps to circle the island following a coastal route. The east coast bays seemed very accessible and inviting and we would visit those during our return from Hobart. First, we would try to find a route down the rugged west coast where roads and tracks seemed thin on the ground.

Our final choice was the best we could do and our success would depend on some faint broken lines on our maps, through the Arthur Pieman Conservation Coast in the north-west. We hoped these would be tracks of substance. If we crossed that area successfully we could link up with Lake St Claire in the centre and travel on to Hobart. We drove from the port to the north-west of the island and then crossed to the northern reaches of the west coast. We were on gravel tracks passing through a beautiful landscape. We felt the thrill of travelling remote places again, camping on our own and relying on Rabia to take us through. We were reminded that this was what our journey was all about.

The route reached higher levels, often weaving through arboreal forests and between deeply folded valleys. When the track reached the Pieman River our hearts sank. There was no bridge and it was too deep to wade. Then we saw the solution, anchored in the bushes by the river bank - a tiny raft which we used to make the crossing. It was a quaint rustic experience, being pulled over to reach the far bank in the bright morning sun. The ponderous crossing reminded us that little had changed here in 150 years since tin mining had prompted a short lived incursion to the area.

We reached Hobart through the centre of the island, three days after leaving the Melbourne ferry. We had been surprised by the variety in Tasmania. A wide range of exquisite scenery had been compressed into a small area, unlike the mainland where days of driving had often elapsed between sights of interest. Tasmania was proving to be an exceptional destination.

Chapter Five:
Closing the loop – Hobart to Fremantle

Hobart was a friendly place. It had a relaxed atmosphere which almost enticed us into staying longer but we were looking forward to travelling the eastern coastline where the raw beauty had an impressive reputation. We were keen to move on.

Our surroundings in Tasmania felt curiously out of place, almost disquieting. We were probably as far from England as we would be anywhere on our journey round the world. We certainly felt a long way from our home in the UK, yet everything seemed strangely familiar. We should have been looking at a strange landscape and grappling with some foreign language. Perhaps rural China would have been more empathetic. Instead, we were strolling through a city built on pretty British architectural lines, enjoying food of European origin and speaking English with a hint of my own Scottish dialect. Worse still, there was a faint drizzle in the air. It **should** have felt foreign but it certainly did not. We were due to make a periodic test call on our satellite phone and dialled a relative in the UK. In Hobart, it was a balmy summer evening despite the overcast sky. In England, we heard, it was frosty and bright - a good winter morning was breaking in Oxfordshire. We were, after all, on the other side of the world.

Of course, we knew of the colonisation that had cast an essential 'Britishness' into Tasmanian history and our east coast journey started where it all began – at the penal colony of Port Arthur. We were pleased to find so much tasteful preservation and accurate history of this amazing place. Along with the harshness and inhuman deportations, there was an effort to rehabilitate, to provide health care and maintain fair justice. Even if some things were misguided, the Port Arthur penal colony was not all bad. We strolled through the prison buildings, the hospital and the church. There was no comparison with the Siberian gulags where all semblances of justice, rehabilitation and fairness were missing. After all, some of those liberated from Port Arthur helped create a new nation!

Over the next three days we explored the beaches and coastal forests of eastern Tasmania. The weather remained fine and we found good routes following much of the shoreline to reach Mount William National Park in the north-east. Wide bays of pristine white sand stretched from one headland to the next, basking under a warm southern light. The inshore waters of the Tasman Sea were of a richer shade of turquoise than anything we had seen in Australia but were spotted with areas of deep blue where the sea floor had been colonised by giant kelp. Frequent outcrops of rounded granite added form and colour to the shore. On these boulders, a distinctive orange lichen glowed in the bright sunlight. Further north, the Bay of Fires stretched for 15km through pure wilderness, an enormous area of white sand and forest. Captain Tobias Furneaux named the bay in 1773 when he saw a great number of fires from settled Aboriginal communities on the shore. We were unable to drive round the bay in its entirety, reaching only the mid point. We did not want to retrace our route and checked our Tasmanian maps. There was no way through the inland forest from here to rejoin the highway north, but the Garmin digital map on our laptop showed a link. That was strange – in Australia the Garmin maps had been mainly inaccurate and out of date since their information was based on old British survey maps. Every historic cattle station was shown and the old drover trails, but the highways and roads were often unreliable. Here was an old track recorded from earlier times which was uncharted on newer maps. We took a risk, logged the track's waypoints into our navigation system and searched for the start of the old route in the woods behind the beach. It was amazing- the forgotten track was still there, winding through the ancient forest and across grassy clearings to give us the link we needed.

We reached Tasmania's most north-easterly point, Eddystone Lighthouse, which was constructed from local granite in 1889. This had been a dangerous spot for sailing boats. We turned west from here, travelling inland through higher ground on our way to visit Cradle Mountain in the middle of the island. We camped in a high forest that night. The following morning was cold and the valleys held an incandescent mist, which glowed in the early sunshine. On open grazing land, high-pressure sprays fired their jets skywards and great plumes of water drizzled onto bright green slopes.

We reached a high vantage point beside the road before Scottsdale where we met Tom and Sandy who were breakfasting in the bright morning light at this lookout. Their Land Rover was the only other car here, complete with raised roof tent. Their journey from Switzerland had been a two-year adventure and had incorporated only one sea passage from India's Madras port to Darwin. We joined them for breakfast and shared our stories of overland travel. We had always enjoyed these surprise meetings with other long distance travellers and this was a new friendship that would endure. We nearly met up again later that year in South America.

We followed the line of the Great Western Tiers to reach our destination in the higher mountains. It was late when we arrived and we camped for the night in the lower valley. There were indications of a clear night and maybe, just maybe, a bright morning ahead. We rose early to catch the sunrise at Cradle Mountain. The air hung cold and still in the early hours and button grass glistened with a dusting of white frost in the darker confines of Soldiers Creek on the way up the valley. The Dove Lake car park below the mountain was deserted at 8.00am. Only a few people had responded to the emergence of a clear day and the prospect of enjoying Cradle Mountain in startling clarity. There were, on average, only 32 days of sunshine in the

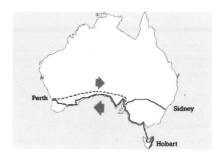

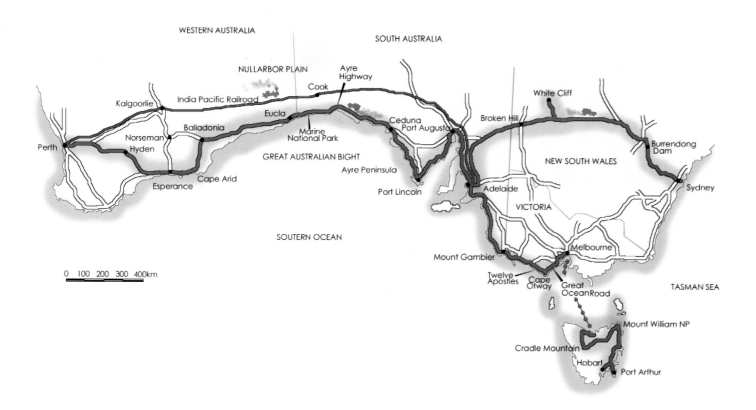

Chapter 5, Closing the loop - Hobart to Freemantle

Rural Tasmania

Plate 21

Wineglass Bay, Tasmania

plate 22

Cradle Mountain Tasmania

Plate 23

The twelve Apostles

plate 24

....and our Opal find!

The old opal fields above ground.....

The Library

Our bedroom   The Lounge

JP's home below ground

The Office

Plate 25

Wave Rock

plate 26

Mitre Peak, New Zealand

Plate 27

year at this place and we sensed the onset of a 'diamond' day. We had stumbled into a few special places in the world where the collective effect within a landscape added up to be greater than the sum of the separate parts. They were rare moments but there was never any doubt that some element of magic was at play; a special ingredient that would coalesce the pieces into something truly awesome. You would be arrested into silence, left elevated in a way you could not adequately explain. The Bungle Bungle at dawn was one such place and there had been others in the northern hemisphere.

Cradle Mountain and its surroundings were to acquire a special significance for us in that morning's sunshine and stillness. There was something more than the peak, the mirror-flat lake and the surrounding slopes. Combined together in that rare brightness, there seemed to be a subtlety that defied description as we wandered round the lake. Above us, Cradle Mountain's granite slopes glowed in different shades as the sun rose higher although some deep crevasses remained in shade, adding form to its striking profile. At times, the faint zephyrs died to reveal stunning reflections on the mirror-flat lake beside us. It was cool and some shady corners retained a veneer of white frost but elsewhere the landscape was washed in fresh shamrock green. Even the heads of the spiky pandanus pines seemed soft and delicate against the rising light that morning.

By mid-day the high sun began to flatten the scenery into something less appealing and we left to follow a route to the ferry through small villages and a pretty landscape of rolling hills, forests and mixed agriculture. The sky remained clear the whole day and we felt sure we were seeing Tasmania's rural scenery at its best. Despite its small size, the island had impressed us. Within its boundary we had enjoyed a variety of landscapes similar to those we had encountered during four months of travel on the mainland. True, there were no massive expanses of red desert to numb the mind but there were exotic forests and beautiful deserted coasts. Rolling sand dunes, rugged mountains and remote lakes were all here. The beaches were, in some ways, more spectacular than those we had already seen. No doubt about it, this was where to find a microcosm of Australia's best places if time was short.

Catching the ferry to Melbourne that night presented few problems. Perhaps we had just been unlucky on our crossing over to Tasmania. After disembarking, we left the city to join the Great Ocean Road on our way to Adelaide. Soon after leaving Melbourne we saw why the route had acquired a reputation for some dramatic scenery along the way, perhaps even ranking as one of the world's most spectacular drives. The road held tightly to the contours of the Otway Range, often high above the coast but occasionally descending to the ocean shore. When the road was built after World War One there was little concession to bridge technology during construction and it still weaves through difficult terrain. The morning was clear and fine and beautiful vistas opened up round each new headland. From our elevated vantage point we saw high waves forming well out to sea. Their progress into each sweep of bay looked slow, almost ponderous, building finally into a turmoil of surf which thundered onto wide beaches. Looking down, tiny black dots raced hither and thither on the advancing crests. Other surfers drifted idly on the open sea, waiting to catch their own personal 'big roller'. It was another gem of a day in Australia's surfing capital.

Gion's Story

When we parked at Cradle Mountain, Gion appeared beside Rabia and knocked on the window. There was no doubt he wanted to chat. His appearance had that haunted look of a long distance motorcyclist. A red bandana sealed his neck from dust above a heavy black leather jacket. Green padding wrapped his legs above his heavy boots, capped with menacing steel studs. The weather-beaten face told of many lonely miles of travel, but under the unshaven appearance, there was a broad smile.

We chatted awhile - his travel story was awesome. He had ridden from Switzerland overland to Australia on a 20-year-old Yamaha single cylinder motorbike, currently parked by Rabia. He had followed an amazing route. After reaching Singapore he had travelled overland through Indonesia and the islands to reach Darwin. No one could reach Cradle Mountain with fewer miles over water from Europe.

Long distance bikers usually have a bad experience somewhere, but Gion was the exception. True, his fellow biker had crashed in Pakistan, leaving him to continue on his own but, apart from changing two front and three rear tyres, he had been free of mechanical problems. He carried one box of tools and spares and one box of clothing on the side of the bike. His personal effects were carried in another bag strapped to the front with his tent and sleeping bag behind him on the pillion seat. This was an impressively light way to travel the world. Gion's personal outlook on life had changed during his 60,000km of travel, in a similar way to our own. "Life should be simple," he said. He had a calmness that comes from seeing the world's poorer regions and realising how lucky you are in the scheme of things

After rounding Cape Otway the Great Ocean Road entered a different landscape. We knew of the sheer cliffs under relentless attack from the boiling Southern Ocean but the reality was even more impressive. Powerful forces were at play here between the ocean's vigour and the fragile limestone coastline. Huge seas thundered onshore, scouring the high cliffs of substance. Over time, that process of erosion had formed the Twelve Apostles – a curious but dramatic set of isolated rock stacks along the coast, rising majestically out of the ocean. Given sufficient time, the giant pillars will become unstable, collapse and decay through the same forces that made them. We were reminded of the 'Flower Pot Rocks' in Nova Scotia where tides and time had formed similar works of nature over millions of years.

We waited in vain on the nearby cliff top hoping for the evening light to catch the profiles in the glow from a low sun. It was windy and grey banks of cloud scudded over the western horizon. 'Grand, majestic and dramatic' were words that came to mind to describe the view but all failed to express their impact. We camped nearby hoping for clear weather in the morning but it was not to be. We woke to rain, light but definitely more than mist! The sky was leaden to the south, dampening any prospect of some startling morning views over the Apostles shoreline. We stuck to the plan, enjoying a few kilometres of cliff walks, despite the flat and uninteresting light.

The coastal route to Adelaide beyond Mount Gambier passes through some sleepy places, which are probably attractive on a good day, but the weather remained overcast and there was little to stop us from making quick progress. Besides, we had a young nephew to visit in Adelaide who was working through his own adventurous gap year in Oz. He had found work in town and was living in a backpackers' hostel. His father and mother had not requested a report about his progress but we had a tacit understanding that we would do our best to perform our role as Uncle and Aunt dutifully and check on his well being.

'Idling to Adelaide' sounds more like a book title than a description of our progress. We reached the city and found the Backpacker Oz Hostel near the centre. The place was friendly but an out-and-out backpackers' residence, filled with the hustle and bustle of young people on tight, low-budget programmes where you could feel the driven enthusiasm, the hallmark of youth on the move. We loved the place but could not check in until the following night – it was just too busy. We shared a few beers with Stephen and exchanged news. He was selling electricity contracts on commission and doing well, he said, earning enough to continue his travels in a few weeks. We left to check into alternative accommodation nearby but arranged to meet again the following evening.

The next day we found the city a pleasant, easy place to explore with a user-friendly street system and a welcome sense of space which is often missing in a large city.   We were in a relaxed mood and in fairly high spirits as we walked up Hutt Street. We had a day free of driving and Rabia was safely parked. Our mood was about to change.

Eileen saw the van nearby, in the car park outside a bank. It had to reverse out, over Hutt Street's pedestrian footpath to reach the road and we were walking along it at the time. The driver's exit was reckless, a high-speed reversal which disregarded our presence in his direct path. Perhaps he was already upset – we will never know. Without Eileen's shouted warning Peter would have been run down. The van reversed on to Hutt Street and paused. Eyes met and a few words of protest were shouted at the driver. A 15 stone brute stormed from the van. We wondered if the driver's determined stride towards us was to apologise, perhaps even to give a friendly handshake. There was no warning of the physical attack that followed. Some powerful punches to the head floored Peter. The attack moved up a gear and kicks to his back left Peter confused and in pain. It was all over in seconds. The driver sped off leaving us both emotionally shocked and dazed. We had the foresight to record the vehicle's number and the police arrived quickly. Two witness statements from shocked onlookers helped to complete the process of Oz justice and we heard six months later that the driver had been caught and sentence had been passed.

We tried to pick up the threads of our day in Adelaide It was sad to think that we had travelled safely in some atrociously risky places around the world and it was somehow ironic that we faced out first physical violence in the relative sophistication of Adelaide on a busy Monday morning. This, of course, added weight to one of our global generalisations, that life is really quite unpredictable but with less risk in rural areas.

Despite our shock, there was a humorous aspect to the attack. We checked into Backpack Oz to await the return of our nephew after his hard day at the office. Stephen turned up well groomed, neatly dressed in shirt and tie, with all the hallmarks of a smart young adult. In contrast, his uncle looked dishevelled, somewhat scruffy after his close encounter with an Adelaide street and worst of all, sported a black eye and a maturing set of facial bruises - they had developed that purple hue that suggests some nasty brutish encounter! The next day, an email reached Stephen's parents with just a hint of youthful mischief, reporting that his uncle was recovering from a street brawl in downtown Adelaide. He hinted that he would keep an eye on his uncle during his remaining time in Backpacker Oz, to avoid further mischief.

Beyond Adelaide the Ayre Peninsula protrudes into the Southern Ocean, looking strangely similar to the outline of a miniature India. It forms a kind of geographic punctuation mark in the landscape before the Great Australian Bight sweeps across the southern shore of the continent. The final challenge of our coastal circuit would be to cross the Nullarbor Plain, an expanse of arresting emptiness with few equals. But first there was the peninsula's coast to follow, hoping to find some hidden surprise. Mind you, we could have by-passed mini India by heading west from Port Augusta to the start of the Nullarbor crossing but we were mindful of our plan to drive Australia's coastline and dutifully headed for Port Lincoln at the bottom of the peninsula.

Perhaps with sunshine things would have been different but a persistent rain made this a dull place. Under leaden skies the landscape was flat and miserable. There was little to impress us on this long detour and rather than camp in these poor conditions we rented a cabin at Port Lincoln for the night. To call the room spartan would elevate the décor well above the reality of our surroundings. Occasionally, during our travels, one of us would raise a simple question that would drive to the core of our predicament at that moment. Eileen said quietly, "What is it that encourages two people, relatively well off in the scheme of things, to sleep on the floor of a Portakabin?" "Wisdom and good judgement to shelter from rain," seemed the only meaningful response. The mood was light and we both saw the humour in our meagre refuge.

Low cloud swept from horizon to horizon the next morning, a boundless expanse of depressing grey. We were pleased to make a swift departure, just to be back on the road and covering distance. The west coast of the peninsula was starkly arid. No rain had fallen for at least two years and wide swathes of dry pasture spread across the country which looked strangely derelict. The dusty yellow land was littered with fallen trees, ancient, gnarled and misshapen corpses, bleached and weathered as if modelled into grotesque beasts for a sci-fi movie. Rain fell in cascades, sweeping over the barren fields in great waves. This was a foreboding place but we should have realised the special significance of the day's weather. This was the end of the drought the community had been praying for and already, the uniform dullness was transforming. Washed free of dust, there was a freshness and sparkle to the place. Within days there would be a hint of green.

The Ayre Highway follows a coastal route over the Nullarbor Plain for most of the way. The journey from Adelaide to Perth is a demanding 2700km, but the arid centre, the region that justifies the Nullarbor's name, is the 1000km at the top of the Great Australian Bight (*Nullarbor* is poor Latin for 'no trees'). Despite its boundless emptiness the highway has a great pedigree. Named after the explorer, John Ayre, who made the first crossing in 1841, the current route follows much of the original alignment of the telegraph line built in 1877. The highway was not fully surfaced until 1976, although the first car had crossed the Nullarbor in 1912. It probably qualified as Australia's first trans-continental highway in 1941, prompted by urgent wartime needs. It developed rapidly then but only as a rough grit track. The timing of the highway's rapid wartime development was in common with that of another wilderness route – The Alaska Highway through the Rockies – which had been constructed in haste by the USA following Japan's attack on the Aleutian Islands. Despite the road's current condition, the crossing still needs careful preparations. The longest gap between fuel stops is a modest 200km but the problem would be the discomfort, inconvenience and expense that would arise in the event of vehicle failure.

We joined the highway at Ceduna and travelled 160km to reach the Nundroo Roadhouse where we hoped to take shelter for the night. The place was run down, almost derelict but for A$85 (cash only) we could have a cabin. There was something not quite right here and we moved on. We were crossing the Yalata Aboriginal Reserve and within an hour we arrived at Yalata Roadhouse, which was also in a sad state, but here there was a cheery atmosphere and the young team of staff were friendly. After eight hours and 600km we were tired and hungry and needed somewhere to shelter from the storm forecast for the night ahead. Contrary to all our earlier information, there was a curious lack of cabins and motel rooms but Dave, the proprietor, rented us a staff cabin overnight in a secure compound to the rear of the main building. We dined with the staff that evening and heard about the underlying problems for the Roadhouse.

This young team from Adelaide had recently leased the Roadhouse from the Aboriginal Community, hoping to inject new life into the venture. Previous management had let the place decay almost to a point of closure. No one stopped here anymore! The Nundroo Roadhouse, back down the road, was currently in receivership as it had gone bust, also through poor community management. Alcohol abuse seemed to be a major problem on the reserve and this Roadhouse, by law, was a grog-free area. Six police had raided the roadhouse some weeks earlier and staff would have been sacked instantly if alcohol had been found. Were we really in Australia or back in Saudi Arabia we wondered? The Roadhouse had a remarkable history and at one time it had been the local pub for those employed at the Woomera Atomic Bomb site further inland.

In the small hours that night Rabia caused us profound embarrassment. Her alarm system, which had been fully armed, signalled an assault. Her strident call invaded the encircling emptiness and woke all the slumbering roadhouse staff in the locked compound. We danced around her in the wet mud, wrapped only in a duvet, trying to find the cause of the hellish noise but nothing would stop her relentless complaint. This was that single event that everyone hopes will never happen to them in a public place, especially at night. It was seriously embarrassing! We disconnected the battery to stop the noise and traced the problem the next day to a tiny switch on her engine bay lid. We needed her to signal an intrusion accurately and a false-positive alarm would not do. This was downright anti-social behaviour for a lady with good manners!

The next day, we would cross the very heart of the Nullarbor and we hoped the character of the place would reveal itself in some pleasant way. Perhaps we would see miles of giant sand dunes or maybe unending gravel planes. We did not know what to expect but we were excited at the thought of what lay ahead. When we left the Roadhouse we could not have guessed at the exceptional impact of the first rains for many years.

Before we reached the arid centre, we saw thick bush washed clean by the overnight downpour revealing a blaze of colour. The earth, darkened by rain, glowed a deep red. Olive green salt grass contrasted with the symmetrical arches of powder blue button grass. Ragged eucalypts rose through this low vegetation, their white stems and fresh green foliage glistening in that morning's sunshine. There was a striking analogy to the form and shape of a subterranean coral reef but here it was in shades of green and blue.

We left behind this landscape after a few hours and entered the treeless plain that was to surround us for the rest of the day. Huge skies and an encircling flat horizon stretched around us, broken only by the occasional lonely tree or by the dust plume from the truck thundering towards us. It was a scene almost entirely without feature. We had not seen such emptiness since the southern plains of Oman. But there was something new developing. The weather was worsening and the sky was lead grey. Low rain clouds rippled towards the horizon threatening to spoil our day.

We reached the Marine National Park where the road passed close to steep cliffs at the head of the Great Australian Bight. Nowhere in the world had we seen such a powerful interface between sea and land. Vertical cliffs dropped directly from the Nullarbor's flat desolation. There was no warning, just a sharp edge before the rock face plunged several hundred feet to pounding surf. The views east and west were fearsome, brutal - an unbroken wall stretching in a straight line, a bleak barrier between ocean and land with no equal. Twenty miles along the coast, the wall vanished into misty obscurity. This was not a place to be shipwrecked!

By mid afternoon we were seeing flashes of sunlight through the cloud, descending in laser-like shafts. Occasionally, the brick red ribbon of the old Nullarbor track, abandoned thirty years ago, came into view weaving a tortuous route through the bush. We had already seen the Nullarbor under unusual conditions, but there was a further strange transition to enliven our day. After Eucla, long streaks of cloud appeared to the south-west, but at ground level. They were initially picturesque but quickly swept over the near landscape in threatening bands of low mist. The Nullarbor darkened and the horizon vanished into obscurity. Drifting wispy grey fingers gave an almost ghostlike appearance to our surroundings.

When we were well into Western Australia, the sky cleared to a deep blue with just a few cotton wool clouds hovering overhead. Things were looking up and we selected a quiet spot deep in the bush near the old road for the night. We looked back on the day and were pleased with our progress. We had covered 500km and it had not been a barren waste, nor had it been lifeless or sterile. The red dingo and its youngster by the roadside had ambled off warily when we stopped. We had seen emus hovering in the bush and there seemed to be more bird life. The 'roo body count at the roadside had been high and reminded us that marsupials were always around us - we were never completely alone on the highway. Road trains appeared occasionally in our rear view mirror, perhaps 5km behind. Soon the monster would thunder by Rabia leaving us submerged in a turbulent dust cloud and briefly sprayed with gravel.

The stars developed with amazing haste during twilight. Orion burst through directly overhead in the growing dusk. To the west, through the stark silhouette of the nearby trees, the horizon glowed bright scarlet. Finally, the full ensemble of southern stars flared into being. A satellite raced from the northern sky, distinctive in its speed and brightness. We retired to bed, sure that the day had given us of its best.

We would complete the Nullarbor crossing the next day but we were not sure where we would be at its closure. We would leave events to evolve at their own pace, but we knew of some interesting 'sink holes' which were worth exploring. These were subterranean cavities formed like inverted mushrooms. The process of erosion was similar to many other limestone caves but the bell shaped inner confines were smooth and rounded in quite a different way. We had seen similar places in the deserts of Arabia and exploring their recesses had been fun. We found one such dark hole near the highway. There was a compulsive attraction into its mysterious confines. The descent to reach the floor three metres below was easy, where cold air flooded from the oily black cavities which radiated from the bottom into the gloom all around. It was comfortable here! The sun was high and a narrow shaft of light reached the drifting dust by my feet. Something moved. A large mound of glossy black and yellow twisted slowly. Something primeval and sinister was unwinding in the silence. In the dim light the form of a large snake took shape at my feet. Basic human instinct took over at that point. I was trapped in these confines with bad company – this was definitely not a photo opportunity. I made my exit not as an organised ascent but rather as one of frantic flight, defying gravity. Had that been a tiger snake I wondered, safely back on high ground?

The next 185km to the old Balladonia Telegraph Station has the distinction of being the longest straight section of road in Australia – possibly one of the longest in the world. The boredom was broken by the occasional dash of kangaroos over the road and the odd sighting of huge wedge tailed eagles, mighty birds with a two metre wing span.

At Balladonia Roadhouse we checked our route options ahead. We could continue east on an inland route to Norseman, remaining on tarmac. Alternatively, we could head south for 150km across open bush to reach the coast but we needed a local input on that option. The garage proprietor offered help. "The track to Cape Arid is open but the far end is soft sand," he confirmed helpfully. This was a great 4x4 opportunity, probably our last in Australia. We set the GPS coordinates as best we could to follow that route and headed south, leaving the Ayre Highway for the last time.

Somewhere down the track we followed a diversion that sealed our fate for the day. We were not exactly lost but were not on the route we intended. More by instinct than planning we reached the coast, passing through a rather blank part of our Australian map. We were to the west of where we intended, but within an hour of sunset we were parked up on a beach, glasses in hand. We thought it was Duke of Orleans Bay but were not sure and frankly did not care: it was a beautiful spot. The last traces of the bad weather front had passed through leaving a clear night. Later, the three-quarter moon glowed brightly through our bedroom canvas and we rose to walk the beach at 2.00am. It felt the right thing to do at that moment. The breaking surf and ash-white beach sparkled with a cold luminescence. Overhead, dark bubbles of cloud, edged in gold, tumbled over the sky in full flight towards the Nullarbor's northern wastes. Why was it that Australian beaches held such an appeal to us? Their remoteness and beauty were a part of it but it was not a complete explanation. We were pleased that these particular shores, before Esperance, were our last indulgence, a fitting end to our coastline journey. They were desolate wild places, full of Southern Ocean vigour, but somehow more welcoming than the brutal ruggedness of the Bight. We had followed the continent's shore within the limits of safety and access for 30,000km. It had taken six months and that plan had proved to be a worthy objective during our time. Our lives had been changed by the experience and we had no regrets – it beat watching travel programmes on TV any day!

From Esperance, we travelled inland to Hyden half way to Perth. We had come here to visit Wave Rock, another work of nature whose oddness held a compelling attraction. None of Australia's geophysical features had disappointed us and this formation sounded too unusual to be true. Other places such as Geekie Gorge and the Pinnacle Desert immediately conveyed a feeling of wonder but also perhaps one of deep religious significance. Wave Rock just aroused a sense of curiosity in us, about how its amazing form had happened. Here was a 25 metre high rock, half a kilometre long, preserving precisely the shape of a giant wave about to break. The streaky veins of colour set vertically into the granite added to the authenticity. All that was missing was a surfer, carved in stone, embedded into the profile to complete its all-Australian freakishness.

There was nothing holding us now and we drove quickly through the south-west wheat belt, across a ravaged landscape beaten into yellow sterility by three years of drought. We crossed Perth and somewhere on the street close to Jezz and Tracey's home north of the city, we completed the circle. It was the 26 February and we had left here on 13 April the previous year. That night we shared a barbecue with friends in their back garden and talked about our travels around the coast. Privately, we felt relieved. Looking back we had taken a few risks, met some truly outstanding people and seen some wonderful places. But, once again, it was time to move on.

You might well ask how we intended to reach South America, our next port of call. After all, we were on the wrong side of the continent to ship Rabia conveniently. But we had a plan! The next day we drove to Perth's railway station. The Indian Pacific railroad crosses to Sydney in three days and is one of the world's classic rail journeys. The route is impressive. It crosses the Nullarbor, but inland from the coast, through the desert's wilder places. Rabia would travel outside on a flat-bed wagon while we indulged in some days of luxury. She would travel virtually free of charge as part of our first-class ticket. This made a perfect way to travel back to Sydney.

We had no doubts when we stepped aboard that the train journey was going to be special and would be more than a comfortable conveyance between two places. We immersed ourselves in the experience from the outset, feeling supremely indulgent. During the first hours we sat quietly in our private day cabin watching the Swan Valley's landscape sweep by. It felt strange to cover distance without any responsibility for progress, just sitting quietly or perhaps being able to read or chat as the mood took us.

The Golden Kangaroo dining car was a unique experience. The décor was luxurious without being gaudy and there was just a hint of discreet historic grandeur. Dining in its confines was a culinary experience. Elegant china and fine glassware complimented the inspired cooking. Eating and sightseeing on the move was new to us, almost surreal. We could watch a pair of wedge tailed eagles glide over the barren Nullarbor during lunch and later, during dinner, enjoy a beautiful scarlet sunset develop, before the world outside slipped into darkness. This was an entirely new travel experience without equal.

Our fellow passengers shed their inhibitions quickly and conversation flowed easily. It was strange, we thought, that this conviviality was missing in other long distance travel. When did we last chat to someone in an aircraft? Perhaps there was something about the hostile scenery outside and our cosy comfort aboard that built a common bond. The staff contrived to mix us socially through their own version of musical chairs and seating plans for meals changed so that each passenger dined with new company at each meal. It was fun! We dined with Joe and Joell, American quality control specialists with a US pharmaceutical company, John an accountant from Yorkshire and a mathematician and his wife who were on sabbatical from Las Vegas. Then there was Wello from Switzerland, travelling on his own. "You need a special relationship to travel with a partner," he said with, perhaps, some past insight. We could only agree with him.

During the train journey we crossed two time zones in Australia, totalling two and a half hours. We could recall that the steps had not been convenient full hours. The train would pass through these time zones but had an elegant solution to avoid awkward clock changes during the train's progress east. The solution, we thought, was quite splendid. 'Train time' was simple. Each night when we retired to bed (and only then!) we were requested to move our clocks forward by one hour. This left an odd half hour to sort out at the end of the journey. But who cares - at least we all had the same time each day during the journey.

Our daytime private lounge changed function mysteriously whilst we enjoyed evening dinner. Through some wonder of mechanical design and nimble work by the staff, our room was transformed to become a bedroom for two, nicely made up with fresh linen. The gentle clickety-clack of steel wheels rolling on rails was soporific and we slept well. Morning tea was served discreetly before we rose. No doubt about it - this was good old fashioned travel and we enjoyed it! We could have become accustomed to this without much effort.

The Indian Pacific stopped at interesting places. There was a short pause at Kalgoorlie with enough time to visit its super-sized gold mining pit in darkness which, in reality, was too vast to comprehend. We halted at Cook, an abandoned town in the heart of the Nullarbor, one of the most isolated places in Oz. Trains don't stop here anymore (except ours). Train staff no longer change at Cook and maintenance and refuelling are not needed. Consequently the community has dropped to four souls. The town's dereliction was both sad and fascinating. Homes lay deserted. The hospital and school, crumbling into decay, were silent reminders of a thriving, by-gone community. The swimming pool was filled with sand and abandoned rubbish but was still surrounded by green Astroturf which looked strangely fresh amongst the debris and decay. How sad it was to see the whole place in terminal decline. But someone cared – a large sign, painted by hand, threatened a terrible fate awaiting anyone who stole relics from the old settlement.

After Cook, the landscape changed to soft red sand piled into rolling hills. It looked like the country's Red Centre. Occasionally some scraggy trees and puffy shrubs added form and colour. Travelling first class had all the appeal of the original Orient Express and until recently a piano played quietly in the lounge during cocktail hour. It was a strange feeling, relaxing in the cocktail lounge, beverage in hand, watching that harsh landscape drift by outside. We felt like voyeurs. There was a sense of isolation, as if disconnected from the world we were crossing. We were distant from it, separated in a way that was quite different from travelling in Rabia.

Rabia's height was a constraint, even with our roof bedroom removed for the journey. She could not continue on the Indian Pacific beyond Adelaide because of low bridges and we disembarked there to complete the short crossing of New South Wales to Sydney by road. Before leaving Adelaide we spent a weekend with Stephen, our nephew, camping in the Barossa Valley and exploring the many vineyards. Wine tasting was fun, a moment of light recreation, but someone had to draw the short straw to be 'skipper' for the day's driving. Australian people had impressed us as direct, no-nonsense communicators expressing themselves freely without too much rhetoric. It was strange, therefore, to see the seriousness with which wine tasting was taken around Barossa. The truth was that everyone was here to enjoy some free wine, have some fun and share a few laughs at the expense of the cellar's profits. Maybe we would spend a little if something impressed the palate. Most of the wines offered were not the winery's premium vintage but the cellars were filled with ponderous discussion about the relative merits of those on offer. Perhaps the British were not the premier wine snobs after all. It all seemed strangely out of character with the Australia we had come to love and enjoy.

We moved on to Sydney expecting an uneventful journey. Broken Hill, although clean and tidy, had seen better days. The surrounding countryside had a thin green veneer, following the rain that had fallen two weeks earlier. Soon, there would be a lush transformation but we would not see that. We had been recommended to visit the old opal mines at the historic settlement of White Cliffs. Local advice had never disappointed us so we diverted north, over rough terrain for 100km. We had stayed in some unusual places during our travels but we had never slept in a cave or worse, in a mineshaft. The thought of sleeping in dark and damp spaces lacked the charm and appeal of a Motel or a Backpacker Hostel or even a Port Lincoln portacabin. However, we were still willing to try something new and had booked ahead to stay at JP Underground at White Cliffs.

Some 10 years back, Peter and Joanne Pedler had tunnel vision. Driven by some inner obsession they decided to make a living out of the old opal workings at White Cliff. Any yield of opals was an inadvertent (but valuable) extra to their plans and what emerged from their work was a beautiful underground home, to be shared with others through their B&B hospitality. Now, 10 years on, the B&B has become of world-class interest and we were lucky to check in to one of their five delightful cave bedrooms. This was a unique interlude in our travels. Their home was decorated to the highest standard offering wonderful cordon bleu meals. The rooms and interconnecting tunnels were painted white and, with a constant 21°C throughout the year, there was a comfortable and pleasant ambience. But you could get lost here! Intricate passages connected neat cut-out rooms and the library, the lounge, dining room and Jacuzzi were all located in their own quarried capsules. Nestled in the corner of the family office was an Internet connection. We had sent e-mails from odd places but never 30ft below ground.

After dinner, Peter's party piece was to take guests through Bedroom 2 and into the network of real mine shafts under his adjoining land. In these tunnels, his mining claim still yields a worthwhile crop of opals, harvested from the thin veins 40 or 50 feet below ground. Some were displayed in his home and sold to guests. White Cliff's heyday during the late 1800s has long gone, leaving a small community which offers a fascinating glimpse into the real outback and its lusty past.

Some claims still remain legal but, unlike gem mining areas elsewhere in Oz, fossicking for opals is not forbidden. Our small opal find at sunset, raking through a spoil heap, gave us a small hint of the excitement which must have overcome many miners all those years ago when real opal veins were discovered down dark and dusty shafts.

The next day, we drove directly to Sydney from White Cliffs. Before we left the drier regions of New South Wales we were privileged to see the continuing effect of the rains that we had endured two weeks earlier. The ground was erupting into fresh life now. Patches of new grass already carpeted the desert in green and trees were showing new growth. The journey seemed to speed quickly to its conclusion. We crossed the Blue Mountains, under heavy skies again. Our last night's camping in Oz was at the beautiful Burrendong Dam and Lake. It was an idyllic place to finish camping but it was a shame that the lake was empty!

Diary Note 6 March. Looking for Opals.

We chased rainbows today. More specifically, we ambled through the old opal claims, looking for the elusive blue flash of a forgotten shard of opal. The tailings from each of the 14,000 small mine shafts remain undisturbed since first excavated over 100 years ago. Viewed from the air the landscape looked like some forgotten World War One battlefield pockmarked with holes, each hole surrounded by a ring of rubble. We knew that this was very different from Alaska's gold mines where the spoil heaps have been sieved through two and three times. Here, the high ring of soft sandstone and soil round each deep shaft has remained untouched.

Opal mining during the late 1800's was simple. You dug down to find a thin seam and followed that lode until it was exhausted. Discarded soil from the dimly lit caves frequently contained missed fragments. During the present time, if no claim remained near the hole (the old wooden posts with a metal tag were the clue) anyone could explore the old workings. Unlike gold mining, the search for opals is direct. There is no intermediate panning stage - what you see on the spoil heaps is what you get! But this is not without its dangers. Slipping down the soft gritty incline into one of the hundreds of square black holes could be a terminal experience. Walking the old mines that afternoon felt much like exploring a battlefield, but it had its rewards. After the recent rain the tailings had been washed clean of dust for the first time for three years. Over the mine fields, many new opal fragments would now be exposed. The reward for several hours of fossicking was a selection of three nice pieces, all with potential. They were found by the briefest of blue flashes amongst the jumble of rock and soil. We retired to the cool comfort of the local pub to chill our hot bodies and celebrate. We were sure many miners must have come here before us to become comprehensively refreshed, after more meaningful finds during the last 100 years.

We were guests of Vic and Heather again during our preparations to ship Rabia to South America. What wonderful friends they were. No visit to Sydney would be complete without climbing the Harbour Bridge. Heather joined in with the exploit - a brave move for someone who suffered seriously from vertigo. But surmounting the bridge's high spots had special significance. Within days of our climb, Heather was to abseil down the tower of the bridge, despite her vertigo. This exploit was a birthday present from a friend. (Think about that - a *present* from a *friend*!) We wondered if this would cure the vertigo, like an arachnophobic handling a tarantula.

We booked Rabia's sea passage to Valparaiso in Chile. Contracting the freight with the shipping company was uneventful but finding a route through the port's bureaucratic maze stretched our skills. We had encountered many unexpected problems when shipping her over oceans and, with persistence, we had found easy solutions. In Sydney, none of the difficulties were new to us but we had more people to deal with, more layers to work through and some heavy-duty red tape to cut. Beside that, we had our own exit to confirm. We had found that it was essential to be at Rabia's port of arrival in a new country after her ocean crossing as unknown problems could arise with which an agent could not deal. Because of her schedule, we would spend a month in New Zealand whilst she made her sea passage and then we would join her later.

On the morning we left Australia we watched Heather's potentially suicidal descent down Sydney Bridge's southern tower. The tiny abseil rope dangled down the stone wall, a ridiculously fine spider's thread against the massive structure. Heather appeared over the parapet. She was no more than a tiny dot high above us edging over the rim. We looked for the signs of someone grappling with vertigo and saw none. Her descent was skilful, almost graceful, bouncing off the face in rhythm with the abseil descent. We said our farewells there and a few hours later we looked down from our aircraft on the same bridge pillar. It was a nostalgic moment.

On another flight, nearly a year earlier, when we were starting our Australian odyssey, we had wondered what lay ahead. We had been unsure of the country. She would be entirely new to us, perhaps a place of opportunity. We just did not know Australia. These feelings had been captured in a few lines sitting in the dark stillness travelling from Singapore. Those words in our diary had come close to capturing our mood. Now we had the answers.

The immensity of her lands had challenged our travels. She had exerted her youthful strength but we had never grown to hate her. She had been kind and we had learnt to love her. She was indeed a passionate being.

"In Australia alone is to be found the Grotesque, the Weird, the strange scribblings of nature learning how to write. Some see no beauty in our trees without shade, our flowers without perfume, our birds who cannot fly, and our beasts who have not yet learned to walk on all fours. But the dweller in the wilderness acknowledges the subtle charm of this fantastic land of monstrosities. He becomes familiar with the beauty of loneliness Whispered to by the myriad tongues of the wilderness, he learns the language of the barren and the uncouth, and can read the hieroglyphs of the haggard gum-trees, blown into odd shapes, distorted with fierce hot winds, or cramped with cold nights, when the Southern Cross freezes in a cloudless sky of icy blue. The phantasmagoria of that wild dreamland termed the Bush interprets itself, and the Poet of our desolation begins to comprehend why free Esau loved his heritage of desert sand better than the bountiful richness of Egypt."
Preface to Adam Lindsay Gordon's
Sea Spray and Drift Smoke, 1876

Chapter Six:
Chile – The start of the Inca Trail

Planning a route through South America was a comprehensively challenging experience. It would have been easy to drift through the continent without an objective. We could have ambled north without a definite plan. It might be fun but that was not our style. We needed something specific that had a beginning and an end, a complete expedition through the continent that, when finished, we could look back on with pride. Many travellers had been attracted to the Pan American Highway from southern Chile, up the coast west of the Andes to reach the border with Panama. Some hardy folk had continued through Central and North America to complete the journey in the cold wastes of Alaska. Apart from one short piece of dense jungle, called the Darien Gap, that route is surfaced all the way.

The Pan Am did not appeal to us. Although it matched our intentions of making a south-to-north journey in the continent, we wanted to escape from its sterile grasp. There was too much to see further inland through the Andes, where the route would be more robust, perhaps offering more variety and scenery typical of the countries through which the expedition would take us.

These ideas evolved to be a proposal to cross Chile, Bolivia, Peru, Ecuador and finally Colombia and Venezuela, but where was the best route? Just as this seemed an impossible dream the final solution popped out from the maps and books with total clarity, a route so obvious that it screamed out "drive me!" It was the Inca Trail, developed by that civilisation to unite their new empire from Santiago to the Ecuador border with Colombia. True, the original traffic had been on foot and with pack animals, but many sections had been so effectively routed by the Incas, so well chosen to link valley with valley through the core of the Andes, that it had remained in use until the present day, at least in a fashion. There was no doubt that parts would be a difficult 4x4 challenge. Many passes were high - over 4000m - and very remote. Other regions were harsh desert where no rain had been recorded. Some sections looked doubtful but dotted lines on our maps where the Inca Trail should be suggested that a route of sorts could be found. These regions were supreme wilderness through spectacular landscapes and often between places of historical importance to the Inca culture.

It was settled. The Inca Trail would be the 'route of choice' at least to Colombia. Close friends, with whom our safety was a genuine concern, asked pointedly about crossing Colombia and Venezuela. What about the guerrillas, the isolation and the increasingly unstable politics? Wasn't the plan risky, a bit bold? Were we not reaching into a place too far? Yes, we agreed but we were becoming more pragmatic about generalised perceptions of safety in specific countries after the robbery in Fremantle and assault in Adelaide, where we might not have expected problems. There were however two very real issues to confront and the first was timing. Rabia would arrive in Chile in April, autumn in South America. Sleeping in the open in the winter was quite impractical. In any case, we had already been travelling for four months and needed a break. We would store Rabia and start the journey again in September, during Chile's spring. That would be an ideal time to travel through the Andes.

The second issue raised more profound questions about whether to continue with the expedition. A number of pressing matters had arisen in England and Eileen had said that she would prefer not to make the South American journey at that time. This meant reducing the team and the expedition would continue with a single driver. There was no doubt that we had worked well together and the proposal to continue on this basis needed careful thought. A new arrangement would require adjustments to navigation, catering and other aspects. Personal safety would be more challenging. I realised how much encouragement and support we had offered each other. Could I tap some extra strength of my own? Would loneliness become a factor? Who would share the good and bad times with me? But there was a burning passion to continue, to see the expedition through. Finally, the decision was taken together. I would make the journey on my own with Eileen's administrative support in England.

To ease you into a sense of perspective here, the plan was to drive 15,000km during three months, largely through the longest chain of mountains in the world. Rabia had passed her tenth birthday a year earlier but was, as far as I could tell, in robust form. (As a point of record, "we" means Rabia and Peter for the journey through South America!). We would drive at a height similar to our earlier crossing of the Himalaya into China but on this journey it would be on a regular basis. To round off this summary - and you need to think about this last point carefully - the driver had no Spanish, not one word. At times, after reaching the decision to continue I had the somewhat tardy thought that, at my age, I was beginning to lose good sense. Others no doubt had reached that conclusion long before I did! Perhaps some self-doubt was a good thing. Maybe even a healthy ingredient of the plan for the solo passage that was to follow.

Rabia reached Valparaiso port on 13 April, coinciding with our arrival from New Zealand. Eileen and I would be in Chile for only a week and had to clear her through customs, make her presence in Chile legal and place her in storage for the winter before returning to the UK. We used a customs agent to help clear formalities. Vinko was a delight to work with and he knew the routine and where to find help on specific points. It was essential to have an international Carnet de Passage to enter Chile and later we would find out how important that document was throughout the continent. Valparaiso's port buildings were tired remnants of an earlier age. The dilapidated customs hall was typical - yellow walls towering to ornate ceilings that had seen better days. Grey linoleum floors, acres of old files gathering dust and old

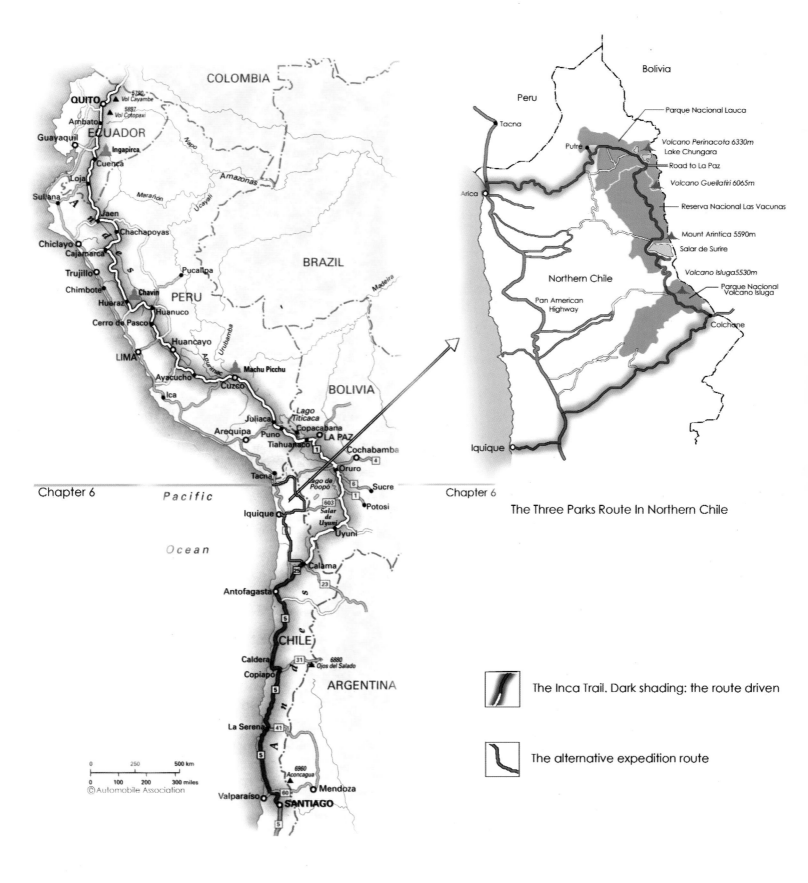

COLOMBIA

QUITO
Ambato
Guayaquil
ECUADOR
5790 Vol Cayambe
5897 Vol Cotopaxi
Ingapirca
Cuenca
Loja
Sullana
Jaen
Chachapoyas
Chiclayo
Cajamarca
Trujillo
Chimbote
Huaraz
Chavin
Huanuco
Cerro de Pasco
Huancayo
LIMA
Ayacucho
Ica
Cuzco
Machu Picchu
PERU
Napo
Amazonas
Marañon
Ucayali
Pucallpa
Madeira
BRAZIL
Urubamba
Apurimac

Juliaca
Arequipa
Puno
Tiahuanaco
Tacna
Iquique
Lago Titicaca
Copacabana
LA PAZ
Lago de Poopó
Salar de Uyuni
Uyuni
Calama
BOLIVIA
Cochabamba
Oruro
Sucre
Potosi

Antofagasta
Caldera
Copiapo
La Serena
Valparaíso
SANTIAGO
CHILE
ARGENTINA
Mendoza
6880 Ojos del Salado
6960 Aconcagua

Pacific

Ocean

Chapter 6

Chapter 6

The Three Parks Route In Northern Chile

Peru
Bolivia
Tacna
Putre
Arica
Parque Nacional Lauca
Volcano Perinacota 6330m
Lake Chungara
Road to La Paz
Volcano Guellatiri 6065m
Reserva Nacional Las Vacunas
Mount Arintica 5590m
Salar de Surire
Volcano Isluga5530m
Parque Nacional Volcano Isluga
Colchane
Northern Chile
Pan American Highway
Iquique

0   250   500 km
0 100 200 300 miles
© Automobile Association

The Inca Trail. Dark shading: the route driven

The alternative expedition route

Chapter 6 . Chile - The start of the Inka Trail

Crossing a pass at dawn

The swag

Plate 28

Camping in the Valle de la Luna

Plate 29

The Oasis of Quillagua

Crossing th Atacama Desert

Plate 30

Vicuna at the edge of the Salar de Surire in the Three Parks

Driving through the Three Parks, Northern Chile

Plate 31

Wildlife, in the Three Parks

Plate 32

Volcan Isluga, the Three Parks

Plate 33

Volcan Parinacota, the Three Parks

Plate 34

manual typewriters, clattering noisily in old-fashioned offices. Finally, the job was done and Rabia was released from the port to the city's cobbled streets. We felt that familiar flutter of excitement when arriving in a new place for the fist time. Driving on a new continent was always revealing! You quickly feel the tempo of the place, catch the mood. You are perhaps more aware at that point of finer details, the things that are different. Familiarity soon dulls that initial sensitivity and Chile made an impact on us quickly.

The traffic flow was fast and daring, almost dangerous, but woven into the cut and thrust of Chilean driving we found a subtle courtesy and discipline. It was not a driving code of wilful aggression. We tried to adapt quickly and tune our own driving to match.

There was a conspicuous contrast between the poor and the rich of Chile which was immediately apparent. The public face of both wealth and poverty was very visible, clearly signalled by dress and manner. We had not seen these extremes since the cities of Asia and perhaps this went some way towards explaining the high crime rates in South American cities. We would have to be on our guard.

There was a good and bad aspect to our language problem which quickly became obvious to us. On the one hand, English was little used and we knew virtually no Spanish, so direct communication was a challenge. On the other hand, Chileans (and indeed all South American people) displayed a very graphic use of body language. They are expressive people, given to subtle use of hands, eyes and facial expression to convey a point. Elsewhere, we had found only one race, the Chinese, who were unable or unwilling to express themselves this way. But in South America this was highly developed and complex and we found some immediate clues to understand a point through body language. We would watch, as well as listen, carefully.

During our first night with Rabia in Chile we checked into a hotel in Vina del Mar, the better suburb of Valparaiso. The crime rate near the port was dreadful and we had been recommended to stay out of town. You will recall that we were robbed on our first night in Australia and so we were on our guard. We set Rabia's security system overnight but, despite our care, history repeated itself. We heard the short burst of her alarm at 7.00am but it stopped quickly. We rushed out to find that her rear quarter window had been broken. The vibration had triggered a short warning alarm and the thief had not opened the door as he intended. Instead he had tried to drag some items through the shattered glass, but with little success. The attack had failed and later that day a small wooden panel was fitted to replace the glass. It had been a useful lesson and the security threat was obvious.

We travelled inland to Santiago and met with the staff of Ditec, the Chilean Land Rover Agency. They seemed interested in the journey and over coffee we discussed how the challenge might work to our mutual benefit. We would help with a press release to promote the Discovery and send periodic articles for their Land

Rover Magazine. In return Ditec would care for Rabia until the spring. It was a good arrangement.

We enjoyed a few leisurely days around Santiago in sunny autumnal weather. This would be our last time together on expedition travel before January of the following year. Behind the city to the east, the saw-toothed peaks of the Andes rose into blue skies and seemed astonishingly close. The snow would arrive soon and Chile's ski resorts nearby would open for business. We flew home to England not sure of what lay ahead for Peter in September when the journey would restart. But beyond those doubts and concerns there was the prospect of something special.

I returned to Santiago on 4 September. It was an arduous thirteen hour night flight from Madrid, made worse by a fractious mood in cabin class. Somewhere over Argentina a glint of scarlet light rose over the eastern horizon. The thundering machine failed to outpace the dawn, drawing out the event for two hours. We crossed the Andes which were still deep in snow and the plane descended quickly. The jagged peaks seemed to rise to meet us. A quilt of mist, the *camanchaca*, had made the usual morning invasion over the coastal plain and its advance was halted only by the wall of mountains, the *cordillera*. The plane dropped through this sea-like carpet to be enveloped in a grey void. It would be a dull morning in Santiago.

The full might of Chilean bureaucracy had disrupted our plans during our time in England. Some obscure by-law concerning car importation had required that Rabia be placed back in quarantine at the port. I caught a bus to the port where I would complete formal immigration for Rabia all over again. Things had not changed. Feral dogs still loitered in the cobbled street outside the office of Pablo, the customs bureaucrat. If anything, his room looked even more dusty and decrepit. Files lay in the same disorganized chaos over his mouldy desk. It became increasingly likely that formalities would not be completed that day, despite Vinko's renewed help. Pablo was in no rush and the clatter of his manual typewriter was frustratingly slow. He looked up from his ancient machine. "Go find a woman for the night and come back tomorrow morning," he said, dismissing us from his office.

The Brighton B & B provided a room for the night. The small hotel was a beautiful place, painted bright yellow with a red tin roof. The balcony of the old building was perched high above Valparaiso's main square and commanded a fabulous view over the city centre. Colourful shacks ascended a steep slope behind the town, stacked on top of each other in ragged disorder. At sunset the broader view was lost in inky darkness but the city below came to life with noise and light. Well after dark, music erupted from a nightclub somewhere below and the evening breeze flooded the town with the smell of the Pacific. By 4.30am a medley of bad music was still disrupting my night. In the early light the *camanchaca* was descending on the shacks which were soon lost to view.

By the afternoon I had worked through some new requirements with challenged patience. Finally, I had access to Rabia and was free to leave. I found her confined in the darker recesses of a damp customs warehouse, buried under a coat of grime. She looked awful, but she burst into life at the first turn of the ignition and we made our exit through Valparaiso's wet and dismal streets. We took the motorway back to Santiago, to reach the small and secluded Posada del Ingles to the east of town where Eileen and I had stayed in April. I had returned here for three days to complete Rabia's routine maintenance and to attend the forthcoming press meeting arranged by Ditec.

I settled in, lost my jet lag and made steady progress through a list of tasks. Some bushes were replaced - Oz had battered Rabia's suspension mercilessly. The GPS aerial was repositioned outside for better reception, but the worst task was left to the end. Rabia's air conditioning circuit was not working well and the problem was a small part, a tiny valve in the circuit. The replacement had cost next to nothing but the work meant a complex dismantling operation. The steering wheel, instrument pod and front facia would all have to come out, along with the central console and then finally the heater unit. All this to change something the size of my thumb! After the job was done, late on the second afternoon, I retired to the lounge to enjoy a Pisco Sour, one of Chile's best kept secrets.

I had a restless night. I was still unsure of my motives for being here. I knew relatively little about the journey ahead despite all the research and study. The inescapable truth was that things could go badly wrong in the more remote areas ahead. Perhaps the lack of company and my poor Spanish were also eroding my self confidence. I needed movement to dispel these dark thoughts. The journey should start quickly now.

After the Ditec press conference the next day we left Santiago. There was no appeal to stay longer and, in any case, Chile was playing Peru at the town stadium that night. Emotions run high in South American football and there was no telling what might happen if Chile lost. We drove round the ring road to join Highway 5, the Pan American Highway. The sign over our exit read *La Norde*. After all, I thought, there were only two directions in a thin country! Turning north was a strongly emotional point, a private moment, broadly similar I guessed to that of a single handed sailor leaving shore. The mountains to the east rose through the city's appalling smog. The peaks seemed to be disconnected, not quite part of the landscape and removed from the drab buildings in the city's outskirts but soon, Santiago's clutter was replaced by green fields and spring flowers. The landscape was full of feature and reminded me of Switzerland in May. It was a startling thought that the High Andes would be with me constantly for the next two months until I reached the Caribbean. Perhaps it should not have surprised me. It was, after all, the longest chain of mountains in the world. I hoped that familiarity would not breed contempt.

Chile, trapped between ocean and mountains, extends for 4300km from the Straits of Magellan to the Peruvian border and is, on average, only 200km wide. The Atacama Desert lies at the heart of the country and is often described as a landscape of repetitive brutality. The Inca Trail follows a coastal route as far as Antofagasta before diverting east to start its winding path up the Andes. Up to there, before it leaves the coast for good, it coincides with the Pan American Highway, the 'Pan Am'. We would follow that route but break free from its confines into surrounding landscapes when there was something of interest near the highway.

We covered a modest 400km that afternoon to reach a camp site, my first in South America. Chile and Peru lie on the Pacific's 'Rim of Fire'. In consequence, a chain of volcanoes blister through the earth's crust, some extinct and others dormant. But another consequence of this instability is the less well-known (and less lethal) chain of hot thermal springs, often in remote and beautiful surroundings. Their location was well documented and the first was Termas de Socos where I camped that night. Over all, I was to camp by five hot springs before leaving Chile and they held a strategic importance. Their hot pools offered a convenient solution to personal bathing and cleaning laundry along the way!

The *termas* was important for another reason. I was camping on my own and had decided to abandon Rabia's roof-top bedroom for something more basic and I had brought with me from Australia a unique contrivance known as 'a swag'. This was the first time I had used it and I was excited to see how well it would work. The construction is a difficult concept to convey, but could be described as a high-tech canvas sack fitted with a mattress. Both ends have loops of glass-fibre rod to hold the whole thing in shape. Put simply, you crawl in, complete with sleeping bag, and zip the canvas closed overhead, leaving the world outside. It became an important part of my journey and was to be known affectionately as 'The Coffin'. It turned out to be one of the most amazing things to come out of Australia, much simpler than a tent, requiring only to be rolled out on the ground and pinned at each end. (Plate 28).

That night's introduction to the Coffin was, quite frankly, pleasant. A full moon rose over the tall cactus on the hillside nearby. Mars, at its nearest point to earth for some time, stood out like a diamond in the clear night sky and the wind died completely, leaving my camp site suspended in silence. I felt infinitely small in the scheme of things and crawling into such flimsy canvas protection was an unnerving experience. I lay there watching the starscape before zipping the thick canvas overhead closed. The end panel was open; giving a good airflow and the comfort inside soon dispelled any sense of claustrophobia.

I rose just before the sun crept over the horizon. It was cold. The air was still and the noise of early stirrings seemed invasive - the farmer's call to his flock of goats, the clatter of horses' hooves on stone, the strident crowing of a distant cockerel. I stood still for a moment and let the sounds wrap around me. White cactus flowers were opening to the morning's warmth. Small birds foraged nervously amongst the spines, searching for berries and insects. Overhead, a pair of hawks swirled and danced in the morning light, flying in perfect unison, an orchestrated performance of outstanding beauty. The sun's warmth soon reached the camp site. It was time to move on and we rejoined the Pan Am to travel north.

September is the season of *camanchaca* fog, which is produced by the Humboldt Current's swelling up adjacent to the Chilean coast. The thick mist surges inland during the morning hours to form a solid wall of cloud which roles inland swiftly. Over the flat coastal plain the fogs progress is curious but unremarkable. South of La Serena however the coastal mountain range, the Altos de Talinay, creates a more dramatic effect. The mountains form an unusually abrupt barrier rising from the Pacific, a 700m high impediment to the *camanchaca's* morning progress. The deep banks of fog rise steadily up the coastal wall during the morning until finally, by mid-day, it floods over the ridge and cascades down the eastern slopes like a tsunami.

I saw the fog rise over the ridge from the Pan Am that morning and diverted up a steep dirt track to ascend through the racing mist. At the summit I found a strange place, something quite new. The mists provide sufficient moisture, equivalent to 1000mm each year, to support a cloud forest here. This was an ecological island, a place of hanging mosses, epiphytes and strange trees. The mists raced up from the ocean and over the crest to dissipate down the leeward slope in a spinning dance. I briefly walked through the forest. Fingers of mist crept through the trees below the canopy; lichen dangled haphazardly from branches in a wiry tangle catching the life-giving moisture and damp leaves glistened a shiny green. I was the only person here that morning and I could have been on another planet. Parque Nacionale Fray Jorge was created to preserve this forest and is now a World Biosphere Reserve. During his travels in the region, Darwin had missed the place by a few kilometres. He had passed further inland, through the region to which I was now heading.

I returned to the Pan Am but soon diverted east through Ovalle, where a dusty track took me over the lower slopes of the Andes to reach Vicuna in the Elqui Valley, away from the fog-bound coast. The GPS navigation system was working well and I was finding road junctions and villages where they should be but, in Ovalle, I headed out of town to the mountains on the wrong side of a wide river bed. I could see the track on the other side but where could we cross? After 15km we could go no further. I descended to the boulder-strewn river bed, engaged low ratio and crawled 100m over the river bed, sometimes wading in the shallow but swift flowing current. I had walked the river first, confident that Chile has no crocodiles!

I joined the track at the tiny village of Samo Alto to continue east up the Hutando Valley. I was now more relaxed and could enjoy the scenery. Spring had reached the valley and cherry and almond trees were in blossom. River and stream beds, flooded just weeks earlier, were now a riot of spring flowers. I camped in a clearing and made an early start before sunrise the next morning hoping to see the valley in good light.

The rough track twisted and weaved erratically holding the contours of the valley wall. I passed through a tiny village, the last before higher ground. The brightly painted walls on some hovels were flaking to reveal their mud-block construction. Soon the green valley narrowed and the track ascended in a complex assembly of hairpin bends and ledges carved into the rock face. We dropped to 20kph and then 10kph to snake up the impossibly steep slope. The Chileans, I decided, are good at making road signs which understate the obvious. Even on this remote track, barely qualifying as fit for traffic, there was a sign that informed me of rocks on the road for the next 10km. "Very true," I thought, as I edged Rabia over the next boulder field. Then, out of nowhere, an old rusty sign prohibited driving at more than 50kph. This was priceless – I was in low ratio with differential lock engaged. Even Rabia would disintegrate at sustained speeds over 30kph here.

We peaked out at 2033m. The ridge summit was basking in bright sunshine and I made breakfast under an impossibly blue sky. To the north, the track descended to the Elqui Valley some 40km away. The snows on higher peaks glistened and sparkled. I looked down on a blanket of *camanchaca* where the coast should be. On the side of the track at the summit, colourful artificial flowers covered a small shrine. It was built in the form of a small clay oven, a monument to a lost life. A name was inscribed in the clay and inside there was an ancient unopened bottle of beer, a half burnt candle and some dusty personal mementoes to someone's past. I began to sense that the Chileans had respect for the dead that went beyond pure Catholicism, perhaps to something deeper and older.

Descending to Vicuna was slow but less demanding. Soon, the silver dome of the famous El Tolodo Observatory appeared high on a mountain pinnacle away to the north-west of my route. Its four metre telescope was the largest in the southern hemisphere, until astronomers built a new giant one north of here. Away from the coastal fog these Andean foothills have a crystal clear atmosphere, ideal for astronomy and a new range of overwhelmingly large telescopes are planned.

The Elqui Valley was green with vineyards erupting into spring growth. The crop from the valley is used to make Pisco. The method has evolved from earlier brandy distillation technology and was used in both Peru and Chile following the Spanish influence in South America. There was a rivalry between the countries and Chile renamed a town in the valley as Pisco in a political move to claim the moral rights to the brand.

I found a camp site outside the town and returned to Vicuna for some urgent shopping. My search for cooking gas failed since the cylinders did not fit the Chilean recharging connections. I needed a solution quickly, but it would not be in Vicuna. A procession of children down the narrow main street stopped my progress. School had closed for the term that day and there was something vaguely disquieting about the procession – 300 metres of little children in crisp uniforms marching in step to drums. It all seemed very military.

The observatory above Vicuna was open to the public that evening. A convoy of cars set out after dark to drive to the building on the high plateau above the town. Soon the whole sky was jet black and Mars came into vision long before the constellations. The observatory staff were enthusiastic professionals and conducted the tour of the night sky with passion, picking out interesting places in the cosmos through the telescope. I could not grasp fully the idea of a star's distance measured in tens of millions of light years. It was too perplexing to observe something so clearly, which was outside my own frame of time and space. I had come to enjoy the constellations of the southern hemisphere and it was fun just watching from the grassy bank outside the dome. I could now understand the story I had heard the day before, the tale embedded in Aymara mythology, predating the Inca civilisation, that if the stars of the Milky Way fell to earth the sky would collapse. Hadn't I heard this earlier in Oz as an Aboriginal story? By 11.00pm the moon was rising quickly to obscure the finer details and I returned to my camp site.

The next morning we returned to the coast down the Elqui Valley, through fields of papaya, avocado and maize. We turned north at Serena, onto the Pan Am. There was a thousand kilometres of the Inca Trail ahead to reach Antofagasta, through the Atacama Desert. The next two days were unremarkable but for one travel innovation, prompted by the shortage of gas. Cooking was becoming a challenge and the business of sorting a menu after a hard day's drive was a chore. All I wanted was to relax, eat quickly and enjoy my surroundings before sunset. I knew I had lots of heat in the engine during the day but how could I capitalise on that? I had the top of a used disposable barbeque in Rabia, a section of wire mesh perhaps 18" x 12". This was bent to make a frame over the hottest spot in the engine, directly above the exhaust manifold. There was enough space in the U-shaped mesh to hold food which could cook there and 'Engine Compartment Meals' (ECMs) were born.

I initially tried wrapping meat in foil but that failed. Too much heat was reflected. Plastic bags also failed – they simply melted leaving a mess of food on the exhaust which smelt of tantalising flavours inside the car before turning to carbon. Finally, oven bags worked well and were sufficiently resilient to the heat. I soon found that slow cooking enhanced the quality of the meat, tenderising it and adding flavour as it braised in its own juices beside Rabia's hot engine. This was similar, I thought, to Moroccan tajine cooking. But ECMs needed some planning. The bag containing the meat-of-the-day, some olive oil and spices, was placed in the engine late morning to cook slowly during the day's drive. Later in the journey, even after solving the gas supply problem, ECMs remained the cooking method of choice in South America, becoming ever more sophisticated with vegetables, rice and pasta and the choice of meat became more exotic as the journey moved north. Beyond the everyday choice of steak, chops and sausages, more interesting ECMs evolved using goat, guinea pig and even alpaca. Often, in remote Peru and Ecuador, the type of meat in the local market was not obvious. My Spanish never overcame that challenge, even with the help of animal photos in my guide book. In one very poor remote place in Venezuela I was sure I bought donkey or mule meat but could never be certain. It tasted fine the following evening, cooked with herbs in copious quantities. I thought that if a community was selling its donkeys it must be, in some measure, wanting.

I move too far ahead! Returning to the Atacama, I left the Pan Am again to reach the deserted silver mining town, Chanarcillo, in the hills. I was hoping to cross from here into the Rio Copiapo Valley, where there was an isolated Inca copper foundry which was not often visited. I wanted more exposure to these places, to try and understand the people whose road I was now following. Pablo, the only resident in the remains of Chanarcillo, lived there with his goats and gave me a friendly welcome. Not many people came here. We had no common language but he indicated trouble ahead on the 30km track to the adjoining valley. I camped above the ruins and knew there could be no-one, apart from lonely Pablo, within 20km. The next morning I struggled for a while but the track was too dangerous on my own and I returned through the ruined town. I passed Pablo tending his flock. He was a regal figure standing there, his ebony faced capped by a wide straw hat. My thumbs-down sign brought a broad smile to his wrinkled face and his body language was clear – I told you so!

At Capiapo the Pan Am turned inland to an area of bleak desert. This far north, the track became narrow and often potholed. There was no sign of life, no occasional shrubs and no hint of human presence. Small shrines were numerous by the roadside, often ornate structures painted in bright colours. All were adorned with loving tokens and mementoes from the life of the person who had died. Trees were planted by some shrines – a curious innovation when you remember that the Atacama is the driest desert in the world. No rain falls here – ever! The trees survive because people stop to top up a small container tied to their trunks. At their bases, a tiny hole drips water onto the roots. Some trees were mature, perhaps five metres high, and had been there for many years, maintained only by passing drivers. My concern though was why so many people had died on this desert road. Boredom and tiredness must have been part of that explanation.

We reached the outskirts of Antofagasta in two-and-a-half days from the Elqui Valley. From here the route of the Inca Trail turned inland permanently, through the heart of the Atacama to cross the cordillera into Bolivia. I drove to Calama before climbing quickly into the mountains. But first I diverted south from the town through the desert to San Pedro de Atacama, beside the vast expanse of a dried lake, the Salar de Atacama.

On the way I stopped briefly on an empty plain under huge blue skies. A wild dog suddenly appeared from nowhere to watch me with doleful eyes. I shaved, ate a late breakfast and prepared the ECM for that evening. Fido lurked closer. It was surreal – she and I seemed the only living things in this infinity of desert. She was heavily pregnant and her sad expression and emaciated body demanded immediate and comprehensive sympathy from me. Not for the first time (or the last) in South America a pitiful dog artfully begged my meal for the day. Driving on, Delius on the cassette player seemed out of place and was replaced with something more vigorous and harsh. We crossed a ridge and saw the road tapering to a point 30km ahead. The white thread glistened brilliantly within a boundless emptiness. By noon the heat had risen. Dry scorching earth loomed up and lost itself in a heat haze. A truck far ahead glided silently in mid-air above a shimmering mirage.

We reached an altitude of 3400m just before San Pedro and diverted into the Valle de la Luna for the night. I fumbled around for a while, disoriented in a strange moonlike landscape surrounded by fearsome ridges and rugged peaks, to find a good place to sleep. (Plate 29). That night I slept fitfully feeling the pulse beat in my head, just on the edge of a headache. I dreamt with amazing clarity in full Technicolor and in complex detail. These were the first minor symptoms of altitude sickness. I needed time to adjust or the soroche would hit me. A high altitude headache would be no fun.

The Valle de la Luna is a major attraction for visitors to San Pedro, a place of exquisite ruggedness and soft sand dunes full of colour and form. But its popularity is at sunset when crowds climb the dunes and perch on high crests to watch the sun go down over a wild barren landscape. The next morning the place was deserted before dawn. The air was cold, just above freezing, but I saw the sunrise on my own from the same vantage point which had been crowded with 200 people the evening before. To the south, the Salar de Atacama's massive plain of dried salts glistened like a snowfield in the sun. Nearby, the pinnacle of Volcan Licancabur's 6000m summit dominated the view. The profile that morning was dark and seemed to be a place of smouldering malevolence. I looked down to see Rabia as a tiny dot in a pandemonium of rock and sand. It was beautiful!

The town of San Pedro had been an important crossroads for over 2000 years, right at the apex of cross-desert commerce. More recently, when the mineral mining industry was developing in northern Chile during the 1800s, cattle for the mines crossed the Andes from Argentina to reach San Pedro where they revived before they were herded over the Atacama. Tourism now dominates the town but it remains a quaint and placid oasis of adobe homes where electricity is only available after sunset for five hours. I felt at home here and could relate to the place. I called Eileen from a phone booth, visited one of South America's finest museums and swam in yet another pleasant hot stream high above the town. I saw a flock of flamingos on pools beside the salar and joined the colourful festivities in the tree-lined town square. Chile's annual holidays had started that day and were the reason for splendid parades, long speeches and military music performed in noisy but disciplined order.

I left San Pedro to return to Calama before my ascent to reach the Bolivian border, but there was bad news. Problems were developing in Bolivia. Farmers were protesting, roads were blocked and people were being hurt. I had only one option – to travel further north in Chile to Iquique, slow the pace and assess options in a few days. If Bolivia returned to normal, I could cross from Iquique and join the Inca Trail.

Later in the day, travelling the upper wastes of the Atacama, Quillagua appeared from nowhere. (Plate 30). One moment there was a barren wilderness by the road, the next a green valley appeared over a lip of sand. A stream that originated in the snows of the Andes, ran through the oasis providing sustenance. I could not recall a more striking contrast between two landscapes. But perhaps one of the great virtues of driving through emptiness is that you get disproportionately excited about something quite normal.

That night I camped off the highway in another oasis called Pica, well into the Andes. I found a restful spot in a lemon grove overlooking the massive desert I had just crossed. The town was in festive spirit. The plaza was quiet but was poised to celebrate the holiday season later that evening, probably until sunrise. It would be a night of boisterous music and dance. I ambled through the plaza's manicured gardens and was reminded again that Chile has a passion for signs. Each plot of greenery had a small plaque with a simple but direct message. "Don't pick the flowers." "Do not walk on the grass." Then one said, with splendid simplicity, "Do not urinate on the greenery." I was beginning to understand Chile. Pinochet's legacy of discipline still prevailed.

I reached Iquique the following day, over a deadly stretch of the Pan Am littered with deep un-repaired potholes. I diverted off the road to relieve the day's stress and to see Chile's most famous geoglyphs. Massive figures of animals, deities and birds were etched into a hillside. Hundreds of these forms rose to 200m along a slope perhaps 2km long. They had been formed during the first millennia by a civilisation that pre-dated the Incas and who saw artistic value and meaning in these shapes. It was an impressive display and, as far as I could tell, their significance was not fully understood.

I passed a few days in Iquique waiting for Bolivian politics to settle and whilst there I learned to paraglide. I had always wanted to fly and, on my last day, made a solo flight soaring over the slopes behind the town at 1000m accompanied, not by eagles, but by a number of large vultures. Maybe they knew something about hang gliding here that no-one had told me! Things did not improve in Bolivia. Roadside battles were regular occurrences. Social unrest had moved forward a notch or two and people were dying in the struggle. Along with that set back, some border crossings were closed. In a curious turn of fate a rewarding plan developed for onward travel. After driving north within Chile I would join the Inca Trail again at Lake Titicaca in Peru. This plan had a bonus, one of those opportunities that happen by accident. There were three National Parks in the very north of Chile, each an area of pure wilderness in the High Andes. Their borders adjoined but access to each park seemed to be through tracks which ascended from Chile's coastal plain and was only possible with a 4WD vehicle. What if a route could be found to link all three parks but from south to north, staying in the Andes? That would be a fantastic journey but maps were not helpful. No route seemed to exist or, at best, was vague. There was an additional complication. From Iquique I would travel over 400km before the next petrol station. Was there somewhere on the route where I could buy additional fuel?

The information about the parks described a wilderness, an irresistible attraction for me. The Altiplano was a broad plateau with an average elevation over 4000m set amongst a chain of spectacular volcanoes. The three parks had been set aside as wild life reserves largely to protect the unique and plentiful supply of surprisingly docile wildlife: vicunas, alpacas and llamas which were all related to the camel family. Even the South American ostrich, the rhea, roamed the plains and flamingos nested during the summer months on the Altiplano lakes. Scattered throughout these vast plains were unique wetlands including desolate salt flats, brightly coloured mineralised lakes and marshy *bofedales* – meadows of bright cushion plants set in damp valleys. Yes, I thought, that route north would be an adventure and a fitting climax to my time in Chile, provided I could find a route that linked the parks.

We drove east from Iquique to Colchane, a spartan adobe village cocooned in High Andes peaks. The journey had been tough, crossing the Atacama and then ascending into the mountains. Llamas roamed the street, oblivious to traffic and it was cool. I found the local petrol station! A mature lady in colourful clothes sold me 20litres of petrol from a drum stored in a shack beside her home, measuring out the precious supplies with a five litre jug. I set off to explore the first park, Parque Nacionale Volcan Isluga, to probe for a route through. Soon, I reached Equela, a partially deserted village beside a *termas* rising from the volcanic plain. I camped here, swam and washed in the *termas* and dined on 'Casserole a la Volcan Isluga', an ECM which had cooked to perfection. At sunset temperatures plummeted in the manner of things at 4000m. Volcan Isluga, towering above the Altiplano, burst into colour in the sun's final glow. Escaping fumes and steam bellowed high into the cold air. I had never camped beside a volcano before. (Plate 33).

It was a freezing night but by the *termas* a measure of warmth permeated the ground under the Coffin. In the morning I was apprehensive and disproportionately concerned about finding a route to Salar de Surire that day. During the morning we passed abandoned but beautiful terraced hillsides which had been adopted quickly by brush and cacti. Some small villages were deserted and their decay added to my feeling of isolation. *Bofedales* swept over sheltered valleys turning them into lumpy pastures. Herds of llamas and alpacas grazed in bright yellow grasses, unconcerned about Rabia's passage close by. Pairs of large Andean geese lurked on the *bofedales*, warming in the new sunlight and preparing to set up home for the season. A long tailed rabbit bounced over the track. I was not alone after all, the place was seething with wildlife.

By mid morning we had passed into the park's northern limit. A track of sorts continued north through a terrain of boulders and steep inclines. We carried on not sure if this led anywhere. After some time the route reached a pass at 4700m. To the north the flat white basin of the Salar lay some 10km ahead in the next park. It seemed we were through! The view was stunning. Towering volcano cones dominated the horizon in all directions, some gently puffing smoke. To my right I saw snow in a shaded gulley. The Altiplano between the peaks was vast, a landscape of subtle green and yellow under a sky of overwhelming blue. From this elevation I could see the herds of wild animals grazing in the wide emptiness below and I thought the African veldt could not be more impressive.

We descended to the salt flat. Rabia told me through the quiet resonance of her engine that she was not stressed by the altitude. I felt relieved, confident that I could now link the remaining parks. I had never been so isolated in South America but I felt elated. The place was casting a spell over me.

On the shores of the *salar* a herd of tiny vicunas scurried over the track, each looking as close to Bambi as any member of the camel family could. There was another *termas* at the east end of the *salar* where we stopped for the rest of the day. The turquoise water of the pool was a comfortable 60°C and steamed in the cool air but it was blustery and it would be cold that night. I hoped to find more shelter elsewhere.

I left the pool, driving over the salt flat to reach the edge of the *salar* 100m away. Disaster struck! Rabia's left rear wheel broke through the salt crust into black oozing mud. Her descent was halted only when the chassis rested on the crust. I had little understanding of the physical structure of the *salar* and knew nothing about the fragile crust. Other vehicles came here regularly but Rabia's two and a half tons was too much. The expression 'skating on thin ice' took on new meaning. Then her front wheel started sinking and I knew instantly we were in serious trouble. It was getting dark and cold. A strategy was required urgently. I emptied Rabia of most heavy things and set out the Coffin for the night in the shelter of a small wall by the *termas*, leaving further work until daylight.

It was a long and dreadful night. To add to my anxiety, I heard a smuggler's vehicle driving by along the shore without lights, travelling on a mountain route from Bolivia into Chile. The cargo was probably drugs. The temperature had dropped to minus 3°C and in the morning the Coffin was white with frost. At first light I rose to face the drama. The air was still and the steam, rising from the hot waters beside me, was spiralling skyward to become a frozen dancing haze. It felt like a cold version of Dante's Inferno. I had planned a way to release Rabia during the long night. Expressed in simple terms, I jacked up her chassis bit-by-bit, supporting her on a frame of stout planks built from a dismantled picnic table which had been near the *termas*. I then had access to Rabia's axles and jacked up each of the sunken wheels to be supported by lava blocks taken from the wall I had slept by. Then I removed the wheels giving access to the black mud into which the wheels had sunk. I built a narrow road of sorts under the water and mud using more lava blocks from the wall then replaced the wheels and removed all the supports below the axles and chassis. Rabia's wheels dropped down onto the rocks. Before they could sink further I reversed quickly taking her onto a firmer crust. Altogether it took six hours of hard work. I had relieved the numbing cold from my body by immersing myself in the *termas* periodically. At the end, there was black mud to clear from my clothing and from Rabia, as well as reassembling the sturdy picnic table. I could not leave it in ruins.

The journey continued through a landscape of increasing grandeur. Volcan Parinacota's snow-capped peak appeared far away over the horizon. That would be my destination that day, where I could leave Parque Nacionale Lauca by the main road from La Paz to the coast. Volcan Guallatire appeared nearby adding to the late afternoon's panorama. Following instinct, I turned on to a tiny trail, no more than wheel tracks, aiming for Lake Changarra by the highway. According to the GPS, that would be more direct. Meanwhile, Parinacota rose in size to dominate the view at the end of a long and hard day. We reached a pass high on the Altiplano at 4700m. It was desolate, remote and spectacular. A herd of llamas, numbering in the hundreds, paraded by to reach a sheltered area for the night. Below, the lake was covered in flamingos, flocking noisily in the late afternoon sun. I had covered only 120km that day. I felt fully acclimatised to the altitude, almost elated by it and, despite the arduous start, it had been the best drive in Chile.

We descended to the lake, joined the highway and turned east. I stayed for the night at a *Refuge* near Volcan Parinacota, sharing the small wooden building with two volcanologists who were there to check, along with other things, when the snowy peak would next erupt. The temperature dropped to minus 15°C that night and I was glad I was not sleeping out of doors at that altitude. We chatted quietly by a small stove into the late hours. I was enjoying my first night indoors in a bed since Santiago, sixteen days earlier.

Chile's border with Peru was only a few miles away to the north but we had to descend to Arica on the coast to make our crossing at a formal border post. On the way down to Putre the next day I had a warm sense of satisfaction. The crossing of the three parks had worked well. It had only been 250km from south to north but I had seen a fabulous wilderness in ideal weather. I had been reduced to speechless wonder at the wildlife and I was certain I had enjoyed one of the best 4x4 routes in South America.

At Putre I met with Barbara Knapton, an American biologist who had lived there for twelve years, providing a specialist guiding service for visitors to the

Altiplano. I had refrained from drinking any alcohol during my journey above 4000m altitude and whilst savouring my first Pisco Sour for four days, I told Barbara of the mysterious vehicle at the Salar, which had passed like a phantom in the night. "It was definitely a drug shipment," she said. "Probably a million dollars passed you and they are ruthless people," adding that someone had been killed by smugglers at the same hot springs the previous year.

I dined out at Putre, also a 'first' since Santiago. The alpaca meat was tough, not as tender as an ECM, but the sauce was inspired.

We descended down to Arica and camped on the beach before making the crossing into Peru. I had time to reflect on my journey through Chile. Her people had surprised me, seeming not able to confront their past political turmoil. Perhaps they were numbed by events during Pinochet's time, or perhaps they feared the latent force of the military which still lurked in the background of power and who had not yet deferred to the new political hierarchy. I did not know the answer, but no-one would freely express a view. Chile had indeed been a long and thin place but with breathtaking scenery and the journey had flowed through it with a natural rhythm. I had been sad to see the dilapidation of country-side villages. I was pleased that I had been forced away briefly from the Inca Trail but I would rejoin it in Peru. Chile had revealed much to me over three weeks and I was content. The Sunday crowds returned to Arica and left me to enjoy the thunder of an incoming Pacific tide.

"I was never less alone than when by myself."
Edward Gibbon's
Memoirs of my Life and Writings (1796)

Chapter Seven:
Peru, Ecuador

I was glad that the border crossing into Peru was quick and trouble free. We had a difficult day ahead which would involve some serious driving in order to rejoin the Inca Trail and we needed to get underway. In my impatience to start the ascent, I got lost in my first Peruvian town, Tacna. The GPS had got us to the centre but then I failed to find the correct exit road into the lower Andean mountains. Peru, I concluded, lacked the Chilean flair for road signs. I crossed the city's maze-like streets with growing frustration until I saw the scar of a route rising up the slope behind the town and managed to trace its origins.

There were three waypoints on our route plan to reach Lake Titicaca where I would link up with the Inca Trail. The first of these was 170km from Tacna as the crow flies and for the next two hours that distance remained tenaciously between 170 and 160km as we edged higher up the mountain in second gear. The route, designed essentially to gain height, spiralled backwards and forwards, failing to take us east but rising impressively out of the Peruvian coast. By late afternoon we were seriously high again and making encouraging progress but I could not believe the figures. We had risen from 500m to 4500m in three hours. I was at 15,000 feet, 2.8 miles high. The air was cool and thin, the scenery rugged and barren and the mountains still rose ahead in all shades of opaque blue.

A new challenge entered our journey that day, the third dimension of elevation that would dominate much of our route north in Peru on the Inca Trail. We would have to get used to it – the mountains would not go away! Just before sunset we were crossing a vast open plain at 4600m. There was no prospect of reaching Lake Titicaca before nightfall. The route ahead was still rising and looked too inhospitable. One of our golden rules was not to drive in the dark and anyway dinner was ready. I camped by a desolate hut hoping for some protection during the night ahead.

At sunrise the temperature was still below freezing but during the night it had dropped to a startlingly low -10ºC. The Coffin had a coating of white frost and despite my warm Canadian sleeping bag, it had been chilly. My first night in Peru had been memorable! We broke camp and drove on quickly, to enjoy breakfast in the sunshine later. We reached the lake that morning, passing scattered adobe homes in sad decay in the mountains. Farming at altitude, it seemed, had lost appeal against the attractions of city life. It was depressing to see these little homes with their stone enclosures so neglected. Near to the lake however, things were different and the communities were still thriving. This was my first real encounter with life in rural

Peru and several things caught my eye. Someone was making new adobe building blocks by the roadside. How similar that was to Yemen! Straw was mixed into a pond of mud with bare feet. Even the wooden moulding frames looked similar and the finished blocks lay in disciplined order to dry in the sun. Ladies dressed in brightly layered skirts gossiped on village streets. Their bowler hats were too small by any standard! Men rode on ancient bicycles and children, late for school, played roadside games. Herds of domestic llamas roamed the slopes by the lake, which glowed a vivid turquoise in the sun that morning.

We reached the main highway and turned south, driving a few miles to the border between Peru and Bolivia. Had we stayed with the Inca Trail from Chile we would have crossed into Peru at this point. We had skipped the Trail's entire length in Bolivia but we could now join it again where it enters Peru. I looked over to the Isla del Sol, a tiny island set in a clear sea, where legend suggests that the first Inca Emperor was born to the world. The traditional creation site of the Inca people was a beautiful place and I felt a transition here to something new. We were entering the heart of the Inca Kingdom and our journey along the shores of that huge inland sea, Titicaca, was taking us to the capital, Cusco, just one day away. As we drove along the shore the isolation of earlier days had gone, replaced with the bustle of small communities. The road was not challenging and I had time to ponder the Inca Trail's origins and try to sense how it would have been 500 years earlier. I wanted to understand more of the forces that had led to the road's construction through 8000km, of some of the worst terrain in the world.

In the 13th Century, the area by the lake up to Cusco was the territory of the Quechua speaking Indians, whose leaders were called Incas. In 1438 the ninth Inca ruler, Pachacutec, came to power. He introduced an expansionist strategy and embarked on a campaign which led to the rapid growth of the Inca Empire. The resulting imperial dominion stretched from Colombia in the north to the present location of Santiago in Chile. Those conquests were followed with social and political reform that united the nation. A common spoken language was introduced and, although there was no written language, a form of communication based on knotted strings helped speed the flow of information through the new empire. In keeping with other early civilisations, a system of runners was used to support the government, adding enormous importance to good roads. Two 'royal highways' were constructed, one on the coast and the other through the Andes, which was the one we were currently following. It was paved with flat stones and was six metres wide over open terrain but narrowed to as little as one metre through difficult mountain passes. Traffic then, of course, was limited to people and pack animals, although horses were used on the route later. In 1524, 100 years after the Kingdom was formed, the Spanish nation, greedy for gold, invaded the young empire. Unfortunately, internal strife at that time had left the nation vulnerable to attack by the conquistadors and,

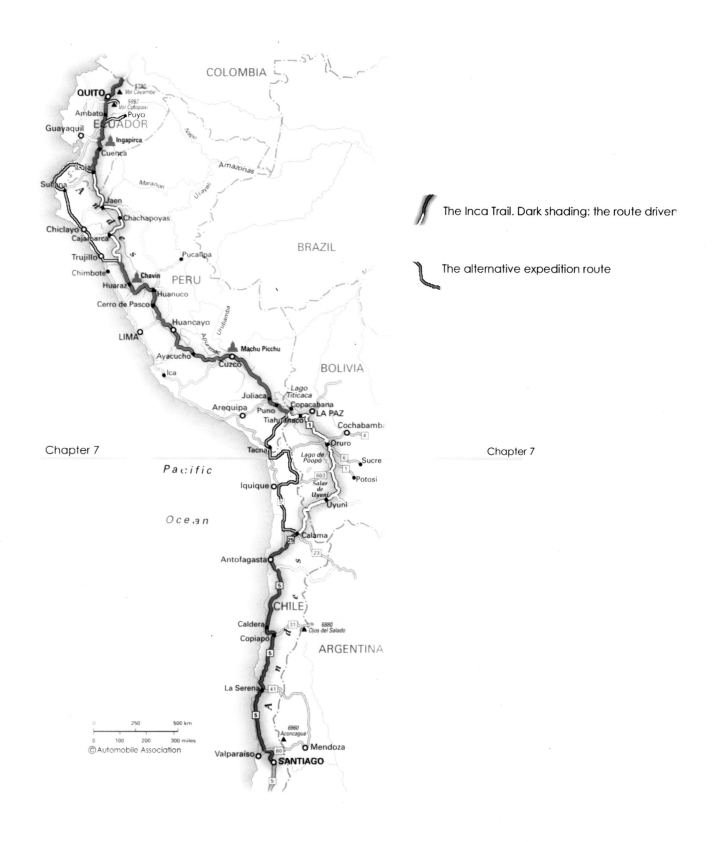

The Inca Trail. Dark shading: the route driven

The alternative expedition route

Going to school on an Island

The floating islands, Lake Ticicaca

Plate 35

Inca wall, Cuzco

Plate 36

Machu Picchu at sunrise

Plate 37

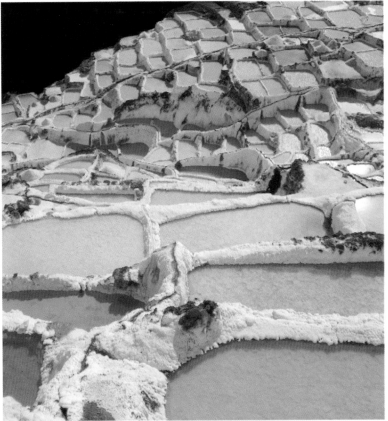

The Inca salt mines

Plate 38

The Inca Trail to Huaraz

Plate 39 LAND ROVER sponsored

Ecuador wildlife

Plate 40

At the snow line on Volcan Cotopaxi (4800)m

Plate 41 LAND ROVER sponsored

within 20 years, it had been virtually wiped out. But the Andean royal highway remained.

Much of the road has been upgraded since then but its route, selected so long ago by the Incas, remained to service modern day traffic. This section to Cusco was a modern highway but it was on the tracks high in the remote regions that I saw it in a condition not dissimilar to how it was in Inca times. As I neared Puno at the top of the lake I began to realise that the Inca Trail had been constructed largely to meet a political need, providing the flow of supplies and essential information in order to govern. We had come across this before. The Alcan Highway to Alaska was built through wilderness by the USA in frantic haste because Japan invaded the Aleutian Islands. What had motivated construction of the Karakoram Highway from China to Pakistan over the Himalaya? Certainly not general trade. The road should not be there by all civil engineering standards. Maybe, I thought, the best wilderness journeys in the world were on roads with political origins.

Puno was a place of small streets, confining traffic and noisy people. It felt cramped as I drove Rabia's obscenely large volume amongst the taxi tricycles, carts and donkeys. But through the chaos it was colourful and lively and finally I found a small hotel with secure parking. I had come here to explore Lake Titicaca the next day before driving on to Cusco.

Lake Titicaca is 230km long, 100km wide and, at an elevation of 3800m, is the highest navigable lake in the world. But beyond the figures there is a rich history that shapes the lives of those who live around and on the lake. I was especially drawn to the colony of floating islands, pulled by a compelling curiosity of something quite unique in the world. The Uros people escaped from inter-tribal feuding (and Inca taxes) by building islands from reeds. In time their life style evolved and they became self-sustaining and independent from the mainland, relying only on the Tolora reeds and fish in the lake. The islands are of ancient construction and are two metres thick. Each year 20 centimetres of new reeds are laid on top to compensate for the rot below. The floating islands are home to 400 people who harvest the lake's reeds to make homes, boats and other items from the material. Fishing provides food and income through trade. In all respects they lead normal lives. One island carries the school, where children arrive in smart uniforms by reed boat each morning. Another island carries the shop. Tourism has added to the economy of the islands and I wondered how that income had helped prevent the demise of this strange community. I was curious to know if the islands truly floated, or were perhaps sitting on the lake bed in shallow water. That notion was dispelled when the island I was standing on visibly rippled in phase with the bow wave of a passing ferry. There was no doubt. We were definitely adrift!

Puno was bustling with activity when I returned that evening. I restocked with food and shopped for ice which seemed harder to find in Peru. We were ready to move on, leaving early the following morning through streets already busy with preparations for the day's market. I had felt quite at home there, enjoying the higgledy-piggledy street stalls and lively atmosphere. Despite the clutter and disorder things worked! We nudged our way through the early rush of *collectivo* and tricycle taxis to reach the open road north.

The day passed quickly, driving over wide Andean landscapes below a sky full of life. Solid columns of cumulous boiled sharp and clear against a dark blue sky in the high altitude. Some way through, a train passed close by, chugging over the Altiplano to reach Cusco from the coast. Set in a ring of snow-capped peaks, it was an evocative image. I could imagine it bearing Butch Cassidy and the Sun Dance Kid who had made this train journey to reach Bolivia in their flight from US justice. I passed it again, as it climbed slowly over the Abra la Raya pass at 4300 metres and later, as I camped on a hidden ledge high above the road in a young eucalypt forest, one of the last sights in fading daylight was the blue passenger train rumbling and hooting below me. It would reach Cusco after dark.

At first light the village below me was still silent and listless before another vigorous farming day in spring. Some tiny figures scurried to the fields early, herding their drowsy beasts to places of choice grazing. The far slope of the valley was now in sunlight. Fingers of green eucalypt plantations clawed their way up the slopes, rising higher into the deep valleys and gullies. In the still air I could hear the river flowing down towards Cusco, that unmistakable rumble of water over rocks.

I reached Cusco early, just as the traffic into town was becoming heavy, so I delayed my entry and found a garage to change Rabia's engine oil. She needed new life blood. The young mechanic was curious. "Can I come with you to Ecuador," he enquired, casting wistful eyes at my spare seat.

I was at the nerve centre of the old empire now, right at its centre of gravity. I needed time here to probe the history but finding a modest hotel with secure parking was proving difficult. Seeing my plight, the manageress of the Hostel Saphi offered a unique solution. "Bring your car into the foyer," she said. This was someone with good powers of lateral thinking. Rabia was driven through the wide entrance doors onto the hotel's marble floor by reception, where she stayed during my time in Cusco. She looked incongruous, somehow out of place, but I was grateful.

I spent two days in Cusco visiting the Inca sights, looking for features that would somehow reveal the place to me. At the outset I stood quietly in the Plaza de Armas, at the heart of the city, where the Inca temples had been built and the ancient roads had come together in one mighty focal point – the 'Times Square' of the old civilisation. In that moment I recognised in myself a feeling of disquiet and growing unease. The ornate cathedral towered beside me and the immensely ornate church, the Iglesia de la Compania, dominated the other side of the square. Looking behind the impressive religious architecture around me there were signs of the destruction of a sophisticated culture carried out in the name of Christ but underpinned by greed. Probably the largest Inca building, the Temple of the Sun, had dominated the square but the temple had been destroyed and the church built on the spectacular stonework of the original walls. That seemed to me an act of symbolic violence, of gratuitous vandalism in which the Church was implicit. The intricate and beautiful Inca masonry remained only as foundations to many religious buildings but nothing could be seen of the former glory that had previously graced the square. (Plate 36).

As my wanderings continued, I understood more of the rise and disastrous fall of the Inca community. There had been a rape of a society previously stable and well developed, but momentarily vulnerable through civil unrest. The conquistadors, acting jointly with the Dominican hierarchy, conspired to destroy all aspects of Inca traditions and beliefs, the very essence of the culture. That process had been completed in the name of the Christian faith. Throughout that time, of course, the real agenda was the theft of the nation's wealth of gold and silver. I wondered how that process, probably one of the worst acts of human subjugation, could have been performed in the name of religion. What criminal arrogance!

Compared with other colonisations, I saw something different in Cusco which had been wilful, systematic, cold and ruthless. Nowhere in the religious buildings or historic institutions that I visited did I see a hint of compassion for the people whose lives were destroyed, whose culture was being obliterated. Dozens of churches were built in the 1500s to impose a new set of values on top of another that had functioned perfectly well. Meanwhile, the nation's wealth was pillaged comprehensively. I learnt that even the local clothing, which we now identify as classic South American dress, was imposed as a mish-mash from all over Europe. The small bowler hats and layered dresses had nothing to do with traditional clothing before 1500, but it had been introduced as another aspect of the strategy.

I wondered what might have been the outcome if two Inca half-brothers, each claiming the throne, had not been feuding in 1532 when Pizario had set out to plunder the Kingdom, and had played one faction against the other. Perhaps South America might have developed into one powerful Kingdom, using Inca riches and social reforms. Perhaps the Incas might have eventually risen to international eminence and been a real power in the modern world.

Cusco's façade, of course, is beautiful. The quaint streets, the people and the splendour of the place combine to offer a unique tourist destination. But I had seen enough of the years of encroachment. The old clerical finery dripping with jewels and laced with gold fittings no longer impressed me. I was disturbed by what I had learnt, thrown off balance and emotionally drained. No where else in the world had had that impact on me. Perhaps Auschwitz would if I ever saw it. Maybe the normality and attractiveness of Cusco had made that impression more macabre. I would leave for Machu Picchu the next day.

It was Sunday and I drove to Pisaq where a traditional market would be open that morning. It was on my route and I could have breakfast there. By mid morning the place was too busy and I moved on, up the valley towards Machu Picchu. At

Ollantaytambo I could drive no further. The police in the village agreed to watch over Rabia and I caught the train to Aquas Calientes, a town below the Inca ruins where I would stay overnight.

The small hostel was surrounded by noise. Rain thundered on the tin roof and a dog howled in an unseen canine drama below my window for much of the night. At 3.00am a rooster crowed its heart out, seriously out of phase with sunrise. Soon after 5.00am a faint grey line appeared over the summits surrounding the village and I caught the first bus to Machu, up the steep slope to the settlement. Before sunrise, I had climbed to a shelf above the ruins know as The Caretakers Hut. Machu was below me, shrouded in mist, but this would be the best view if the morning clouds cleared from the mountains. I was on my own but soon a group of walkers reached my ledge after trekking all the way from Cusco. The footpath finished at this spot where the hikers hoped to watch the ruins appear through the clearing mists. Their emotions were high after four days in the mountains.

The clouds began to drift away revealing the grey peaks that surround Machu's tiny plateau. Then the mists shrouding the ruins began to dissipate and their vague outline, the image so well known to the world, began to take shape and detail below. Finally, the whole place cleared and we looked down on the green terraces, the stone buildings and the massive profile of the rock pinnacle, Huayna Picchu, rising behind the village. Thick cloud still lurked in the lower valleys to the north and south of the plateau, giving a striking focus to the ruins. The 30 or 40 people on the ledge beside me were all lost in speechless wonder. Someone nearby cried on the shoulder of a friend. It was a view filled with feature and made even more striking in the knowledge that it had been lost to the world for 400 years until it was rediscovered in 1911

It had been an exceptional morning. Sometimes the mists don't clear and that infusion of morning cloud, ruins and mountains are not revealed at sunrise. After wandering the ruins I felt that Machu was a place best admired from a distance in its entirety and without the crowds that descend on the place from Cusco daily. The view down from the top of Huayna Picchu was equally splendid and made more rewarding by the demanding climb to reach there.

By midday Machu was busy with visitors. I had hoped to find something new about the Inca people but it seemed there were more questions than answers. I had gained further respect for their engineering and construction skills, but not much more. The place remained a mystery, a scenic gem viewed from afar but close up it did not reveal a great deal of its historic significance. Much rebuilding had occurred and empathetic as that was, it made the ruins less authentic. I descended to catch the train and rejoined Rabia by 6.00pm. Breaking a golden rule, the journey in the dark to my destination, the Inca salt mines, was demanding and at times quite threatening. To reach there, a small track snaked through a desolate landscape high in the mountains under a sky of velvet black filled with the wink and glitter of stars. By

7.30pm the narrow trail led to the end of the road by a few buildings. My GPS told me I had arrived! In the blackness I could not tell but a group of three local villagers joined me for a beer and, with some difficulty, we chatted for an hour.

By way of explanation let me describe the salt pans that had drawn me to this desolate hillside high above Cusco. Before Inca times the flow of hot water from the slope was especially rich in salt and must have scarred the adjoining hillside with a pure white crust, like some giant residue of burnt candle wax. The Incas had tapped into this resource and through a cunning engineering scheme had built terraces which cascaded down the slope in a series of ponds fed by carefully routed channels. The flow of saline solution was managed so that the ponds were primed with liquid periodically, then left to dry out depositing an especially pure form of crystalline salt. You need to understand the scale to appreciate the aesthetic appeal. The pans stretched for two kilometres along the hill and the terraces dropped steeply for half a kilometre until the flow ran out. But the ultimate attraction, the magic of the place, was that it had remained as a flourishing salt mine for 600 years, using the methods and ponds as they had been designed by the Incas. This was a living remnant of those times, something that connected directly with the people. (Plate 38).

I rose before dawn and looked over the ridge beside Rabia on to a splendid scene of intricate terraces cascading down the slope. Some small figures moved through the network of pools below, starting work early. Even at that time, well before sunrise, the slope was full of subtlety and delicate colour in the soft light. I met up with Carlos, working his area of ponds for the day. At 5.30am he had already carried six bags of salt for half a kilometre up the steep slope to reach the donkey track. I could barely lift the bag, never mind carry it up an incline. "I get four Sol (£0.60) for each 50 kilo bag mined and carried here," he complained. He would be old and infirm by 30. "When the sun comes up be careful," he warned, showing me the woolly hat that he would pull over his head and eyes to protect him from the glare of reflected sunlight at this altitude.

I roamed the site for several hours, absorbed by the intricate workings, the delicate controls and the careful maintenance. Nothing had changed over hundreds of years. Only the chuckle of gently flowing rivulets broke the silence but, occasionally, a few whistles resonated round the valley. Carlos had said that the workers had a code to communicate in this way over the long hillside.

The sun finally rose over the high ridge above the valley and the terraces glowed with a new radiance. It was time to leave. I drove out of the valley, over the opposite shoulder and looked back. Far away, on the road above the pools, three donkeys were being loaded with Carlos's bags, to move the salt through to the next link in distribution. I wondered who would make the profit in this supply chain; certainly not Carlos.

The Inca Trail north of Cusco ascends again into the spine of the Andes and remains there for 2000km up to the Ecuadorian border. There are a few remote towns on the route but it is characterised for most of its length by raw wilderness, narrow gravel tracks and, the third dimension, the ascents and descents between high passes. There was a frustrating predictability to the track's frequent route backwards. It would climb one side of a valley only to reverse direction along the opposite side, to reach the high pass into the next valley. Gaining height was everything and the expression 'auto-mountaineering' (plate 51) came to mind as a good description of the process. Maps failed to show these meanderings and the distance travelled between places would be three times the line-of-sight value, as the track snaked over the landscape. The statistics gave the best clue to the unfolding struggle. Each day we would drive a modest 180km to reach a destination only 60km away from the previous camp site. In one day we might make the punishing ascent to 4000m twice, before dropping through an equally dramatic descent to the next green valley at 2000m. We were unable to drive faster than 25kph, maintaining low ratio to keep optimum power available for Rabia's engine.

During the second day from Cusco one of Rabia's rear tyres was punctured, our first for the Michelin tyres in the southern hemisphere. But the conditions were very rough and I was not surprised. At the next village some hours later, I tried to organise the repair but modern tubeless tyres were not the norm in these poor communities. The small repair yard had no power tools for the job and breaking the bead away from the wheel was difficult. I stopped the work just before an attack on my precious tyre with the blunt side of a pick-axe! Later that day, I found a yard in the next village equipped for heavy truck tyre repairs. It was dark when Manuel finished the repair and I edged Rabia onto the adjoining spare ground for the night, amongst some trucks which had succumbed to the fearsome mountain roads. I shared my dinner with a tiny pregnant dog that appeared forlornly from a stack of old tyres beside me. This was a camp site with a difference - a truck and tyre graveyard.

By our third day the journey developed a natural rhythm, climbing between altitude extremes. We crossed the Rio Bamba, a mighty tributary of the Amazon, in a pleasant green valley. It was hot and the river banks were filled with bright bougainvillea, banana and wild figs trees. It was almost tropical but we soon climbed out to the north. Within an hour we had risen from the valley to cold open tundra well above 4000m. The temperature had dropped by an astonishing 20 degrees. At one point the track had been swept from the hillside leaving a scarred earthy banking which listed downhill at a crazy angle. On a 4x4 test track this would be fun but we were a day's drive from any help with a sheer 2000 foot drop below and crumbling rock above the track. There was no avoiding my feelings – I was simply terrified, almost locked rigid by fear. I walked the 200 foot gap several times assessing the odds. Our centre of gravity was low and we had good treads to make it safely. Finally, we edged over with enormous care.

My camp site that night was not a happy place. I was exposed on a high meadow and had grappled with the terrain for eight hours. I was tired. The ECM had cooked too long and my Mince al la Cusco had burnt to a cinder. If there was going to be a moment of doubt about this extreme section of the route it would be that evening but, despite these minor problems, I was content knowing that I was enjoying some very special landscapes in South America.

The small communities at altitude were poor beyond measure – just a collection of rundown adobe shacks, a few tiny herds of animals and some plots of potatoes to support a tenuous existence. Perhaps life had always been that way here. I had heard in Cusco that the people of the Peruvian mountains from Cusco to Huaraz, a strip of land 1000km long, had suffered most during the years of Conquistador domination. I had been told that 90 million people had died of disease and slaughter during their resistance and I was dumfounded by that figure. I tried not to drive through these poor settlements conveying an air of imperious grandeur. Perhaps my journey through these remote Andean places was a kind of splendid indulgence by comparison with the lifestyle of the people I was passing, lives of deprivation and endurance.

There was still restlessness amongst the people, something cold and remote. No doubt they had been treated badly and probably ignored by recent governments. In this region of relative isolation I found it strange that the old buildings were often daubed with political slogans. Then I remembered! I was in the heartland of the *Sendero Luminoso* – The Shining Path Party that effectively brought this area in particular, and Peru in general, to its knees in the 1970s. This was a no-go area until the 1990s when the problem was resolved.

I reached Ayacucho, an attractive place despite the clutter, dust and chaos of the streets. I had learnt some tricks to cope with not speaking Spanish and had noticed that every Peruvian town had a plaza at its centre. Asking for directions to the town's plaza would lead to the core of activity where I would find the information office, money changers, internet and food shops. This was a quick solution to urban navigation which served me well. The process was easy - just ask for the plaza and follow the hand signs until the square appeared!

Over the next week we made good progress north. Rabia ran well through the Altiplano but at Ayacucho we had taken on some poor fuel, probably well below 85 octane. She struggled at the next pass, telling me with an occasional splutter of her distaste for shoddy supplies. I promised to try harder for better fuel in future.

We descended towards Lima over the Cordillera Occidental but soon regained altitude to join the Inca Trail before the Huaraz Valley. The valley, although at a modest altitude, was flanked by the Cordillera Blanca and Peru's highest mountains. Snow-covered peaks rose sheer, glistening under blue skies. Huascaran's 6768m was a powerful feature capped by tumbling glaciers and made mysterious by drifting cloud which ringed the middle slopes. At the town of Huaraz, at the centre of the region, I halted progress to catch my breath and enjoy the town's atmosphere. Walking through the centre in the evening I passed a dance school, a small place busy with teenagers but the waltz and quickstep played no part in proceedings. I loitered at the entrance watching the passion and beauty of South American dance flow from these young people. Their movements were full of a sensuous passionate rhythm executed to the accompanying guitar music. Their faces conveyed something quite neutral, leaving only their arms, legs and bodies to express all the passion of flamenco. I was captivated.

Later, I found a covered area lined with tiny cubicles displaying an odd selection of hanging carcasses. It could have been an abattoir rather than a meat market. One cubicle with a sign pronouncing it to be 'Carnakia Mary' provided me with a slice of meat of unknown origin and my shopping prize, a guinea-pig!

The next morning, sunlight flooded through the window of my cheap hotel room. Long-distance buses revved into life in the street below and people scurried around starting their dusty day in Huaraz. I took breakfast in Rabia, safely parked in a secure yard nearby. We drove north along the valley but turned east on a poor and dangerous looking track. The ascent was one of auto-mountaineering unequalled in South America. We rose quickly to a place of glaciers, tumbling snowfields and jagged peaks. I left Rabia at 4700m to walk briefly. The air was still and cushions of cloud drifted silently round the slopes beside me. Fingers of mist broke away to corkscrew into a skyward spiral where they diffused quickly in the morning sun. Huascaran's powerful presence dominated the view with a kind of brooding malevolence. I had promised Eileen to steer clear of terrifying situations unless they led to something spectacular but thought my surroundings justified my somewhat risky ascent here. I felt an expanded sense of purpose in the journey. The success of high altitude driving during the previous two weeks had somehow imbued me with a fresh appreciation of my vehicle. Far below, two turquoise lakes sparkled on a high ledge where I planned to camp after making the descent.

By late afternoon, the 'Guinea-pig a la Huaraz' had cooked nicely for dinner in a cocktail of herbs and tasted like a gourmet meal of tender chicken. It froze overnight on my high ledge and the Coffin was coated with white frost. Ice had even formed on the inner surface from my breath, but it had been a good site. By first light I descended quickly to enjoy some heat away from the sombre shadow by the lake. Yungay lay at the bottom of the track and some distance above the town the landscape looked strange, almost lunar, and quite barren. I noticed the frequent memorials dotted over the slope and the huge statue of Christ in the midst of the desolation. Then I realised what lay before me. It was the remains of a huge avalanche, triggered by an earthquake in 1970. The path of the massive slide was quite clear and the slope below was, in fact, an immense grave. Eighteen thousand people had been buried under the rubble.

Some way up the valley towards the border with Ecuador, I checked the maps again to plan our crossing. I knew from earlier correspondence with the British Embassy that there was no formal border post where the Inca Trail crossed from

Peru. Once again I would have to descend to the coast and I had to decide where to head west. There was another important factor. Between Cajamarca and Jaen the Inca Trail followed remote valleys dedicated to growing coca and most of the crop was used for drug manufacture. I went by my instincts and turned west to reach the coast road (and the Pan Am again) before Chiclayo.

My final days in north Peru were not an uplifting time in my journey. For the first time travelling the world I found that a police force can be wholly corrupt. I guessed that the traffic police in Northern Peru had been supplied with expensive Toyota Landcruisers at the USA's expense to help stop the flow of drugs, but the police had found an attractive and more rewarding option by using their power to extort money from passing traffic. One memorable morning on the Pan Am characterised the problem. Within 20 minutes of leaving my camp site I reached an open road with a curious 60kph limit. I slowed to 55, causing lots of abuse from traffic behind but was soon pulled over to the side of the road by a couple of thugs in police uniforms. I got out of Rabia, smiling and calm. "You were not wearing your seat belt." True – I had taken it off to get out. Then they said "You were 20 kph over the limit," but had no equipment to check this. "The fine will be US$100." A bus immune, it seemed, to extortion swept by at 90kph. I stood my ground pleading ignorance of the process. Finally the pair tired of the exchange and I moved on, knowing that Rabia must look like a moving dollar wallet to these people.

At the next village, five kilometres down the road, the same thing occurred in a 45kph zone where I was driving with immense caution and causing consternation at my slow speed. I pulled over on request from the police at the roadside. You can guess the sequence. "You were not wearing your seat belt," followed by the impossible claim, "You were too close to the car in front of you." Every charge in the book was thrown at me. "You were speeding. The fine is US$100." Then the scam unfolded. Big Carlos in the Landcruiser, who had an expression of criminal brutality, had my driving licence. He muttered that he could be my friend. He said he could help me, as he sat with pen poised over the formal charge sheet. "I won't fine you after all, but you must give me some petrol money." The penny dropped. He wanted a personal payment in cash. Carlos opened at $50. He became bored with the language barrier which I was erecting in haste and finally accepted $30 to give me my licence back.

Another 10 kilometres on, as I crawled through a 30kph zone, the same thing happened. This time I stood my ground, with my window open, door locked, all documents hidden and smiling broadly. I claimed absolute ignorance of the Spanish language, so the demand for documents went without response. I knew that once any important document was passed over the game was lost. The two got angry, huddled together to discuss how they could finesse money in a situation new to them. After 20 minutes they tired of the game. They were missing too many other lucrative opportunities. The next confrontation down the road that morning challenged the effectiveness of Rabia's lights as the opening gambit. Remember it was mid-morning! My plan worked again and I knew I had a solution for the future. I now recognised I was facing pure corruption.

Between Chiclayo and Suliana, the Desert de Sechura ranked low in the scale of attractive deserts. There were no exotic sand dunes, no expansive panoramas of colour and contour; only flat gravel, some sand and a few scruffy trees and shrubs. The remnants of garish coloured plastic bags fluttered pathetically from thorn bushes, forlorn and grotesque adornments that had no empathy with desert surroundings. It would be an enduring mess that could never rot or decay in an already fragile landscape.

I drove the coastal route to the border, stopping at a small hotel on a beach to prepare a newsletter to friends. The border was a confusing place, located in the middle of a busy market town which straddled Peru and Ecuador. I missed the small cabin, surrounded by loitering dogs and boys and had to reverse to complete formalities. It was very strange; traffic seemed to be flowing freely in both directions, unrestricted by the border. It was essential that my documents showed that I had left Peru and entered Ecuador legally and I was glad I had not gone with the traffic flow any further.

By a strange coincidence Rabia mutinied just after the crossing, spluttering her protest and losing power. Her record was exceptionally good during previous expeditions, failing on the road only twice in seven years. But she had chosen her moments well. In 1997 she had also come to rest on a border crossing, between Jordan and Syria on that occasion. The fuel pump had failed but after 100,000km this had perhaps been predictable. Was my present predicament caused by the same problem I wondered? She was either starved of fuel or had no ignition. The electrics seemed in good order but without the ability to be in two places at once it was difficult to check fuel flow in the engine bay. The fuel pump had operated for 90,000km and my instinct was to change it. Reaching the pump through the floor of the car was a long tedious task. I was parked by the road side near a family of charcoal burners, who watched me curiously whilst I removed all Rabia's contents. I hated the thought that my guessed diagnosis might be wrong and some other more dramatic failure would spoil my day. After two hours the replacement was fitted and, for good measure, I had also changed the fuel filter. I turned the ignition not sure what to expect. After a hesitant start her engine ran sweetly again and my spirits rose. My guess had been correct and the family of charcoal burners whooped excitedly, sharing in my moment of success.

I drove to higher ground in Ecuador, to rejoin the route at Loja in the Andes. The landscape was different here, more green and lush with a jungle-like quality. Other things impressed me quickly. There was more prosperity and in Loja I bought chocolate and ice in the supermarket – supplies I had not found for some time. A bus passed me inscribed *El Gran Lenon* – The Great Lenon. The bus was named after either the iconic communist or a past pop star. I did not know enough about Ecuadorian politics to guess which.

I headed north on National Highway 35, symbolised on my maps of Ecuador incorrectly with the wide and solid red line of a trunk road. Why was I not surprised to find a gravel track? Three days of beautiful scenery passed quickly after Loja, driving through green hillsides and rolling mountains. The scenery was more soft and subtle than Peru but the route was populous, making it difficult to find a good camping site. That evening we reached Ingapirca, picturesque under a powerful sky, the last of the preserved Inca ruins on the trail. Angry cumulous boiled around me and sunlight swept over the ruins through the racing banks of clouds. The site's most appealing feature, the intricate Inca masonry, was intriguing. The mortarless polished stonework had the same remarkable quality to that at Cusco and Machu but was made more dramatic because there had been no restoration. The custodian was kind to me and let me camp in the ruins, where I enjoyed the fiery sunset in that ancient setting.

The next day the road rose steeply to the town of Riobamba passing high meadows and beautiful pine forests. There was a strange similarity to Scotland in the landscape, although we were only two degrees from the equator. I halted the journey briefly at Riobamba - I needed a break and some strange new feelings about the journey entered my consciousness. They were not especially deep or profound and I was sure I was not confronting some form of mental 'brick wall.' Nor did I feel unduly stressed. It was more a vague feeling of disconnection, perhaps a loss of momentum after eight weeks of travel on my own. But something was eroding my enthusiasm and I felt emotionally stalled. I decided that something different was needed, perhaps a complete break from travel that would reconnect me with the journey.

I took a local taxi early the next morning out of town then up a track, reaching the road end below the snowline on Volcano Chimborazo, Ecuador's highest mountain. It was a barren and desolate place but in the snows high above, at 5000m, the climber's refuge stood out clearly. The scramble to reach there was easy, over the volcanic ash made firm with time. I had adapted well to altitude and loitered at the hut chatting with a few people and enjoying the view. But the weather closed in after a few hours and it began to snow heavily. How strange it felt to be only 160km from the equator in a raging snow storm. I returned to Riobamba, relaxed and ready to move on, my enthusiasm renewed. The mood had been broken.

There is an aspect to Ecuador that endears the place to you. Travelling the central highway is a majestic experience, flanked by mountains and volcanoes. But two options arise for those who tire of this splendour. You can turn east to become lost in dense Amazonian jungle within a few hours. Alternatively, turning west leads to a beautiful tropical coastline. Where else in the world, I wondered, was the choice of exotic beach, snow-capped mountains and tropical jungle so readily accessible. It seemed to me that Ecuador was the hidden gem of the travel industry.

Both these options were tempting me and I turned east after Riobamba to reach Puyo, a staging post to explore the jungle. Shortly after leaving E35, we passed through Banos. Towering over the town Volcano Tungarahua was in restless mood, belching fearsome black clouds into the air from its unstable summit. In 1999 seismic activity was so bad that the government ordered evacuation of Banos. A year later she had still not erupted and in frustration people forced their way through the army blockades back to their homes. The town was still on red alert – Tungarahua could blow at any time.

Puyo was a typical jungle town. My guidebook recommended the Organisation of Indigenous People who could provide guidance for a short jungle visit, but the office had gone – just a burnt out shell remained where the building had been. I tracked down the new office on the outskirts of town and heard about the recent drama. "Our old office was burnt down by the oil companies," said the secretary with resignation. It seemed that passions were high over exploration rights on local tribal land. I met with Ingaro who offered to accompany me during the next day if we could use Rabia. I left the office to find a place for the night but finding a camping site in the jungle was curiously difficult and I was caught off-guard. The lush greenery was impenetrable and the few clearings I found were always damp and soggy. Rain was almost certain that night so I finally took a room at a safari lodge outside town. It poured overnight, raining in a way I had never experienced. The deluge thundered on my cabin, cascading off the roof in floods to form rivers of mud on the ground. Lightning flashed and thunder clattered around the surrounding forest. I should not have been surprised – after all this was a tropical rain forest in the Amazon Basin!

I joined up with Ingaro the next morning. He was a quiet young man from the Quichuas people and he had spent three years in New York canvassing support with the UN for the Amazon's remaining indigenous tribes. We drove through narrow muddy tracks to reach small villages deep in the forest. The variety of exotic trees and plants was strange to me. On the way, Rabia waded some streams made vigorous by the night's rain. We left the car to walk for some hours through a tangle of lush vegetation and along noisy stream beds. His knowledge was profound and he pointed out plants of interest. "Here is one offering help for cancer of the stomach.... There is a plant to relieve a sore throat.... That other plant, made into an infusion, helps prostate problems and this one, boiled briefly, makes an excellent shampoo.... Use the stem of that plant to brush your teeth!" We dined in a Quichuas village, sharing the harvest of the nearby jungle, surrounded by animals and birds that had adopted the clearing as their own home. After lunch we sped down the Puyo River in a dugout canoe, a turbulent passage when we were often on the edge of capsizes. It beat river rafting for excitement! Ingaro was in his element. All too soon the day was over. I had enjoyed my 'heart of darkness' experience and could have stayed longer.

We drove from Puyo to rejoin E35 and to head north again on the Inca Trail. Shortly, Volcan Cotopaxi rose to the east of the Central Valley. The symmetrical cone towered to a dormant summit, capped by snow and ice. We drove east into the National Park which surrounds Cotopaxi, not sure if the weather would be kind. A doughnut ring of cloud hung round the peak's middle slopes and I took refuge for the night in the lower of the two climbing huts below the mountain. As I arrived, a group of twelve was leaving to make an ascent during the night. They hoped to see the sunrise from the volcano's cone. The weather cleared and at sunset the snows above me were washed in pink light. After dark I had the derelict cabin to myself. During the night I looked up from my sleeping bag, through the open wall, to see a ghostly pyramid set in a black sky, glowing under the light of a full moon. High on the snows tiny lights twinkled as the climbing party crossed an open snowfield heading for the summit.

Before first light I broke camp. Rabia had signalled to me in her own way that she was ready for her final auto-mountaineering adventure in South America and we followed the pair of wheel tracks up to the snowline. She purred quietly, in equilibrium with her high surroundings and at sunrise we had reached 4800m, just below the snowline. (Plate 41). She was at her highest point. I left her there, to climb the steep snowy slope below the first ice fall and reached 5200m, 700m short of the summit. It was still safe to be there without climbing gear – the snow was hard and the morning still cold. The climbers passed me heading down, despondent at their failure to reach the summit. The upper slope had been pure ice and they had not had enough time to cross safely before dawn. It was a strange unworldly panorama from that height. To the north the equator was 70km away over a flat and barren expanse of tundra. The morning sun was low, flooding the view with yellow light. Below me, Rabia was parked in the ash and gravel of earlier eruptions, looking tiny and fragile. Beside me, long icicles glistened in the sun, hanging from a confusion of fractured glacier blocks. I sat quietly under the indigo sky enjoying the moment. I had never been as high in my life and would probably never reach this altitude again. I could not grasp fully the thought that I had been in hot humid jungle the day before. It seemed too strange a contrast.

Suddenly, there was a sharp crack behind me that jolted me from the pensive moment. There had been some movement in the tumbled ice nearby and it was time to descend. The snowfield below me was softening and a heavy heel step made its own indent in the crust providing a slip-free staircase directly down the fall line. I love these conditions! By 10.30am the adventure was over. I looked back from Rabia to the symmetrical cone and glistening snows. A grey blanket was reaching in from the west. It was time to move on.

I drove through Quito and crossed the equator heading for Tulcan on the border with Colombia. Ecuador has some wonderful rural markets full of colour and activity. The Saturday market at Otavalo was in progress as I passed, and I strolled through the streets letting the sights and sounds of the place flood my senses. I reached the meat market where I became submerged in noisy crowds between stalls. I felt the jostle from the two people either side of me. It was unnatural, out of place and seemed too well synchronised. In a moment they were gone, vanished into the throng and I knew instantly that I had been robbed of my shopping cash, buried deep in my pocket. It was over quickly, a precise and orchestrated manoeuvre that must have been well rehearsed. After all, Otavalo was not to be the pleasant experience I had hoped for.

I reached the border town the next day expecting to see nothing new. But northern Ecuador had one final surprise in store, something very curious and unexpected. Tulcan was not a pretty place, serving mostly as a gateway to Colombia. It is, however, the provincial capital of Carchi, the northernmost province of the Ecuadorian Highlands and deals with the burials for the region. I had heard that the local cemetery was special but had no comprehension of how strange the place was.

I entered the cemetery to find long concrete buildings, white rectangular blocks rising three storeys. Set into each face were small cubicles one metre square, banked nine cubicles high below the roof and stretching for 200 metres down the length of the building. (Plate 44). I walked through, passing perhaps twenty of these giant concrete mausoleums. Each small cubicle in the wall was a vault for one body. It seemed that dying was an elevating experience in more ways than one! Thousands of people were incarcerated here. I noticed that many of the vaults were very old but were still 'dressed' with flowers and mementoes, even photos behind glass. I could not help admiring the continuing care of these tiny concrete spaces through several generations. On that Sunday, hundreds of people were visiting relatives who had passed away and the place was bright with fresh flowers filling the air with fragrance. The cemetery also contained a unique topiary collection, beautifully manicured into an eclectic assortment of tall shapes. Many were hundreds of years old and towered 20 metres over the cemetery. It must take an army, I thought, to maintain the topiary display as one of the best in the world.

Other more mundane activities filled the rest of the day. I had Rabia washed free of underside mud but in a brief moment when I was not watching, the enthusiastic operator pressure washed her engine bay, flooding her distributor and other components. I know how distasteful she finds this – it took two hours to dry her electrics.

I stayed overnight in town preparing for the crossing the next day. The first 400km in Colombia would be through an area controlled by FARC guerrillas, bandits by any other name. I had to reach Cali by nightfall, over one of the most risky areas of Colombia. Driving there at night would not be safe. I did not know if the road would be good enough to maintain reasonable speed, or whether I could join a convoy as recommended, nor whether there would be bureaucratic delays at the border before starting the day's long drive. I was restless and ill at ease that night, apprehensive about crossing Colombia and I did not feel in control of my journey the next day. Through those concerns, I had to admit to an excitement about facing something different, the thrill of entering a new phase in the journey. Tulcan marked the top end of the Inca Trail. I had learnt much during the 10,200km from Santiago and enjoyed some great 4x4 driving, thanks to the old road builders. Perhaps it had even been some of the best off-road driving in the world. But it was over and a new challenge lay ahead.

Carved stone heads from Peru's oldest major culture. (Chavin, 1000BC)

CARIBBEAN SEA

PANAMA

Maracaibo

Lake Maracaibo

Palmarito

Merida

Cucuta

Bacaramanga   Pamplona

PACIFIC
OCEAN

Cali

Popayan

Pasto

Tulcan

ECUADOR

Porto Cabello

Trancheras

Caracas

Cumana

Curmanacoa

Pui Pay

Peninsula
de Paria

TRINIDAD

VENEZUELA

River Orinoco

COLOMBIA

Bogota

0   100   200km

Chapter 8. Colombia and Venezuela

The football match, Peru

Plate 42

Market scenes, Equador.

Plate 43

The graveyard, Tulcan, Northern Equador.

Plate 44

Mountain view, Southern Columbia

Plate 45

Reaching the Caribbean

Plate 46 LAND ROVER sponsored

Venezuelan birdlife

Plate 47

Street scene, Porto Cabello

Plate 48

Beach, Venezuela

Plate 49

Chapter Eight:
Colombia and Venezuela

When we chose our route in South America there had been a lingering concern about Colombia, a country with an enduring image of lawlessness. It was not safe and presented a threatening obstacle in our minds. But without including it the plan would be imperfect, somehow lacking in completeness. There was a vital practical reason to cross Colombia and that was linked to our onward travel. We had to ship Rabia from the east coast of South America and Venezuela offered the best port option. In addition, there was an emotional appeal to continuing through the Andes. We had driven the Inca Trail to its conclusion at the top of Ecuador. That route, by necessity, had followed the Andes all the way from Chile but we had met that objective. Why not follow the Andes, we argued, to reach their northern limits in South America. That would make a fitting destination. We would follow the mountains to their final descent on the Venezuelan coast where they slip below the Caribbean. I was sure there would be a beach there, perhaps a tropical paradise that would make a good conclusion to the journey - an emotional 'full stop'.

The popular perception of Venezuela was that it was relatively safe but Colombia was not and would require a different approach. There would be no ambling through country roads, no ad-hoc diversions and definitely no night driving. Camping in remote places was ill-advised and photography could not be allowed to distract from driving. We would cross 1600km from border-to-border in three days of hard driving. The British Embassy had said that the regions of greatest risk were those furthest from the capital, just after the crossing from Ecuador and before reaching Venezuela. But when the Embassy heard of my solo journey plan I was comprehensively disowned by Her Majesty's representatives in Bogota.

I left Tulcan early on the first day, in apprehensive mood. The place was a ghost town at sunrise and I rattled through the empty cobbled streets to reach the border post. It was a beautiful day and the air was cool and clear. Volcano Cumbal to the west of town had a brooding presence, puffing lazy smoke into the blue sky. The crossing was in a valley and I descended to find an attractive set of buildings staffed by friendly officials. I made my exit from Ecuador in a record-breaking four minutes but, a hundred yards along the road, Colombian formalities were more difficult and I waited in a queue for nearly two hours to deal with my entry requirements. Rabia, however, was cleared quickly, the Carnet forming the only requirement. There were no convoys of vehicles forming to drive the dangerous road to Cali and as I was already behind plan I decided to drive on at my own pace. I set the GPS to the first waypoint, the town of Pasto, and eased Rabia onto the narrow road through the mountains.

What a pleasant surprise! We were surrounded by a beautiful and spectacular landscape of rolling hills, wooded slopes and deep valleys, clothed in all shades of tropical green. At a greater distance rugged Andean peaks rose in jagged fingers to reach an inky sky. Surrounded by splendid scenery, it was hard to concentrate on the road but this was a day to make distance, not to admire the views. The small villages challenged the notion of a region locked in conflict with central government. Instead of dilapidation and poverty we passed through neat settlements, tidy and clean places, with bright plants in flower. People made gardens here! It was easy to ignore the reality, that FARC guerrillas controlled this region.

I was becoming more concerned about a greater risk than the threat of kidnapping. Driving standards were beyond poor! Vehicles were passing us on bends, completely blind to oncoming traffic. We had found that each country had local driving conventions which we would try to adopt quickly and I wondered what code of driving conduct these strange manoeuvres complied with. There was no doubt that blind overtaking was a normal practice in Colombia. The question was, how should I respond?

We reached Pasto and edged through chaotic traffic but with a friendly Latin spontaneity, a kindly reception from total strangers. A message of welcome was shrieked at me through the open window of a passing car. We followed a dust cart into town and two labourers, clinging to the back, waved and smiled. Pedestrians shouted a happy welcome from the sidewalk. I was beginning to warm to the place and to feel more relaxed about the crossing. We reached open country again, driving through remote valleys where the steep slopes were soft and green with cultivation. The plantations were fronted with banana and avocado trees but I suspected there were more exotic, and lucrative, crops up the slope hidden from view. I wondered if the region's less impoverished appearance was, in some measure, due to a local economy with its roots in drugs.

The narrow road twisted through the landscape and traffic continued to pass on blind bends. I watched other vehicles ahead of me and began to see meaning behind this strange convention. Colombia's commercial vehicles were old and lacked power so, once speed and momentum were acquired, the drivers were reluctant to hang back in a convoy of traffic which would inevitably develop on the twisting and often steep roads. That was in no one's interests. Once speed was achieved it should be maintained. Those overtaking did not often meet an oncoming vehicle but if there **was** a confrontation, and this is the crucial point, it was expected that the oncoming vehicle and the vehicle being overtaken would both brake to allow the passing vehicle to escape from the impending head-on collision. That was the way things worked! In general, this curious convention made for an efficient traffic flow but often left me feeling out of control of events around me. It was worrying too that sometimes the convention failed and the mangled wreckage by the roadside gave testament to a brutal collision and the inevitable loss of life.

The road north to Cali was locked between the Cordillera Occidental and the Andes and made no dramatic ascents. Those would come later! I was pleased with our progress that day, reaching the outskirts of the town by late afternoon and well before the onset of darkness. I planned to camp, staying close to Rabia and making a prompt departure next morning. Open countryside would not be secure but some 20km before Cali I found Robertali's restaurant which had a grassy area under mature trees adjacent to his building. Robertali welcomed me with a broad smile. "Of course you can camp here," he said, his body language conveying his warm hospitality. Initially, the evening passed with a predictable routine but soon degenerated into happy chaos. Colombians, it seemed, used any opportunity to party. Robertali had summoned friends to meet his strange visitor and his two boisterous children swarmed around me, curious and fascinated by my incursion into their play area. Digital photography was new to them and their images on my camera screen caused whoops of excitement.

I had never seen an impromptu party develop so quickly! Some people arrived, drinks were served and my campsite under the trees soon filled with noisy babble and laughter. My dinner burnt, a cow reached through the fence and ate my vegetables, someone spilled my sundowner and the family dog took up residence in the Coffin which I had managed to lay out on the ground. My precious stocks of Ecuadorian chocolate chip cookies were all gone, gifted to the increasing number of lively children. I resigned myself to the flow of happy events that filled Robertali's garden for the rest of the evening. Much later, after guests had said goodbye and email addresses had been exchanged, I had the garden to myself again. I looked over to the adjoining field to see a myriad of fireflies twinkling in the darkness amongst the long grasses. It was finally a peaceful ending to a long day.

In Colombia the Andes divide to form two separate chains. The western spur follows the Pacific Rim of Fire towards Panama. The eastern chain, the longer and higher of the two, continues into Venezuela before its graceful descent into the Caribbean. My journey east from Cali would take me over both chains during two more days of surprisingly demanding auto-mountaineering. We left Robertalis before dawn, hoping to cross town quickly, but already the place was busy with a strange mixture of traffic - bicycles, buses, cars and the occasional horse and cart - which made progress slow. By late morning we turned east towards Bogotá to cross the first of the Andean spurs which appeared as an impenetrable barrier to progress in front of me. The road ascended steeply through lush mountain forests, weaving backwards and forwards in a familiar way. During one and a half hours we made 15km linear distance east and ascended a remarkable 2000m. This was the only road crossing of the spur and was busy with heavy commercial traffic. The climb for those old Colombian vehicles was taking its toll and we passed twenty trucks, all broken down at the roadside, in various states of disassembly. One lorry had its gearbox out and an engine had caught fire in another. On that ascent the Colombian etiquette for overtaking made perfect sense; once momentum was lost some vehicles would not be able to complete the climb.

I noticed that children on small home-made carts were being towed up the mountain behind trucks. The cart wheels were old truck bearings, the bodies were made from scrap wood and the children carried large plastic containers during the dangerous ascent. A boy on a cart hurtled round a bend towards me, descending at speed and on board the large plastic container was now full of water. This was not a game - a child's sport - to race down from the summit back to their villages in the valley. He was carrying fresh water from the stream high in the Andes back to his home and it was his job that morning to fetch supplies for the family.

I had hoped to cross Bogotá before sunset that day but the mountain traffic had slowed my pace and I was late. I reached the city during rush hour and followed a pre-planned GPS route round the outskirts in heavy congestion. It was frustrating but everyone seemed in good humour, perhaps resigned to this slow progress as a feature of everyday life in the capital. It was dark when I left town, travelling through the northern suburbs on Highway 55.

As part of our security plan for Colombia I called Eileen each evening from the satellite phone. My contact was expected to confirm safe travel that day and I stopped by the highway to call, already concerned about finding a secure place for the night. The phone failed to work for the first time in South America and I tried twice more, further down the road, with the same outcome. I did not realise at the time that the signal was blocked. I was only 5km from the airport and the army was everywhere. I had driven out of Colombia's southern region that day, where the army had no presence, into one with heavy artillery at every strategic place, including bridges, major junctions and village centres. It took time that evening to find an internet facility to confirm with Eileen that progress was good and I wasn't, after all, another hostage statistic. (Seven Europeans had been kidnapped a few weeks previously).

I was tired and driving on into rural Colombia in the dark had no appeal. I noticed a secluded area behind a 24 hour petrol station on the outskirts of town. It was not a salubrious place but it was hidden behind the forecourt's bright lights. There would be staff around all night and I settled in to make camp. As if to justify my curious choice I argued that it really didn't matter where you camp after dark!

The following morning I left early, soon passing into green and forested valleys where morning mists drifted lazily through the surrounding landscape. The sky was powder blue but high cumulus hung in the distance. We started to ascend again, to make the crossing of the second Andean spur. Two lorries had crashed that morning and their mangled wrecks lay at the bottom of a steep banking. The drive became superb – beautiful scenery through quiet roads under clear skies. Wild poinsettias made a splash of red by the roadside, a bright display adding to a scene already profuse with colour. During the rest of the day altitude, the third dimension, played an increasing part in our travel. We descended from 1100 to 600m in ten minutes, ascending immediately up to 1300m from the valley. We found a good route through Bucaramanga but against a GPS distance of 56km to Pamplona, the road sign said 120km. What lay ahead? We made another dramatic ascent within the eastern arm of the Andes chain, to reach a cloud forest high on the steep slopes. It was late afternoon and the place was wet with rain and mist giving no scope for a good camp site. We drove on, reaching a summit in thick fog where visibility was down to 10m and thunder grumbled noisily in the distance. We had reached 3500m and our prospects looked grim. A red truck raced up behind us with no lights and overtook us at a blind bend in the mist. Pure suicide! We descended and soon broke through the cloud base onto a flat moor stretching to infinity. Some cottages were scattered through the landscape, white and clean in a panorama devoid of trees. It was very grey and I imagined myself to be in Scotland's Outer Hebrides.

There was now an urgency to find somewhere to stop. In the first village there was a gas station and I took my lead from the previous night. I was welcome to stay on the rough ground behind the station for the night. I called home, rigged the Coffin and set about dinner but I had little appetite. I was very tired and the meal had no appeal. There was sheet lightning all around, no sound - just the illuminations which profiled the high cumulus with a mysterious cold outline.

I intended to cross into Venezuela the following morning. I would descend to the border near Cucuta which, I had been told, was full of thieves and bandits. The day opened in a style untypical of South America – cold mists enveloped the miserable fields around me. There was no hint of movement in the damp air, no sound of life from the nearby cottages, just a still and cold morning. The horizon was lost in grey emptiness and the nearby buildings stood in ghostly profile. A pig in a nearby enclosure grunted its displeasure at the dank conditions and two tethered sheep, resigned to the bleak morning, watched me prepare to leave. I joined the road and was enveloped in mist and rain during the descent to Pamplona, my first destination.

The road was quiet and I reflected on my Colombian journey, my headlong flight over 1600km through some beautiful landscapes. I had been spurred on with unseemly haste by my fear of an unseen threat, not enjoying any real contact with the country, not feeling its daily rhythm and not seeing its finer qualities. But one aspect of my rushed passage had made a real impact on me. I had enjoyed some brief moments with the people and had found them to be the most spontaneous and friendly in South America. One day, I hoped, I could visit again when stability had returned. I had seen nothing of the country's crime – perhaps, after all, this was a generalisation disproportionate to the reality. True, I had faced dangerous and life threatening conditions but these had been on the narrow and twisting roads. The congestion had caused the greatest problem and had turned the Colombian roads into the most dangerous during our global travels.

On this occasion the immigration process to Venezuela had required more planning for me than for Rabia. I needed a visa and a yellow fever certificate, both obtained in advance. Rabia's entry required only an up-to-date Carnet. By early afternoon we had reached Cucuta's busy border post. The place lacked discipline and people loitered everywhere near the border selling currency and making deals in huddled groups, the nature of which I could only guess. After a trouble-free crossing, I headed for San Cristobal for the night where I hoped to restock and change money.

You know something is wrong with an economy when you cannot use US dollars to buy any local currency legally. I walked the streets trying to swap some precious US currency but even the National Bank of Venezuela was not taking dollars, or any foreign currency for that matter. A red light was beginning to flash in my mind. There was a strange absence of *Casa de Cambios* (Money Exchange) for a border town and I resorted to checking for black market opportunities. I needed cash to eat! I found the bus station, a favourite haunt of money changers but failed. Someone tried to help, "Ask Hosé in the tool shop on the third floor of the Civic Centre."

Hosé was friendly and courteous. Over a counter cluttered with chisels and other wood-working tools, he took my US$500, giving me a good rate to buy Bolivars which was 35% more than the current bank rate (had the bank been selling!). In the quiet confines of his shop Hosé filled me in on the problem. "Our currency is collapsing," he said, adding "our savings are vanishing and the government has stopped all of us changing our money to foreign currency. If the banks can't sell dollars, they also can't buy them – they have no need."

The collapsing value of the Bolivar was very visible when I shopped for supplies. Petrol, never lower than 18 cents per litre anywhere in the world, was a staggering 6 cents per litre, priced in Bolivars. A six-pack of beer (excellent quality as I later found out) was priced at an equivalent of US$1 for six large cans. My 5-star hotel room that night was US$15. Despite the euphoria of cheap shopping I realised that I was benefiting from a currency in free-fall and the people, already poor, were losing everything.

From San Cristobal the eastern spine of the Andes, now called the Sierra Nevada, heads for the Caribbean but turns east before reaching the coast. The mountains then remain parallel with Venezuela's shore, renamed as the Cordillera de la Costa. They lose height and vigour to become the Peninsula de Paria on the coast, just before the offshore island of Trinidad. The peninsula was my final destination but the first step on the journey was to reach Merida at the heart of the Sierra Nevada. I had an invitation to stay there with Ana-Maria Attryde, a friend from our days in Saudi Arabia. The ascent back into the mountain chain was made tricky by tight bends and steep gradients which were sufficiently severe to deter lorries and buses from that route. Consequently, it was quiet and I enjoyed the journey. From high passes I looked down on ribbons of cloud spread through adjoining valleys but the mountain slopes, now bright green and tropical, rose to higher peaks under a clear sky.

Merida is the 'jewel in the crown' of Venezuela's high places and sits in a deep valley between parallel mountain ridges. Pico Bolivar (5007m), the country's highest mountain, rises above the city and is capped in permanent snow. Ana-Maria knew the locality well and had been a member of the local mountain rescue team whilst at Merida University. She accompanied me on a journey up the mountain by teleferique. The installation is the highest and longest cable car system in the world and I was curious to see how the high Andes had changed since I had last explored them in Ecuador. I was now 10° further north after my frantic sprint through Colombia, when I had been surrounded by them but had neither time nor opportunity to appreciate their northerly evolution. The cable car would take me up to 4700m again where I would see the changes first hand.

After two hours rising through the cable car's three sections we walked into a landscape new to me. There were a few brightly coloured flowers in bloom but the scenery was wild and barren, eroded by glaciation and weather. We reached a strange forest of gnarled low trees. Ana-Maria explained that this was a fossil forest - a form of ancient tree species that survived in a high altitude. Mist swirled around making it appear a strange and unworldly place.

We descended to find Merida in ferment! University students had rioted and the city streets were littered with burning tyres. Traffic was at a stand-still and the issue behind the problem was not clear. The incident brought home to me that Venezuela was a volatile place and an important election was due. I could not drive north to follow the Sierra Nevada as planned since the road was blocked by the army. "This is fate," I thought as I escaped the burning tyres and mayhem of Merida by driving south then west. By evening I had reached Palmarito on the shore of Lake Maracaibo, driving through an increasingly Caribbean landscape as the road descended. It was hot and humid as I set up camp on my first tropical coastline, right on the shore, surrounded by coconut palms and a few grass huts. I had come to this place hoping to see the spectacular display of Catatumbo dry lightning during the night.

The lake is the largest in South America and I enjoyed a cool swim as a bright sunset display was forming over the western horizon. It was a restful end to a hard day and a particularly tough piece of beef had cooked to tender succulence in the engine bay. I rigged the Coffin so that the open panel at the head faced west, in the direction of the spectacle that would unfold after dark. I felt a strong compulsion to see this amazing display, a work of nature that remains without a good technical explanation to the present day. The phenomenon is unique to our planet and takes place at the south end of the enormous lake. After dark the sky flashes with vivid lightning and, dry and silent, it dances across the horizon with a macabre blue light. At its most spectacular time, during the dry season, the display exceeds the best discothèque laser lighting but without the noise!

The lightning started on time that evening, intermittently lighting up the distant cumulous clouds above the horizon. Soon the frequency and brightness increased, becoming a continuous ripple of ghostly silent light over the length of the western skyline. The spectacle was the strangest sight I had seen in South America. I retired to the inner confines of the Coffin to enjoy viewing the evening's display in repose. All evening the intensity of the light increased but, by midnight, I failed to question the abnormal accompaniment of thunder.

I slept well but by 2.00am I woke to find the show had travelled towards me and had reached the middle of the lake. It had now become ominous and threatening. At 5.00am the heavens opened and, in an instant, a wall of rain cascaded down and thunder crashed overhead. The Catatumbo Lightning was no longer 'dry' and worse, it was in my backyard. It had turned into a no-nonsense tropical storm and water rattled noisily on my canvas cocoon. I realised I was trapped, entombed in the Coffin for the duration, with no prospect of a dry escape. "This is the ultimate test of Australian technology," I thought, lying in the close confines of the swag. "Tropical storms are short, aren't they?" The clock ticked by and the storm worsened. A glimpse outside convinced me that I should stay put, zipped in and still dry.

By 7.00am, wind had added an extra dimension to the turmoil. I could hear waves crashing onto the banking a few feet away, the earth shaking with each blow. "Can the swag float?" I wondered, marvelling at its impermeability so far. But the confinement had gone on long enough and with a deft flip of the roof opening I made a quick exit. I closed the swag, dashed for my swimming costume and saw, to my horror, that the lake was overflowing on to my patch of paradise. Water ran in tidal waves through the sand underneath the swag. "What a welcome to the Caribbean coast," I thought. Soaked and naked but still in control, I dragged the swag through soggy sand underneath a canopy of a deserted beach restaurant nearby. Rain cascaded off the shelter's roof in a solid wall of water. I unzipped the Coffin to check my pillows and sleeping bag, expecting problems. To my surprise the inside was completely dry! Not even the lake's overflow had penetrated the bottom to soak the inner mattress. The contraption had held at bay two hours of tropical rain, a soggy beach and driving wind but it had still been an unnerving experience, to be inside such a small space whilst the world was in chaos outside. Despite the hardship I would not have missed one moment of the Catatumbo Lightning that night.

Palmarito was wet and forlorn when I left. Streets were flooded and neatly dressed children huddled under shelters, perhaps secretly delighted that school would not open that morning. I rejoined the route north to reach Porto Cabello on the coast. Rabia would be shipped from there, when the South American journey was over and I wanted to arrange that with a shipping company before continuing along the

Cordillera de la Costa. The weather became bright and sunny but the highway's lethal potholes were hidden below a flooded road.

We drove north rising into the cordillera that day, passing rocky hillsides coloured red and softened with low shrubs and cacti. Huge thunder clouds remained over the distant peaks adding a hint of malice to an otherwise pleasant day. Venezuelan police stopped me twice in an attempt to extort a payment but it was a weak effort compared with Peru and easily deflected. The drive that day was long, over 500km, and I camped on the coast where large flocks of flamingos were feeding in shallow coastal waters.

I had already found two companies at Porto Cabello who could ship Rabia and I planned to visit both the next day near the Plaza Bolivar in the middle of town. The area around the plaza was bright and tidy. Small shops and homes down narrow streets were painted in vivid colours which seemed fitting decoration for a Caribbean coastal town. My first contact was with CCNI, a shipping firm of long standing. A good plan soon emerged and costs were within my budget of US$1000. Shipping, customs and port handling matters were agreed leaving only minor costs for wharfage and storage to be concluded later.

I didn't need a second shipping quote so drove to the hot springs at Tricheras for the rest of the day. It was a place of quiet charm, the old colonial hotel at the site hinting at the former grandeur of the place. High mountains, clothed in fresh colours, rose steeply to enclose it. I booked a room and quickly immersed myself in the pools of steaming water. You could choose to boil at 45ºC in one pool, squirm in the grey, but therapeutic mud of a second, or inhale the steamy vapours through special vents. A few hardy souls were pummelled by high pressure jets of hot spring water - the choices seemed limitless. But it was also a restful place with palms to shade the bathers relaxing by the pools. I alternated between the pool's sweltering heat and the coolness of the rest area for an hour, enjoying the mellow sunlight of late afternoon.

I was relaxed, ready for a few days of travel to reach the end of the journey. The Peninsula de Paria was 1200km away, along the coastal cordillera. The mountains swept east some way inland from the Venezuelan coast and were, in truth, the runt end of the Andes. But they held a soft charm, different from the raw power further south and in their own way displayed a wholly respectable eminence.

I had some concerns which threatened to spoil the mood. Chavez, the country's President, was unpopular and a referendum would be held that week, which had, as its ultimate objective, his removal from power. The economy was in ruins and there were fears that the President was following Castro towards extreme left-wing policies. If the referendum succeeded, there would be a national election in a few months to depose the President. The advice from those in the port was strange but unequivocal – "Get your car out soon." There was growing social unrest and nearly every Venezuelan I met warned me of soaring crime. The beautiful streets of Porto Cabello, after dark, were now deadly criminal areas. I wondered if our past journey experience of safety in rural areas would hold true. I sensed that perhaps the greatest threat to Rabia and me at the present time was here, in Venezuela, rather than Colombia. My remaining camp sites would be selected very carefully.

Driving through Caracas the next day was an experience to be endured rather than enjoyed. I had to change my outward flight plan and visited Iberia's city office. The capital was surrounded by mountains and a thick blanket of smog tenaciously smothered the city, unable to escape. Skyscrapers rose through the haze, their tops seeming to hang curiously in mid air. Caracas was grid-locked at 9.00am and the disgusting smell of trapped exhaust fumes filled the air. It was a miserable place and I was glad to escape over the coastal plain towards Barcelona.

Diary Note, 23 November (to the cave at Guacharo)

Election day! Voting stalls are erected in the centre of towns and villages along the coast. Army personnel loiter everywhere, watching suspiciously. But the mood is slightly festive – God knows why. I suspect Venezuela's future may depend on this referendum and I cannot guess how reliable the outcome will be for the voters.

Passing through some smaller villages on the journey to Cueva Guacharo, I see more lively voting. Here and there some marshal music blasts from speakers rigged on trucks. It scares the hell out of me! The road is bad and although mostly tarmac there are canyon sized pot holes to catch the unwary and good navigation is important this morning. By 9.00am I am rising through exotic jungle. In Curmanacoa the place is really busy. Long queues have formed and there is an increasingly joviality to the day's voting.

I have mixed sentiments about this ascent into the tail-end of the Andes. The mountains are benign. The uncompromising virility of the chain has gone, replaced by gentle and beautiful green slopes, almost fragile in their texture and stunningly green in colour. The road meanders through an unchallenging ascent and poinsettias are now in their brightest crimson, set against yellow coleus. But here they are wild, growing metres high and the accompanying bougainvillea add their own flamboyance. It's a wonderful spectacle and it feels like Christmas!

I reached the cave high in the mountains to find that the Andes had one final surprise to show me. The cave is home to 15,000 Guacharo birds, a large blind nocturnal fruit eating species, the only one of its kind in the world. I wanted to witness their mass flight from the cave at sunset – something quite special in nature. I found a quiet corner in the entrance to the cave, not sure of what to expect. Soon a noisy cackle came from deep within and then the entrance was filled with a pandemonium of birds, black silhouettes fluttering like giant bats, leaving to forage for the night. You need a sense of perspective on this to appreciate the moment. The cave entrance was only 50m high by approximately 20m wide. Each bird had a wing span of one metre and navigated only by a radar location system. Six hundred birds were leaving the cave every minute to vanish into the night sky and the spectacle continued for twenty minutes until the cave lay still and quiet. I found a space to camp nearby under a starry sky and was lost in wonder at the display – I had seen nothing like it.

The next day, my last travelling in the Andes, I drove to the Caribbean following the mountain's graceful descent to reach the coast. I hoped there would be a remote stretch of golden sand with willowy palms, a defining point in the journey where I could look back to green mountains tumbling to the sea and say, "This is the end, there is no more!" I was drawn towards this stylised ideal by my Lonely Planet Guide which said of the coast, "It has the country's loveliest beaches between Rio Caribe and San Juan." I found an unpaved and rough track through the coastal jungle and, with a measure of effective GPS navigation and good luck we found our beach near a tiny fishing settlement called Pui Pay. The last remnants of the Cordillera de la Costa reached sea level behind the palm trees. There was truly no more and I had found my beach paradise.

Two friends from Australia, Harold and Carmel, had given me a miniature bottle of Hennessey to celebrate a landmark event on my journey and it seemed fitting to open it there. I was 63° west of Greenwich and a mere 150km from Trinidad and there would be no further progress east. I had travelled 15,000km since leaving Santiago, mostly in the mountains which I had followed. I stayed in 'paradise' for two days encircled by palms, blue sea and fine white sand, enjoying some relaxation, a few beers and the occasional swim. Rabia was made ready for her Atlantic crossing. She would leave from Porto Cabello and I would fly to the UK. My evenings were special times. Surf hissed up the beach beside me, fireflies danced in the darkness through the palms and a confection of stars filled the dark night sky. It was a place of silence except, by choice, for some quiet music by Elgar and Delius.

I was looking forward to sharing time with Eileen over Christmas and then moving on with the journey as a full team again. Playing nomads on my own, I thought, could be seriously suicidal. My time in South America was a splendid indulgence compared with the lives of those around me but it had surpassed my greatest hopes. I finished reading the book '*Between Extremes*' by Brian Keenan and John McCarthy and one part hit a chord with my own solo experience. "Aloneness is something we carry with us at all times, yet how do we understand it and, more importantly, how do we value it."

We returned to Caracas following a coastal route, camping on beautiful beaches along the way. We reached Porto Cabello on 3 December leaving three days before my flight home. In that time, I had to clear Rabia through customs and seal her in her shipping container. The process did not go smoothly but with time and patience solutions were found to handle the bureaucratic delays and confusion.

We finally parted, Rabia safely stored for shipment in two weeks while I returned to Caracas by local bus to catch my flight to Madrid and then to Birmingham. I had come to find that Venezuela was a lawless place. An attempted theft had left Rabia with a broken door handle. I had lost clothing on a remote beach whilst swimming. Camping on another beach, a stunningly beautiful place, I had noticed that it was protected all night by a guard with a Kalashnikov watching the local fishing boats. It had been serious – there had been gun fire from the local village. Asdrubal, my contact at the port, had been viciously attacked and robbed of his car the previous week. Porto Cabello's bus station had a fearsome reputation for crime and, at 6.30am, waiting on a concrete bench for my transport, I was nervous. I clutched my three bags to me and watched the morning unfold.

You see the essence of a place in a bus station, catch the mood and see the flow of everyday lives. A dog with a bent ear and serious limp lay near me scratching contentedly. Relieving flea bites would be the only gratification at dawn and, on a good day, food scraps may come later. Nearby, a trader gifted a cup of runny porridge from his cart to a shoe-shine boy, a scruffy and dirty youth of lower status in the scheme of things. They chatted quietly before the day's hustling started in earnest. There was still time for a friendly gesture.

I boarded the old fashioned bus for the four hour journey, feeling a sense of separation from Rabia - our reunion would be on another continent. Driving back to Caracas it felt strange to cover distance without her. On the journey to the airport I reflected on the vitality and beauty of the Venezuelan people. Their attractiveness and strength had impressed me and was probably due to the diversity of stock. Without much ethnic segregation, European, local Indian, African and Asian blood had mixed to form a powerful blend, a unique and potent gene pool for the future.

The roar of the Airbus engines signalled the imminence of take off and I left Venezuela to the tones of the Christmas carol *'Hark the Herald Angels Sing'* over the plane's speakers. I was beginning to feel in Christmas spirit.

Chapter Nine:
North West Africa

We had to include Africa to add completeness to our global journey. When we planned our route from the Middle East our initial thoughts were to start there, driving the length of the continent from Ethiopia through Kenya to reach Cape Town, from where we could then ship Rabia to Australia. In the end we decided to leave for Australia straight away. The shipping costs to Oz from the Middle East were especially low, US$800, because there was so much empty container traffic going there. We could plan an African route later, after we had driven through South America.

When the expedition reached Venezuela it was time to decide about South Africa. What part of Africa did we want to see? How much time would it take and what were the shipping costs? Another factor had also entered the equation, a crucial point that was finally the deciding factor. From a legal standpoint Rabia was still registered in Saudi Arabia. She had Arabic plates and her Carnet, which had been crucial to our progress, was issued by a Saudi authority. By May, in four months time, we would have to register her in England but we could not do that without returning there. The African journey would have to be finished by that time.

Shipping Rabia to Cape Town would have been ideal, driving through the continent to Europe and on to England. But we had found that a slower pace was best suited to our travels. Driving for driving's sake was not our objective and our style had evolved to give us more leisure time along the way. The length of Africa would be a plan too fast for us before May. Besides, without a direct shipping line, the costs for Rabia to South Africa were high - well over US$1900.

The option was to travel in North West Africa, leaving time for a more leisurely pace and using Rabia for the purpose that she was best suited - to give reliable access to beautiful and remote places that we could explore and enjoy. That plan had merit. We would be there in early spring and the region would be ideal for our style of travel. There were deserts, mountains and desolate shorelines where we could slow our pace to fill the time with interest. We researched the container rates and costs to the port at Casablanca where we could enter the region. As always, we watched for the hidden charges that sometimes surface late in these negotiations. True to form, some poorly explained extras soon began to surface to get her through the port on arrival, none of which I was able to conclude in Venezuela. A better option soon emerged, which was to ship the container to Spain and cross to Morocco by ferry to start the journey.

One problem surfaced when we added substance to that plan. We wanted to include Morocco, Algeria and Tunisia in the route and, perhaps Libya - the Maghreb of North Africa. We would return to Europe by ferry from either Tunisia or Alexandria. Only one border was a problem - Morocco to Algeria - and that was central to the plan. A legal land crossing would not be possible since the border at Oijda was closed. There was a solution to pass that border which meant using ferries to and from Spain and we decided to keep that option available.

By late January Rabia had reached Valencia and had been cleared through Spanish customs. Only one problem blighted an otherwise effortless port clearance. A kind of port 'mafia' was controlling freight handling and an exorbitant charge was made to move her container 100 metres from the wharf to an adjacent area where Rabia could be driven out from her confinement. There was also an additional charge, hidden from the original quotation, to cover two people for half a day to unstrap Rabia inside her container and drive her out. We did that ourselves in ten minutes whilst the staff stood by - but the charge was still levied. In the end the 'extras' in Spain were nearly equal to her shipping costs.

With Eileen back in the team again we drove to southern Spain through Granada, where the mountain tops were deep in snow in early February, to reach the port of Algeciras. There were gales in the Straits of Gibraltar and ferry services to Africa had been halted. The storms increased all day and Algeciras port was a grey miserable place to wait in a ferry queue which was lengthening by the hour. By night time we were reluctant to move out from our place in the queue to find a room for the night but we had a solution! We erected the roof tent and Algeciras port became an unusual camp site.

The storm abated the next day and we crossed to Tangier driving down Morocco's Atlantic coast to Casablanca where, in our minds, we would start our journey. We were back in an Arabic country again and after fourteen years in Saudi Arabia, Morocco's atmosphere felt familiar to us. The evocative call to prayer from shrill speakers on countless minarets, the narrow passageways through lively souks filled with aromatic fragrance and the flowing robes all hit a familiar chord. We had admired the kindness and generous hospitality of Arabia, admired the discipline and commitment to the Islamic culture and wondered how North West Africa would fit into that experience. Although we were not in the Middle East we had a sense of 'arrival', of reaching familiar ground through the things around us.

Our plans were flexible but an outline had evolved which we hoped would give us an unusually wide variety of landscapes as spring developed. First, we would travel down the Atlantic coast to the Western Sahara and then turn east all the way to Erfoud. We would be travelling a region below the Anti Atlas, where the mountains descend to become the Northern Sahara. During February it would still be cold in the mountains but this would be the best time to be in the more southern desert region. By mid March it would be sufficiently warm to explore the High and Middle Atlas and to reach into their more remote regions where we would again call on Rabia's mountaineering talents. There would be many good 4x4 routes to reach interesting and colourful places. As spring gained momentum, April would be the best time to head through the Riff Mountains on to the Mediterranean coast (which we had found positively cold in February). We thought the timing of that plan was good and we could set our own pace on that journey, adjusting to suit the things that interested us.

Major highways had little appeal to us and we found a good route following a minor coastal road from Casablanca to Essaouira, 400km to the south. We left the city's beautiful but neglected architecture and wide boulevards, passing the massive Hassan II Mosque, to head through a clutter of dowdy buildings on the outskirts of the city. We needed to refill our gas cylinders, always a trial in a new country and when we reached Jedida we tracked down an Africa Gaz depot, a small place in a wholly disorganised industrial area. The staff rose to the challenge, finding a make-shift solution to decant propane through a complex and probably dangerous series of connections. We were finding that Rabia's Arabic plates and our basic French were giving us credibility.

Morocco's south Atlantic coast was a delight in February but still cold at night. We camped in the small village of Oualidia, dining on crabs and oysters bought locally from a jovial band of fishermen and oyster farmers. This was sea food heaven! The journey to Essaouira the next day, along the high Atlantic cliffs, was strangely quiet, devoid of people or traffic. Even Safi was a ghost town. At a road block the police were glued to a portable television. I disturbed the staff to ask what was happening. "We are playing Algeria this afternoon," he said, as if to justify their disregard of passing traffic. It was the Africa Cup final and Morocco was a passionate country about football. Nothing brings a country to a stop quicker than sport. On a previous journey, we had driven through Karachi during Pakistan's cricket match in the world cup final. The streets were eerily deserted.

Essaouira was strangely muted that night. Morocco had lost 2-1 and the noisy car horns and loud drums were missing. Arabs, we knew, were exuberant noisy people when their national team won. But nothing could deter from the old town's charm and evocative narrow streets, despite the downcast mood.

The final stages of the route to Agadir, although highway, followed a dramatic coastline. High cliffs overlooked wide beaches where Atlantic surf thundered on shore. We found a quiet place to camp, high on a bluff overlooking the sea, away from the shoreline's noisy rumble. Rabia's inner workings had stood up well to the punishment in Australia and South America but we were careful to watch for early signs of potential problems. Prevention, we had learned, was better than cure. We detected a developing leak in a high pressure fluid line connected with her power steering circuit and traced the Land Rover Agency in Agadir where we hoped to buy a replacement. That spare part was not available so we had the new pressure hose fabricated locally. In the late afternoon, prior to leaving Agadir, we shopped for supplies. We wanted some meat to cook as an ECM but our request for 'Agneau' failed miserably to secure Lamb. Eileen, always skilful with body language, made a melodious lamb-like bleating and secured a knowing smile from the butcher. But her bleat had not been sufficiently subtle and a large slab of goat was hacked off a carcass by the smiling butcher, with an assurance of tenderness.

We could leave the confines of the main road into the western end of the Anti Atlas Mountains to reach Guelmime to the south and then descend to drive a stretch of remote Atlantic coast. The 'S' shape route (route 1 on the map) rose through rugged mountains, passing Kasbahs of ochre red, before sweeping down to the coast after Tizinit. In the afternoon light the steep slopes and ancient mud-block Berber villages took on every imaginable hue. In many ways this region at the western limit of the Arab world held an identical mystery and charm to the high mountains at the eastern limits in Yemen. How strange to find the same tower like architecture, hillside terracing and culture. We camped in a pleasant wadi bed and enjoyed the goat meat and vegetables, cooked to tenderness over the manifold during the day's travel. It was a pity about the bits of splintered bone. The butcher, we thought, had chopped into the carcass with excessive enthusiasm that morning!

On the coast before Sidi Ifni we found a place, quite startling in its remote beauty, where a cluster of small beaches and massive stone arches lay below steep cliffs. We left the coast heading inland over an increasingly harsh and rugged coastal plain, made soft in places by green wadis and a few scattered palm trees. We stopped for the day at the Abianou Thermal Springs outside Guelmime. Contrary to Islamic practice, mixed bathing was permitted in the indoor pool, but only after 6.00pm. Mousa, the owner of the nearby restaurant, was a wily Arab with a huge personality. "The temperature dropped in the pool when they made the new building," he said, as he served us a mountain of Moroccan couscous. It was true – the temperature was quite modest.

We turned south at Guelmime over a desolate treeless plain to reach Tan Tan, passing a landscape of repetitive brutality. We had intended to drive further south, even to reach Mauritania but, with that landscape of boundless emptiness continuing all the way, we called a halt at Tan Tan and planned a route east into the Sahara. We were pleased we rented a room that night – it poured! The first rains after three dry winters caused everyone, except us, to become disproportionately excited about the downpour. There was an African brightness to the dress in Tan Tan – men in Tuareg Blue jellabas and ladies in bright kaftans. The place had all the qualities of a sub-Saharan town but looked bedraggled and out of context in the aftermath of a cloud burst.

The River Draa originates in the High Atlas and twists its way to the coast near Tan Tan. In its upper regions it supports a rich valley of *palmeraie* (date palm plantations) olive and almond groves, a fertile place of Kasbahs and Berber villages set in a green landscape. But the waters rarely reached the coast and, in the lower

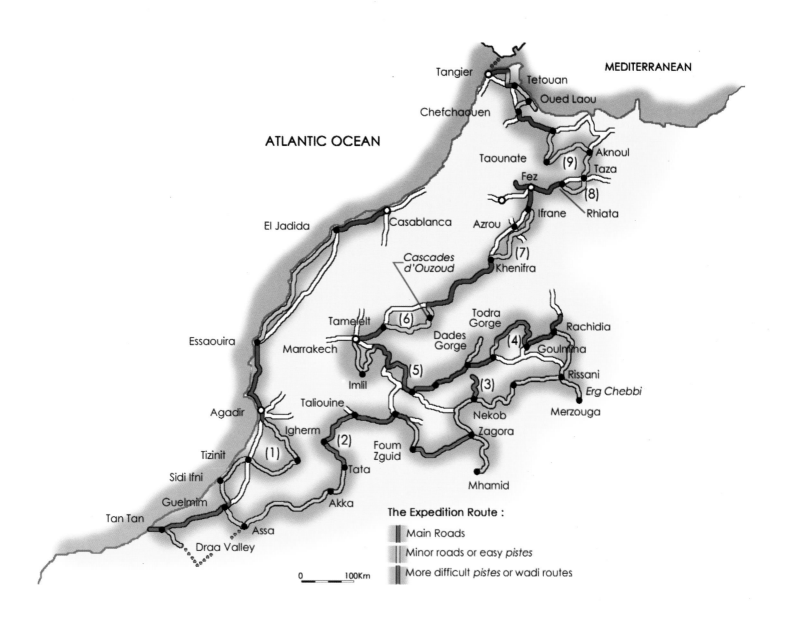

ATLANTIC OCEAN

MEDITERRANEAN

Tangier
Tetouan
Oued Laou
Chefchaouen
Taounate
Aknoul
(9)
Taza
Fez
(8)
Ifrane
Rhiata
El Jadida
Casablanca
Azrou
Cascades d'Ouzoud
(7)
Khenifra
Tamelelt
(6)
Todra Gorge
Rachidia
Dades Gorge
(4)
Goulmina
Essaouira
Marrakech
(5)
Rissani
Erg Chebbi
Imlil
(3)
Merzouga
Taliouine
Nekob
Agadir
Zagora
Igherm
(2)
Tizinit
(1)
Foum Zguid
Sidi Ifni
Tata
Guelmim
Akka
Mhamid
Tan Tan
Assa
Draa Valley

The Expedition Route :

Main Roads

Minor roads or easy *pistes*

More difficult *pistes* or wadi routes

0   100Km

Chapter 9. North West Africa

Sahara Landscapes

Plate 50 LAND ROVER sponsored

Auto Mountaineering in South America

Auto Mountaineering, the High Atlas

Plate 51

The village of Ait Benhaddou

Plate 52

Portraits

Plate 53

Wadi routes

Plate 54  sponsored

Kasbahs and castles

Plate55

The climbing goats of the Anti Atlas

Plate 56

reaches, where the waters seep away in desert sand, it forms a wide stony valley between Zagora and Tan Tan. We planned to drive east in that valley following old tracks which we had researched carefully.

A minor road heads south from Tan Tan to the tiny settlement of Msaid where we planned to start the piste route up the valley. But we never got there, faltering at an army check point 20km down the road. "It's too dangerous – you can't go past here," was the reply to my protest at being stopped. True, Msaid was close to the Mauritanian border but we never fully understood the real reason. We had no option but to turn back to Guelmime, driving over the 150km of barren plain we had crossed the day before. We would try to rejoin Wadi Draa at Assa the next day and, by way of compensation for our bad day, we camped beside a beautifully restored *caravanserai* – an ancient building that served in earlier time as a safe resting place for camels and men at the end of a long Sahara crossing. The old mud-block building towered through the palms and held an enduring charm but had been difficult to find in the heart of a large and derelict palmeraie. It had no proper road access but had been lovingly restored into a museum, an Aladdin's cave of memorabilia which Abdu and his cousin had collected over 20 years.

February 22 was unforgettable – it was the day of the locusts! We drove south to Assa in the early morning light. The day held promise and we descended through rugged escarpments twisted into complex folds of red rock to form whirled hillsides. As we rejoined Wadi Draa we drove into a cloud of locusts that filled the landscape, enormous yellow and brown insects that spanned the palm of a hand. The air was full of them, swarming into Morocco from Mauritania on the prevailing winds which had also brought Tan Tan's rain. They slammed into Rabia, exploding like firecrackers and the yellow entrails splashed over all exposed surfaces. We knew they made good eating, fried in a little butter, but we were disinclined to try.

To our disappointment we found that the piste was now paved all the way to Tata up the valley. There was repetition across the valley's barren plain, singular in appearance. Rather than continue to Foum Zguid through more of the same scenery, we chose a difficult but exciting track into the Anti Atlas towards Igherm (route 2 on the map). Rabia rose to the occasion and we meandered through bright palmeraie and small settlements on the narrow track before a dramatic rocky ascent to reach a high plateau, green with spring grasses after the Atlas winter rains. Looking back over our ascent, the view to Wadi Draa was splendid. At the end of the day we regained a road east at Taliouine and found an Auberge for the night. It was cold and the morning's warmth and brightness brought welcome relief. We decided it was, perhaps, still too early to spend time in the mountains. The wadi back down to the Draa was especially pretty that morning and the rocky hillsides were bright with purple spring flowers. From Foum Zguid we headed for Zagora, 100km to the east, over a rocky and desolate piste. Preparations were underway near the town to upgrade the route but we struggled over eroded wadi beds and along the apparently desolate valley. There were a few people minding herds of goats and camels along the way who rushed over to meet us as we passed. How sad that the opening exchange was always to beg for our belongings.

During that afternoon we bumped our way along the stony piste, becoming more aware of the pick-up truck that was shadowing us a kilometre behind. As darkness descended we set up camp for the night, sure that our desolate location could cause no offence. The pick-up parked beside us and the driver said with an air of authority "You can't camp here, you must move on." It seemed we were in a recently created Reserve for Morocco's rare gazelle and idmi. He was the Berber warden and perhaps our Saudi plates had raised suspicions that we were there to plunder his precious stock for sport, as had happened in the Saudi deserts. We were only half way through the long valley and after some radio conversations with his base he finally relented, leaving us to our remote camp site.

We hoped for a pleasant break after Zagora in the *Erg* (sandy desert) at Mhamid. There we hoped we would find qualities similar to the Rub al Khali or the Great Nafud Desert which we had crossed in Rabia. The Draa Valley turns north here, away from the Algerian border and connects to Marrakech by a good road. Consequently, tourism has transformed the area from a sleepy Sahara backwater of dunes, camels and small villages to a busy commercial place full of carpet sellers, touts and people who claim enduring friendship who could 'help' you. "I have a cousin down the road …" How we hated this rhetoric. It fell terribly short of our expectations and we left quickly to travel the desert route to reach Rissani hoping for better prospects to see the Sahara's finer aspects later. Perhaps we should not have been so optimistic and our disappointment would have been somewhat eased.

We stayed at a small Auberge in Nekob and spent time exploring the high mountain pass into Jebel Sarhro (route 3 on the map). It was no more than a gravel track across the basalt massif. Driven through its entirety it would have made a spectacular crossing between the desert plains and the Dades Valley but we returned from the summit, the Tizi-n-Tazazert pass at 2200m high. As we drove back to Nekob the route was full of ravines and flat topped mezzas which came alive with subtle hues in the evening light while we descended. Young Yousef, a twenty year old cook from the Auberge, had come along squeezed into Rabia beside us. We passed some Berber girls and Yousef took on a manly pose, sporting his carefully tweaked white turban at a rakish angle and wearing my blue sunglasses. The last glow of sunshine dissolved into a steel grey sky spoiling the prospects of a bright sunset. We reached Nekob as the call to prayer rang out over the darkened village and the male population scurried to the Mosque for Friday prayers, dressed in their finest jellabas. The day was coming to a close.

The desert road to Rissani passed through Alnif, the fossil centre of the region and there was a shop of some fame in town. Mohand Ihmadi's place was not large as shops go but he was friendly and his knowledge of fossil hunting was profound. Hearing of our interest to make our own finds, he suggested a wadi bed not far from town, which swept down the debris from the fossil filled mountains close by. After the recent rains new fossils would be exposed in the stream bed. "Go there today, before the children find the new supplies," he said encouragingly. We spent the afternoon in profitable toil under a bright sun, ambling up the wadi and making our own dramatic finds of Precambrian trilobites.

After reaching the busy market town of Rissani, we headed east to reach Erg Chebbi, a drifting expanse of sand mountains close to our preconception of the Sahara. A line of old Kasbahs flanked the eastern edge of the dunes which rose imperiously in graceful wind blown contours. We camped within the peaceful grounds of a Kasbah at the base of a spectacular sand ascent to 1000 feet. Before sunset we climbed the soft slope and enjoyed the view from the summit. The dunes below us rippled south in ridges of contrasting brightness and shade with a delicacy unique to soft mobile sand. The sun, a dull yellow, dropped through the haze over the peaks of Jebel Ougnat and the contrast and structure of the dunes, so beautiful in the low fading light, began to merge and the moment of ephemeral beauty was gone. The wind had exhausted itself leaving the Erg with a stillness and quiet that fitted perfectly with a sandy desert at sunset.

We dined that night on some rough beef cut from the bone in the Rissani market that morning but we smartened our dining area under the vast desert sky with a table cloth and candles. Later, at the onset of the desert's coolness, we retired to the Kasbah's light and warmth for the rest of the evening. Christine, a fellow guest, was in despondent mood. Travelling on her own, she was writing articles for magazines and had endured four days from hell – she needed to unload. She had been systematically 'milked' by a Berber family who had initially offered her home hospitality during the preparation of an article on rural life here. It was a gruelling account of deception and false friendship, not pleasing to hear.

Rabia was running well and, like children playing on a beach, we were tempted to reduce her tyre pressures to drive her for a while through the sands around Erg Chebbi. We had crossed The Great Nafud Desert during earlier travels, spent time in the Rub al Khali, but we noticed the difference between Arabia's disciplined and relatively predictable dune patterns and the random, almost chaotic structure of the Sahara sands. The slip faces, which always faced the same direction in the Nafud, were not aligned in any order here, making vehicle route selection along the ridges and over slip faces more difficult. Perhaps the reason was the varying wind direction in the northern Sahara. We reluctantly decided against the idea. We had no sand ladders and we were on our own. It was an adventure that was too risky and we made do with long walks, feeling the therapeutic pleasure of warm soft sand between our toes.

One predictable aspect to Morocco's landscape was the disciplined alignment of the three chains of Atlas Mountains, the Anti-, High- and Middle Atlas which ran in regular order from south-west to north-east. We had driven 1700km from Tan Tan following a route below the Anti Atlas, along the Draa Valley. We would leave the desert and travel back to the west between the Anti and High Atlas following the Dades Valley to Ouarzazate. There we would turn north across the mountains to reach Marrakech by mid March. It was getting warmer and we would probe some high mountain pistes along the way, hoping that the Atlas would reveal something new to us.

When we arrived at Goulmima we stayed overnight at a small Auberge set in a pretty palmeraie shaded from the hot sun by arching date palms. It was a restful place and the French owner, hearing our intention to explore the Todra and Dades Gorges to the north, offered some local advice. "You must go to Todra by the northern piste which leaves from here," adding that the route would pass through some remote mountain villages along beautiful and less visited wadi routes. We always took local advice seriously and checked our maps. There it was! A barely discernible line ran north into the High Atlas from Goulmima then swept round to join the top of the Todra Gorge (route 4 on the map).

For the first few hours we followed a narrow piste between steep cliffs glowing red under a clear blue sky. At the top, before the village of Amelego, the piste had been washed away by floods and had been abandoned in favour of a rocky but discernible option up the middle of the wadi. (Plate 54). Between Amelego and Assoul a patchwork of emerald green spring crops in tiny valley fields softened the view of sheer ochre red cliffs to rugged ridges. It was late in the day when we finally descended into the Todra Gorge which was, by then, cold, dark and sinister. We camped and, at first light, walked up a donkey track near the gorge to see it at its best, before the buses and tourist traffic reached this popular destination.

Another piste linking the Todra and Dades Gorges through the High Atlas caught our imagination but there was still snow there. We travelled down to the Dades Valley instead, turned west then ascended again, snaking through small villages with ancient Kasbahs and finally round tight hairpins to enter the canyon. Dark cliffs rose sheer in the narrow slot and daylight appeared as a ribbon of blue above the foreboding walls 300m overhead.

Our detours into the High Atlas were pleasant and, in places, offered exciting driving through exquisite scenery but the experience was tarnished by a sad and disquieting aspect to rural travel in Morocco, which was outside our past experience on the Global Discovery Expedition. We had failed to dispense pens and other gifts freely to village children and this had excited some to retaliate. Stones had been thrown and water squirted through Rabia's open window along with shrieked verbal abuse. We learned to watch for the child running to meet us but stopping momentarily to pick up a stone to throw if, after all, we failed to dispense a gift. It was a worrying aspect and we had only come across this in two places in the world before – Egypt and Yemen – but on a lesser scale. We could understand how it had developed through misguided and indiscriminate gifting by earlier travellers but presents were now expected, almost demanded as a right of passage, and it seemed you could be a legitimate target if you did not comply. The Atlas in many respects was similar to the Andes, but smaller, lower and more crowded. Unlike the Andes, there were never any real risks from the mountains and pistes themselves, only it seemed from a few wild children.

Over the next few days travelling down the valley and crossing to Marrakech our lives were filled with interest and variety. We saw the most beautiful Kasbahs in Morocco at Skoura, scattered through the surrounding palm groves. (Plate 55). Viewed from a higher vantage point, ornate lookout towers rose over the green palmeraie growing red in majestic profile against snow covered mountains. At Ouarzazate we enjoyed the French ambience at this peaceful crossroads between early desert and mountain trade routes. At Ait Benhaddou we stared in wonder at the cluster of six-storey ochre Kasbahs and towers rising up the pink sandstone slope of Wadi Mellah, seeming to be built on top of each other. Their restored walls looked exquisite in the late afternoon light. The fortified village is now a UNESCO World Heritage site and has been used as a stage set for films such as Gladiator, Ben Hur and Lawrence of Arabia. It was easy to see why. (Plate 52).

From here we followed a demanding 4x4 track (route 5 on the map) breaking away from the highway. The views were typical of the High Atlas – deep canyons and rocky plains, crowned with high peaks. Two ancient Kasbahs lay at the end of this route, Anemiter and Talouet, both in a sorry state of decay after an illustrious past. We rejoined tarmac here and headed for the main highway. Soon the road ascended through a dizzy series of hairpin bends to make the main crossing of the High Atlas at the Tizi-n-Tichla pass.

We delayed our descent to Marrakech and headed west instead, keeping to high ground to reach Morocco's premier ski area at Oukaimeden near Imlil. The chairlift was still operating and the skiing was good, tempting us to halt briefly in our travels. Jebel Toubkal, the highest point in the Atlas Mountains, rose majestically still in deep snow. Whilst the ski pistes by the chairlift lacked the sophistication and length of European resorts, they were in good condition and provided a few hours of fun at absurdly low prices for equipment hire and day passes. We camped amongst the pines in a nearby forest, beside the remnants of the season's snow which lingered below the village.

We were guests of our niece in Marrakech. Jennifer's home was in a quiet leafy suburb and was a restful retreat for a few days. We roamed the city, caught up with some practical details and enjoyed eating out, as one must in Marrakech, sampling the delicious titbits sold from steaming stalls in the night market of Djemaa el-Fna.

At this stage in our global travels we had driven Rabia in every continent, finding that entry and exit from a new country followed certain prescribed patterns.

Whilst we were not exactly blasé about this, we were confident about the process, sure in our minds that we could always find a route through any particular bureaucratic maze that may confront us. China had been an induction of fire, taking two years to resolve. However, one aspect of roaming with Rabia was still a problem. Sometimes we needed to leave her for a while, when she would stay in the country whilst we departed temporarily from it. This was usually made difficult through the lack of clear rules that would apply. Chile had turned into such a problem and Morocco was about to throw the weight of her customs regulations at us.

We needed to leave Morocco briefly but we would be back in one week. We reached the airport and at the immigration desk the officer took our passports, consulted his computer screen and asked, "Where is your car?"

"It's not in my hand baggage" I felt like replying but a facetious remark would not be smart. It became apparent that a departing foreigner could not leave a car behind, which was temporarily imported to the country, without paying duty (which is the purpose of the Carnet). Would we get through this by keeping calm and smiling we wondered? In the end there was a provision to handle the problem and her Carnet, keys and all of her documents were placed in the immigration office safe whilst Rabia was impounded nearby in the airport car park. That seemed to deal with the underlying concern that Rabia would be sold on the black market without paying import duties (which were very high in Morocco).

The landscapes of southern Morocco had transfixed us with their variety. We had seen the barren splendour of the Draa Valley which hinted at the Sahara's greater vigour further south. The Anti Atlas had been majestic and rugged but mellowed in places by the greenness of spring agriculture. The pistes of the remote areas in the High Atlas had made exciting detours. The route had been a good choice, driving from south-west to north-east then doubling back along the southern slopes of the High Atlas to Marrakech. We would now reverse direction to complete the giant 'S' pattern of our travels through the country, following the Middle Atlas to Fez and then crossing the Rif Mountains. Perhaps some new insights into Morocco in the warmer weather of late March and early April would emerge.

After we returned to Morocco we rejoined our planned route from Marrakech, leaving the highway just after Tamelelt, driving into the northern slopes of the High Atlas. We found a good loop (route 6) which rose to Damnate before reaching the Cascades d'Ouzoud. The waterfalls were impressive. Heavy rain and mountain melt water had turned them into a thundering tumult in March and we probably saw them at their best.

At Khenifra on Highway 24, a side road led off into a beautiful area of ancient cedar forests, lakes and green rocky plains within the Middle Atlas (route 7). Lake Azigza resembled Canada's Lake Louise in colour and setting but on a smaller scale. We saw the source of the Rhia River, a curious place of tumbling pools in a rocky valley. The cedar forests offered restful and quiet camping in grassy clearings between giant trunks, probably 300 years old. It felt like camping between giant Roman columns in a colosseum. Looking up in early morning, the weak sun filtered through the cedar canopy in a crazed patchwork of daylight and shadow. We felt really small and insignificant with the tree tops arching 50 metres overhead. After leaving the area we held to high ground by crossing Highway 21 south of Azrou to join the 'Lakes Circuit' – a tourist route to Ifrane but attractive and full of charm in spring.

Fez beckoned! The tannery, the narrow streets and cluttered markets, all cast their spell on us as they had done for many people who had stopped here for a break whilst travelling through Morocco. The Medina's maze and tiny walkways were busy places which challenged our navigational skills. We became comprehensively lost looking for the stinking but immensely colourful tannery. In the end we accepted our failures and wrote the Crichton precepts of Medina route finding! 1) No matter how hard you navigate, all alleys lead back to where you started. 2) A wide central thoroughfare, followed in a straight line, will eventually degenerate to shoulder width. 3) When reaching a junction, nine times out of ten a large heavily laden mule will appear round the corner. 4) Retracing what you believe to be the route you have followed will never lead back to where you started and no alley stalls will look the same.

The ancient tannery of Fez had a magnetic appeal that transcended the earthly individuality of the place. The Inca Salt Pans in Peru had the same qualities, freezing in time an authentic activity which had remained essentially unchanged during hundreds of years. There was no artificiality to the equipment or methods which preserved something just to be a tourist spectacle. Men toiled in difficult conditions following traditional processes simply because the methods worked well, needed little input of mechanical power and gave meaning and status to the lives of those employed. Tourism was on the periphery of both places, not at the core of the business, and although contributing indirectly, the tannery and the salt mine had been able to continue on the economic merit of their ancient crafts and traditions. Of course, tanning is a vital primary industry in Fez, supplying material to the leather industry in Morocco.

We found our way to the tannery through a tortuous maze of narrow alleys. "Just follow the donkeys," someone had suggested so we trailed behind the poor animals, heavily laden with skins, heading for the tightly packed tanning and drying vats which were surrounded by high buildings in the old quarter. Our noses were an additional navigational aid – the smell of rotting flesh approaching the tannery was appalling. Cluttered leather shops surrounded the vats, each offering a balcony view high above the brightly coloured scene. We were early that morning and Mustafa enticed us into his leather emporium on the promise of a good view. "Go to the roof," he said, "there is no charge." We struggled up his steep and rickety stairs to the fourth storey. The tannery was tightly enclosed below by old buildings, the honeycomb of mud block and tile lined vats awash with rich colours. Skins of sheep, goats, cows and camel lay around in soggy heaps, their hair and flesh removed during the previous stage. Apparently there was some order to the soaking and tanning process but this was lost to us in the overall confusion. "The tanning solutions come from the bark of pomegranate or mimosa," Mustafa told us helpfully. Another set of vats dye the skins after they had dried on the surrounding roofs and balconies. The dying vats radiated the brightest hues but the air, trapped above, was infused with a rancid smell – this was not a place for sensitive tourists!

"We have some amazing natural dyes" he said, now spurred into full disclosure of the ancient art. It seemed that cow urine, pigeon droppings, animal fats and brains all played a part in the craft, along with sulphuric acid and chromium salts. A Health and Safety executive would be appalled! We thanked Mustafa and left the balcony, sure that we had enjoyed a very unique aspect of Fez which preserved an ancient tradition in Moroccan culture.

We had learnt by now that staying in Morocco's cities was not the challenge we had expected. Parking Rabia on a city street at night seemed safe because of the 'guardien' system in the central areas. We paid a few dollars each night to the person who was responsible for watching over Rabia and we never had a problem in Morocco's cities, unlike Australia and South America.

We left Fez heading east towards the final high barrier before the Mediterranean – the Rif Mountains. But before that, a small road left the highway at Rhiata, through the Jebel Tazzeka Nature Park (route 8). It was one of the nicest circuits we found and was not especially demanding. In the lush colours of spring it was a stunning place, full of interest with waterfalls, gorges and lakes. The huge cavern at Gouffre du Friouato was an amazing hole in the ground, best visited without other tourists.

The Rif Mountains were an altogether different landscape. We found a good route, best suited to 4x4 travel, which started from Taza (route 9). We crossed rolling eroded slopes, green with new crops and dotted with mature olive trees full of new growth. The route had a profoundly softer feel but became rugged again at higher levels crossing from Aknoul to Taounate. The descent through the Rif and on to Chefchaouen was as dramatic as anything we had seen in Morocco. But it was the first of April and the weather played April Fool with us. We endured winds, mist and snow during our descent to the Mediterranean. Driving through snow in Africa during April was not what we had expected!

Kif was being sold at the side of the road by aggressive touts and we kept moving through this area, made dangerous by drug manufacture. We found a good piste just north of Chefchaouen to take us down to Oued Laou on the coast, driving on to the beach to enjoy an excellent ECM of camel meat, cooked to perfection during the day.

The coast road along the Mediterranean offered some spectacular views and walks for a few days, but there were curiously large numbers of police and army lookout posts along the cliff tops. Was Morocco at war with France? "We are under pressure from the EU," said the officer. "We need to reduce the drug smuggling from Morocco and this is where it leaves from in small boats."

We had not realised how much the local economy in the Rif depended on hashish trading. None of this spoilt the soft Mediterranean quality of the shoreline. It was a beautiful place in early April and still rural and undeveloped, perhaps similar to the Riviera or the Costa del Sol before their rise to international popularity.

We headed for Tangier, diverting after Tetouan to reach the coast road at the very north of Morocco. Gibralter stood out over the Straits and seemed very close. We crossed to Spain the next day and we reflected on our Moroccan odyssey on the ferry. We had driven 7000km within her borders, enjoying the enormous variety of landscapes which we had hoped for, but one aspect concerned us. We were used to exceptionally open and spontaneous friendship in the Arab world and always responded to that warmly. In Morocco much of that traditional Arab friendliness had become false, nearly always leading to the ultimate 'sting' – the gift you must buy from him…, the cousin's shop you must visit…, the hotel he could take you to… The pressure was often relentless and we were sad that this would distort the view of many travellers concerning the broader Arab world.

We were glad in the end that we had not hurried through the country. The original plan, to travel on to Algeria and along the Mahgreb, would have been a rush and there had been more than enough to capture our imagination. Perhaps we would have felt an unseemly haste which would have made an inappropriate ending to our travels. February was really a little early to start our journey, a month later would have been ideal, but we had been lucky to see the huge variety of landscapes in North West Africa at their best in early spring after a wet winter.

"No man can live this life and emerge unchanged. He will carry, however faint,
the imprint of the desert, the brand which marks the nomad."
W Thesiger (Visions of a Nomad)

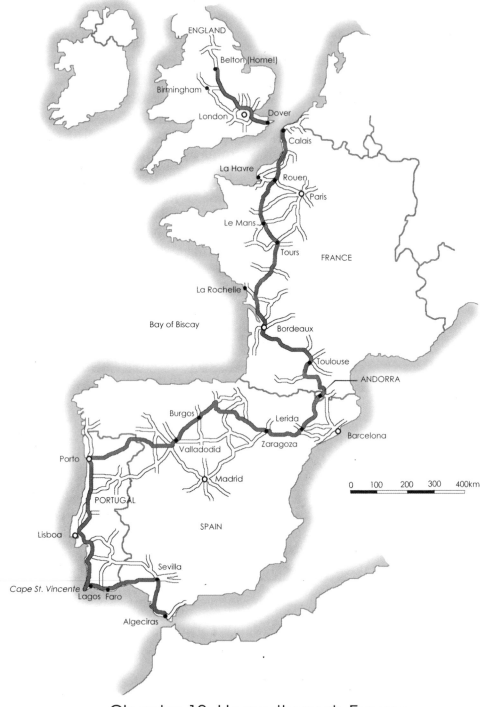

ENGLAND

Belton (Home!)

Birmingham

London Dover

Calais

La Havre

Rouen

Paris

Le Mans

Tours FRANCE

La Rochelle

Bay of Biscay

Bordeaux

Toulouse

ANDORRA

Burgos

Lerida

Barcelona

Valladodid Zaragoza

Porto

Madrid

PORTUGAL

SPAIN

Lisboa

Sevilla

Cape St. Vincente

Lagos Faro

Algeciras

0 100 200 300 400km

Chapter 10. Home through Europe

Chapter Ten:
Home through Europe

The crossing from Africa to Europe brought profound changes into our journey, disproportionate to the ferry time and short distance across the straits. There was the obvious cultural transition, the features that differentiate Islamic North Africa from the sophistication and prosperity of the Iberian Peninsula. But it went deeper than the physical changes around us and we both felt a metamorphosis in our attitude to the journey. We were a few thousand kilometres from home and unsure of our own expectations for our final days of travel. Like many people from northern Europe who travel south by car on vacation, we could scurry along the motorways to home in a few days, making distance, seeing nothing but concluding the expedition efficiently. The alternative approach, compelling to us at the time, was to slow the pace and try hard to probe interesting aspects to the places along the way. Could Spain, Portugal and France reveal something new to us? Could we find things to wonder at, some hidden and unexpected landscapes that we might wander into by chance? We hoped so and slowed our pace, avoiding motorways and major roads. Deep in our minds we realised the excitement of expedition travel was slipping away from us. The risks were gone and perhaps there was a subliminal attraction towards our home which influenced us.

In preference to driving through central Spain we chose a route through south-west Spain into Portugal, hoping a coastal route would provide us with variety and interest. We soon found that rough camping in Europe's remote places was not an option. When we did find an isolated corner in a pleasant landscape, sometimes with Rabia's help, we knew we were probably camping illegally and felt guilty and on guard, losing some of the spontaneous fun of being there. There were many well manicured formal camp sites, sometimes in outstanding scenery, but it didn't feel the same. Rabia's roof tent, an essential resource to our expedition in remote places, was now just a cheap option to motels or camp site cabins.

April was a wonderful time to be travelling in southern Spain and Portugal and we reached Seville the week before Easter. We were not usually enamoured by inner cities but we found Seville impressive. The old Muslim fortress, the Alcazar Palace and the massive cathedral dominate the centre of town. We noticed that, once again, a cathedral had been built directly on the sight of an earlier centre of worship, Islam in this case. Unknown to us, we had arrived during one of Seville's two great annual festivals – the Semana Santa. This was a week long event, filled with religious processions during the final days of Lent but it still managed to be a colourful and boisterous affair.

We dined in a restaurant during late afternoon, a place renowned for its curious selection of bulls' vital parts. We enjoyed the meal even though we were not quite sure what we had eaten! When we left the restaurant we were swept into a surging procession of people leaving the cathedral nearby. The streets were lined with crowds of enthusiastic onlookers who had been gathering for several hours and ahead of us, just 30 metres away, we saw the reason – a massive religious effigy of Christ stood in a bed of red geranium petals on top of a large ornate platform of carved wood. Below the platform, hidden behind a drape which fell from it, twenty or so men held the Icon aloft, staggering under its massive weight. The whole assembly swayed gently in pace with the rhythmic drum roll set by a few people who accompanied the procession. The statue and entourage had just left the cathedral and by a stroke of good fortune we had joined it and were quickly surrounded by people jostling to follow the procession through the streets of Seville. It would be early morning before the statue was returned to its resting place inside the huge cathedral near the tomb of Christopher Columbus.

The old streets were narrow and the procession's route, passing through tight bends and by ancient stone buildings, was complex and slow. The bearers could not see their surroundings but shuffled the platform through delicate manoeuvres which had probably been perfected over centuries. The procession was solemn. Around us, people carried candles and rosaries, some lost in quiet pensive prayer. The task of the platform bearers was gruelling and difficult and every 50 metres progress would halt whilst the team changed. Perhaps, for them, it was an act of penance. As darkness fell the plinth was decked with countless candles and Christ's statue was illuminated in elegant profile against the blackness of the city's streets.

We could tell that something unusual was preceding the platform and we moved out of the throng, struggling to be free, eager to move ahead. On each side of the road two lines of people, members of a local religious brotherhood, walked the route ahead of the statue. The two lines stretched for perhaps a kilometre and included hundreds of participants all swaying in unison. They wore white hoods which rose three feet to a pinnacle and also covered their heads and chests. Two small eye holes provided vision and below the hood each person wore a black cape over a white ankle-length gown. They all carried a large candle mounted on a stave, adding a further curious aspect. It was the strangest sight! Had this not been a religious event, we could have been watching a meeting of the Klu Klux Clan. It was an evocative but unsettling scene and our enquiries about the dress and the religious significance were inconclusive. No-one we spoke with along the route could describe the tradition that lay behind this curious procession of hooded people.

We crossed to Portugal the next day and drove along the Algarve coast to reach Europe's most westerly point at Cape St Vincente. We had become complacent about planning our fuel supplies and found ourselves on a newly built motorway with no petrol stations. Consequently, after circling the globe twice without once running out of petrol for Rabia, our lack of forethought nearly brought us to an unseemly and embarrassing halt on a European motorway! We promised to become more vigilant about refuelling.

We diverted on to the coastal route before Faro to continue along the headlands and coves of the Algarve. The scenery was impressive and before Lagos we searched for a place to stay for the night and chose a camping ground at Alvor, a quiet town set in a splendid sandy bay. We parked Rabia in a secluded corner and probed the features of a modern European camp site, hoping to find a little bistro where we might enjoy some local seafood and a bottle of Portuguese wine. Instead, the camp site's 'pub' offered fish and chips and John Smiths English beer. Crowds of fellow English campers and caravan owners had grouped in the bar to watch the day's British football matches on the huge TV screen, becoming noisy and boisterous in the tradition of football supporters. The bar staffs' amateurish attempt to short-change us failed and we left quickly to enjoy a quiet stroll on the local beach, looking for some finer aspects to southern Portugal that would confirm that we were, after all, in a foreign place.

We made our way to Cape St Vincente the next day, hoping that it would reveal some new feature of land extremities. The Levant wind was blowing strongly but it was a clear day and high cumulus cloud scurried over the promontory. As points of land go, Cape St Vincente was a powerful place. Looking out to sea you could sense the vastness of the Atlantic, the infinity of ocean beyond the horizon before reaching America. We had a similar feeling at the edge of the Sahara looking south from a high point on the green slopes of the Anti Atlas, knowing there was only a hostile expanse of stony plains and sand for 1500km before Timbuktu.

A tall lighthouse, a solid and robust building, stood on top of high cliffs and imbued the point with meaning. Its purpose was not to indicate some safe passage through local reefs or off-shore rocks but simply to announce, "You have arrived – you have reached Europe". We wondered how many people in small sailing boats had seen the regular flashing light at the end of their own water-borne travels around the world and been reassured of their safe return. We wondered if there would be a similar feature during our remaining travels to England that would give the same sense of arrival. We doubted it!

After travelling north for a few kilometres by main road, we diverted west to the tiny coastal village of Castelejo. We had noticed a small and intermittent track on a local map which followed the coast for 30km. We hoped to follow it all the way, knowing this might be our last section of rough-terrain driving with Rabia. The narrow track passed some remote beaches, isolated places untypical of other Algarve tourist destinations that we had passed. The route was rocky and steep over desolate cliff tops high above the Atlantic. We looked down on white surf pounding onto sandy beaches once again and heard the angry roar far below. It felt strangely secluded, out of context with the sophistication and urban development nearby.

Perhaps this was, after all, a remaining wilderness, small but still intact. The cliff top views were amongst the finest we had seen over the Atlantic.

Our luck ran out some way up this remote track and, even with Rabia's off-road abilities, we could not bridge a rocky valley between two headlands. Turning east we found a sheltered clearing amongst pines, where we stayed overnight. It was mid afternoon and we had time to dine well before sunset. Chicken a la Segras, had cooked nicely during five hours in Rabia's cooking frame. It was a peaceful evening and we were in reflective mood. This was our last bush camping location and, in many ways, matched our previous rough camping site amongst the cedars of Morocco.

There was no doubt that Portugal's coast had other beautiful places overlooking the Atlantic but we wanted to reach Porto, to visit a friend of long standing who lived there. We were not in a mood to loiter so by-passed Lisbon to our left as we crossed a notably elegant bridge to the east of the city. The drive north was fast and provided little by way of variety to the day. But the countryside was fresh with spring colours and apple blossom added a bright sparkle to the scenery.

Porto impressed us with its beautiful buildings and colourful history. Driving across town we rattled through narrow streets, still surfaced with worn cobble stones and met with Margaret and Jose. With their help and hospitality we saw some of the city's attractive features on the north and south banks of the Douro River which flowed through the town. There was much to enjoy in the city - the caves, maturing cellars for port wine and quaint buildings. The port's historic 'cask boats' lay at their moorings, but were no longer required for their original use - to bring the product down the river from the vineyards inland. They had been perfectly restored and played an important part in the town's tourist industry. The sun dropped through an angry sky and sunset over the town's estuary was a vivid spectacle, full of fiery colours. After dark we looked up to the old town from the quay and the ghostly shapes of whirling seagulls danced in the cathedral's bright illuminations. It was an unusual sight, seeing birds fly by choice in artificial light. The house of Henry the Navigator was up there in the old buildings, and we thought Porto would be a romantic place to start a voyage by sea.

Our route back to Spain from Porto took us into Portugal's high Sierra Mountains which, by early April, were washed with startling shades of yellow and purple from early flowering broom. The pine forests had also acquired a delicate blush of seasonal green and it seemed that we were following the European spring as we travelled north that year. We reached Bragancy just before the Spanish border and found a commercial camp site in a forest clearing behind town. Apart from our high elevation, we missed the warning signals of a cold night ahead – the sharp drop in temperature after dark, the clear starry sky overhead and the still air hanging in the dark forest around us. We woke to find a landscape coated in frosty white under a steel blue sky. Ice crystals sparkled like diamonds in the low light of early morning.

We were thoroughly off-guard and decamped quickly to find warmth in sunlight down the valley, but Rabia's aluminium tent spars were coated with ice and the canvas tent was rigid. Dismantling our bedroom was a frosty and challenging chore that morning.

We drove 600km through northern Spain during the day, passing towns and cities which seemed to be energised with new commercial endeavours. It was Easter Sunday and although the roads were quiet during the morning, they soon became busy with Easter traffic. With the prospect of another cold night we took refuge in a room at a roadside motel near Zaragoza before we reached the Pyrenees. It was in a strange setting - although in open countryside a national motorway passed nearby and 100 giant wind turbines mushroomed from the fields around us, their huge blades whirling silently in the prevailing wind. We looked through the restaurant window in the fading light of dusk and the structures appeared like an army of alien beings stepping over the landscape from the distant horizon. But nothing in these surroundings could detract from the surprisingly excellent meal in an otherwise bland motorway rest stop that night.

The next day, Easter Monday, brought heavy traffic descending from Andorra to Spain and we were hopeful that the tiny Principality would be deserted when we finally reached there. We were heading for the Pyrenees Mountains hoping for an interesting crossing into France.

Andorra has a timeless charm. Technically described as a parliamentary co-princedom, it is governed jointly by the Bishop of Spain and the French President as Heads of State. Notionally independent, it is still a member of the UN and Council of Europe but, strangely, is not a full member of the EU. We were attracted by the ambience of the place, as well as to the prospect of some enjoyable skiing on empty slopes between Easter and the close of the season.

By good luck snow was abundant, as plentiful as at any time that season and the slopes were perfect. All lifts were open and by a happy coincidence, Andorra's ski slopes had been transformed by a new agreement between the regions. In previous years, embedded hostility between the separate operators had prevented good connections linking the different skiing areas. That year, through good sense, things had changed and with the addition of new strategically positioned lifts, a hugely expanded area had formed over Andorra's mountains. We knew nothing of this when we arrived but guessed that the main skiing villages would now blossom quickly to become international ski centres, raising the country's reputation from one of budget skiing to become a premium destination. Free of queues and with perfect conditions the massive area came as a pleasant surprise.

By a twist of fate it snowed that night. Rabia was coated in a thick blanket of white. Looking down on her from our apartment window, she looked incongruous with her Saudi number plates standing out through deep powder snow. Was there anything more for her to endure we wondered?

We descended into France and broke free from main roads to amble briefly through a quiet backwater on the slopes of the French Pyrenees. Spring had not yet reached these higher levels and, although it was a pretty region, it looked austere under lingering snow. We travelled north to Toulouse, into a landscape vivid with spring colour again. Forsythia was bright with fresh yellow flowers and fruit trees blossomed in every shade of pink in fields washed with emerald green from new growth.

Roadside transport cafes and Auberges in France have a legendary reputation for good food and simple accommodation. We stopped at a quiet place just off the highway, the Relais D'Auvergne, noting the huge but empty parking area around the small building in late afternoon. We did not know it at the time but this was an Auberge with a singular clientele – truck drivers! The parking area, bleak and uninviting when we arrived, was soon swarming with giant commercial vehicles and by sunset we were surrounded by 40 pantechnicons neatly parked in disciplined order. Although many drivers would sleep in their own bedroom behind the vehicle cab, we were lucky to have arrived in time to rent a room. By 8.00pm the restaurant was filled with a noisy band of friendly truck drivers. But they were neatly dressed professionals, clearly proud of their job and discerning about where to eat – this was probably a highlight of their lonely day. The 5-course menu du jour, good value at €13, provided inspired cuisine in good company. We sat quietly at our table enjoying the delicious meal and watching the drivers' friendly camaraderie.Although the evening flowed in boisterous mood we noticed that the liberal supply of good wine with the meal went relatively untouched. Our impression of roadside truck stops and their clientele, already high, moved up a notch or two.

We skirted the Massif Central through a changed landscape coloured with the delicate red of young eucalypt trees in new growth. We reached Mansle, north of Bordeaux and were guests of Carol and Keith, two good friends who we had last seen in Saudi Arabia some years earlier. We shared our respective news and through their kindness we saw some authentic and pleasant aspects of rural France. We were enchanted by the old buildings of soft cream stone, the quaint shutters and cobbled streets. Sleepy rivers drifted lazily by arching willows and soft reed beds formed home to countless water birds. There was a calm feeling to the countryside and the unhurried pace appealed to us.

We had one final act of our journey planning to accomplish, a seemingly simple task to book our ferry crossing from Calais to Dover through the internet. Giving our English address during the process confused the automated booking system and despite our clear request for a one-way crossing from France to England our booking confirmation had, with misplaced logic, reversed our passage to be from England to France. Wouldn't it be nice, we thought, to be able to talk to real people when conducting our affairs?

We were sad to leave Carol and Keith. We had enjoyed the easy pace of our time there but we had a schedule to meet. There was no point in remaining in expedition mode. If we chose to, we could amble through northern France at any time in the future and we changed our approach to be one of focused travel, to make distance and to resign ourselves to reaching the Channel. There was nothing left now, by way of planning, except to navigate through Tours, Le Mans and Rouen avoiding motorway toll roads. Instead, we worked our way north through a network of major highways avoiding the tolls. (Had we taken the *peage* route that expense would have risen to equal the cost of fuel.)

As if to add a final challenge to our journey, fate conspired to make our last overnight camping stop in northern France a damp, depressing affair and deprived us of the ideal site we had hoped for. Dark thunder clouds rolled over our deserted municipal camping ground outside an undistinguished village. We dined in the fading light, very aware that it would rain that night. We could recognise the signs! Our expedition, which had been full of colourful people, drama and excitement, was drifting to a mediocre conclusion. Was there to be no final highlight to the story, no concluding lines full of meaning that would finish the adventure with elegance? It would not be here we thought, in that damp and miserable camp ground, under a grey and threatening sky.

Memorably, it rained all night and the next morning in a cold drizzle we rushed our departure to drive the final miles to the coast. Our ferry to England was the next day and as the weather broke into a late winter storm we stopped early at a Motel before Abbeville. Soon the rain thundered down in a relentless deluge and the wind howled malevolently across a bleak landscape outside our window. We resigned ourselves to dominoes and, whilst we shared a good bottle of wine, we quietly reflected on journey highlights, of the people we had met, places we had discovered and saw some humour in our travels drawing to a close in these adverse conditions.

In that reflective mood Rabia came into to our thoughts. In our minds she had become more than a complex assembly of metal, glass, plastic and rubber parts. In a mysterious way she seemed to have acquired her own character and personality. She could tell us when she was unhappy or ill at ease and we ignored those signs at our peril! Her reliability had confounded us. Even now, at the end of two global circuits when she had been pushed to her mechanical limits, her health was impeccable (engine cylinder compressions were better than those of a new vehicle). It was remarkable that she had failed on the road on only two occasions throughout our journeys and, in one of these mechanical failures, the part was due for replacement in any case (the fuel pump). Apart from some tired graphics on her bodywork she was almost as good as new. She had waded through rivers, crossed deserts, climbed mountains and had been axle deep in mud. She had, in a fashion, housed us and fed us and now looked majestic in her maturity. How could you stop feeling a personal attachment to such a fine lady?

There were few appealing aspects to be found in the Calais to Dover crossing the next day. Perhaps the White Cliffs of Dover, now bright and sharp under a clearing sky, had some meaning to our journey. During our first, northern hemisphere, circuit we had enjoyed a beer below them before driving through Europe to reach the Black Sea. In that respect our arrival in Dover closed a global circle of our own making and Rabia's passage over sea and land had verified again that the world was indeed round!

It was surprisingly difficult to crystallise our feelings driving north from the port at Dover. With two circuits of the globe completed and with no new places ahead to plan for, there was an emptiness which we did not expect and was difficult to define, perhaps a restless feeling of something not quite concluded. But there was also a sense of fulfilment and, as we drove up the M1 motorway to our home in Leicestershire, we both knew that we had reached a point of closure on something that had added meaning and substance to our lives. The adventure was over. The memories would endure and it was time to move on.

"To travel hopefully is better than to arrive, and the true success is to labour."
Robert Louis Stevenson (1850-1894)

Epilogue

We look back on the journey and wonder how we coped! Our resources, although meeting our requirements, were not large and during extended periods we went without much of the paraphernalia of a modern lifestyle. Space was at a premium and, apart from the great outdoors, all we had were two front seats in Rabia and a makeshift bedroom and kitchen. We likened this to sailing a small boat on a long voyage and concluded that the key feature of successful travel, as well as our lives in general, is learning to cope with what you have and to avoid, as far as possible, the relentless pressure in the twenty-first century to consume, to own and to do so conspicuously. The journey taught us that, in the end, life is about attitude of mind.

Our second circuit, these wanderings in the southern hemisphere, added a new insight into the views we had formed during our first circumnavigation through Asia, North America and the Middle East and gave fresh meaning to them. The first had been the amazing ability of human beings around the world to smile, endure and be happy in direct proportion to the hardships they faced in life. The second, linked to that, was the enduring skill with which challenged communities (crudely described as under-developed by the West) preserve and manage resources with breathtaking care and real talent. We have much to learn from them and imposing our western values and standards is an act of gross arrogance. The third point, confirmed often in South America, was the general rule that ethical and family values are at their strongest in rural, rather than urban, communities. We never felt threatened in remote areas, even in those places benchmarked as dangerous. But in cities we felt at risk because of embedded crime and failing moral standards; New York, Adelaide or Caracas, it didn't really matter which.

Our travels were usually fun and our relationship continued to flourish. Maybe this was because we were able to maintain that measure of flexibility that is so important to a successful expedition. Despite strong personal preferences at times, we always managed to blend in the others alternative viewpoint to find a good compromise.

One aspect of travel planning that became important was to limit ourselves to three months of continuous travel at a time. Beyond that, the extraordinary tended to become ordinary, reducing the relative enjoyment and pleasure from seeing things and places. There was a second factor that sometimes encouraged us to break our journey. The timing of travel in a region could be crucial to its success. Choosing the best season often optimised our enjoyment. Sometimes this meant a gap in travel when we left Rabia in storage. If we had not returned to the UK at these times we would probably have chosen to find work locally, perhaps adding another dimension to our travels.

At the end, there were two deeper, more profound insights. Why was it, that human evolution had not given us the sense to learn from past mistakes, to move on, adjusting for obvious failures and human frailties? Around the world, open hostility between different beliefs and religions still leads to wasteful conflict. We can explore space and conduct business around the world at the speed of light but seem unable to bring some ancient weaknesses in our makeup into check in a disciplined manner. Catholics still fight with Protestants, Sunnies with Shiites and despite a common belief in one God, Christians, Jews and Muslims continue in conflict. This hasn't changed in hundreds of years. God, we are sure, is not amused!

We saw a widening gap between the rich and poor in many areas. As sure as night follows day, conflict erupts when excessive consumption by a minority becomes conspicuous to those enduring absurdly low comparative standards.

Beyond these deeper insights during our travels, the simple truth is that life is short and risk to it occurs anywhere! Broad-brush pronouncements about what is safe and where is dangerous can be misleading. We found that the risks during our travels were random and did not follow any preordained rules or current guidelines. In a contradictory way we never understood, our experience often seemed to reverse the prevailing advice. On our first circuit, Northern Pakistan and Siberia had been welcoming and friendly places. On the second circuit, when crossing Colombia at the height of some hostage dramas, there had been kindness and hospitality everywhere. Maybe we were just lucky, but we wouldn't hesitate to face those risks again.

There were of course bad as well as good moments – the 'diamond' and 'stone' days in John Denver's song. In Santiago before the solo passage through South America there had been lingering doubts and black moments. That low mood had passed and a few lines in the journal at that time seemed to capture the essence of why people set out to discover more about our small and fragile world.

"Time shouldn't pass you like a stranger. It should accompany you on your journey through life and, if you listen, the advice will be profound. It will remind you constantly that the days and months it gives you on this planet will not be taken back. There will not be an upgrade to give extended years or a trade-in for a fresh start. And the gift is finite. You are expected to use it with a driven passion."

Appendix One:
Preparations

Before our first expedition through the northern hemisphere the vehicle was checked carefully and suspension bushes, brake parts, shock absorbers and all fluids were replaced. The vehicle was kept to standard specification (for a 1992 V8i high compression Discovery) except for the following changes which, in hindsight, turned out to be worthwhile adaptations. A second battery was fitted with a simple switching system between the two units to manage recharging and the rear springs were upgraded. Rabia's rear seats were removed and a cargo system was fitted, based on stacking crates, ten in all. To prevent movement, these were held in place by tie-down ratchet straps which were mounted to strong anchor points on the vehicle floor. A robust roof platform and purpose-made roof tent were built to our design and the high internal roof cavity at the back of the Discovery (normally dead space) was used to store our folding table and two chairs on a shelf that pivoted from the rear seat belt mountings.

In retrospect, one aspect of our preparations that was very successful was that the vehicles entire bodywork was treated with Ziebart protection. The vehicle remained free of rust and corrosion despite the dust, water and mud that invaded her inner body spaces. We also think it paid handsomely to use the best tyres and we chose Michelin Radial X, fitting only one set on each of our global circuits.

Planning for vehicle maintenance parts meant allocating two crates (of the ten available) to their storage. Of the parts for routine maintenance, the spare fuel and oil filters were important and both were changed every 10,000km. Fuel can be of appalling quality in some countries. Suspension bushes and drive belts were also important stock items. We had owned Rabia for many years and knew the best choice of spare parts to take with us through our knowledge of the vehicle. Our advice to others who may have acquired an unfamiliar model for an expedition would be to search out people, with knowledge of a vehicle of that model and year, to ask for their thoughts when planning an appropriate list of spare parts. However, it was reassuring to find that most of our parts, other than those for routine requirements, remained unused during two circuits of the world (The spare coil, alternator and water pump were examples).

Forget the electric fridge! Somewhere in your journey it will cause you problems. When you need it most – perhaps parked for a few days in a remote area – it will be a challenge to battery power. We used a good quality cool box adapted in two ways. We fitted a small drain at the lowest point and also made a perforated zinc platform which sat 1cm off the base on rubber spacers. This made for effective daily drainage of melting ice water and prevented blockage of the outlet. We did not hold to convention by leaving the melt water to slosh around in the cool box – everything got too wet. We found block and cube ice usually available somewhere and one charge of ice would last for up to five days. Block ice was by far the best. We only used the cool box for meat storage, perishables, a few beers and perhaps some white wine. (The inner bag from a wine box worked better than bottles!)

Some additional changes were made for the second circuit in the southern hemisphere, primarily to deal with wading rivers on off-road routes. Axle, gearbox and transfer box breathers were extended and door seals renovated. We were anxious to reduce water spray in the engine compartment, which might soak the electrics - the distributor was especially exposed. A cape was made to unroll from the bumper over the front grill but in addition a temporary internal canvas-and-plywood jacket was designed to fit round the fan and drive belt area which would contain spray if the water level reached the fan. This worked well in practice, preventing spray reaching the air intake, batteries and all the electrics. We did not fit an elevated air intake, arguing that its best function was preventing dust ingress to the engine when driving in a convoy of cars, a situation we would not be in. If the water level reached the normal intake level we thought we would already have bigger problems to worry about!

One other change was to simplify our cabin electrics. We had to be able to charge additional electronic equipment and designed a simple internal ducting system for auxiliary charging circuits to distribute power to the most convenient place to charge our laptop, standby electric light, camera and satellite phone whilst travelling. We were tired of the dreadful tangle of charging cables inside the car and the new system kept our internal space clear of vulnerable wires. These auxiliary circuits were connected directly with one of our two batteries through a separate fuse.

We also revised our security planning by constructing a hidden place for valuables. We changed the mounting of one of the readily accessible internal body panels at the rear of Rabia, giving us access to discreet storage space for money, passports and other valuable documents. The new panel fixing was designed to release quickly but its alternative function, as secret storage, was not obvious nor could it be released without following a certain sequence. It worked well. Another aspect to our security planning was never tested but had a useful potential. Had we faced a robbery by a group we could not deal with, we would have produced a small locked cash box, chained under the driver's seat. This was authentic but contained, by design, expired passports and credit cards, a large stack of Saudi Riyal notes of low denomination, a few dollar notes as well as some expensive looking (but cheap) jewellery. We hoped this might distract attention giving us time to escape. We called it our 'loss-leader' strategy and it seemed a good idea!

Rabia's range of driving distance on a full tank of fuel was between 340 and 600km depending on the terrain. We carried two 20L metal cans of spare fuel, adding around 200km to that distance. This was adequate and with some care and planning, we never ran out of fuel on either circuit. In hindsight, we were pleased that Rabia used petrol (rather than diesel) because petrol was the fuel-of-choice in many remote places. Besides, the cost saving was less of an issue since petrol elsewhere was relatively cheap, compared with Europe. Storage of the two spare fuel containers, along with our two containers of water, was inside the vehicle at floor level, keeping the centre of gravity as low as possible.

Many sections of our travels were on grit roads. Oncoming traffic, although mostly light on these tracks, was a real threat to our headlights and windscreen. Our windscreen was badly chipped in Russia on our first circuit and we built screens for the second circuit. Two light frames were made up, each covering one half of the windscreen, and these were covered in a fine black nylon mesh which was sufficiently opaque to see through clearly. These were held in place by strong suction pads and, when not in use, these fitted into their own storage location under the roof platform. They worked well when needed on gravel tracks and in strong sunshine also kept the glare and heat off the windscreen.

We avoided headlight damage by making simple Perspex covers held on with Velcro. These were left in place permanently and their value was confirmed by the cracks and chips they acquired in the southern hemisphere.

Appendix Two:
Navigation, Communications, Records and Documents

During our first journey in the Northern Hemisphere, the route was researched through maps purchased from Stanfords of London. These were aeronautical ONC maps, to a scale of 1:1,000,000, which provided a grid reference sufficiently accurate to select waypoints which were keyed by hand into our Garmin GPS. We found that these maps were not always accurate for the road network but coordinates for villages and towns were very reliable and that was our main requirement. During our crossing of China, however, we found that some towns with military significance were sometimes displaced by a massive 30km from their true position, supporting a rumour we had heard that western cartographers had sometimes plagiarised maps released by China years earlier, which contained errors by design.

In 2001 technology moved forward and we loaded the Garmin Mapsource programme onto our laptop. This digitised map of the world allowed us to plan routes, select waypoints and download these as a route plan directly to the GPS memory. There are, of course, more up-to-date navigational systems available now but these only apply to developed regions such as Europe and North America. We found that Mapsource was very good for all regions although the road network was not always current. Towns and villages were always correct, even in remote regions of South America and North Africa and that was sufficient. In a curious way some smaller and more remote tracks, only suitable for 4x4 traffic, were often shown correctly, perhaps because of their older and more historic use. As a good example, parts of the Inca Trail were mapped, despite the old route's dilapidation and redundancy. The down side was that we had to carry our laptop in the vehicle but since we were also using that to store digital pictures it was an excellent trade-off. Our laptop charged at 15volts DC which meant installing a voltage converter from 12volts DC to 110volts AC, then using the normal charging unit. All that equipment was stored neatly under the passenger seat.

Photography was important, augmenting our diary notes with a more graphic record. We used a good Canon camera and lenses with slide film provided by Fuji and we were pleased with the results. However, during the second circuit we also used a Nikon Coolpix 3.0m pixel digital camera and we were astonished at the results. Each image was stored at 1Mb (more would have caused laptop capacity problems) and we had CDs written periodically to clear the laptop. Many of the images in this book were from that camera in preference to the corresponding slide at the same location. Keeping slide film cool could be a problem, especially for exposed material. In warmer regions we usually allocated precious cool box space to store film but that was a nuisance factor we would have preferred to avoid.

Communications in an emergency would have been through our satellite phone and although it was never used in that function, it was reassuring to have it aboard. We felt that our best option for day-to-day requirements was to use internet facilities. Even in very remote places these were available. Our most unusual internet cafes were (a) a shack in rural China, (b) an old red bus in Australia and (c) an underground room in an opal mine! All of our correspondence and backup files were contained on a tiny storage stick which could be inserted into the USB port of any computer we were using and we kept our records up-to-date by downloading incoming mail on to it. The stick also allowed us to prepare emails in advance on our laptop, before accessing the internet.

We found that expedition documents and paperwork needed some thought. On our first circuit Rabia's ownership document had been rejected at the border crossing between Germany and Austria. The belligerent Austrian officer said he could not read it because it was in Arabic and for all he knew it could have been for my speed boat or lawn mower, even though Rabias chassis number was printed in English on the document. Consequently, we had a stand-off for several hours before common sense prevailed. We found that all our paperwork could face the same challenge. Simply having a valid Carnet de Passage, passport and vehicle ownership document was not always enough and there were two good practical reasons for having translations formally authenticated and available. First, it always helped speed things up if we offered a document copy that could be understood locally and this applied especially to the car ownership document. The second was that we became very wary of passing over original documents at roadside police or army checks. It was safer to provide an authenticated copy, especially if these were also translated into the local language. As far as we could, we never even brought our documents to open view and as a last resort pleaded total ignorance of the language to deflect many random requests. But that did not work in Australia!

'Guinea-pig a la Huaraz'

154

Appendix Three:
Cooking in the Engine Compartment!

Engine compartment meals (ECMs) were developed in South America out of necessity – the cooking gas had run out! The initial experiments were successful, using the available heat just above the exhaust manifold whilst driving during the day and by Venezuela ECMs had become the preference, since they provided a ready cooked and tasty meal at the end of driving, when you most want to relax.

An open mesh cooking frame was made and the Mark III version, described below, was simple to build and did a great job. The metal grill from the top of a disposable barbecue was bent to make a 'U' shaped trough, sufficiently long and deep to be wired in place just above the manifold. Plywood baffles were fitted to the front and down the side away from the engine, to which reflective silver foil was glued on the inside. This channelled the heat rising from the manifold to the cooking area and also stopped cooling draughts reaching it. Placing food in foil or normal plastic bags failed. The foil reflected the heat and plastic melted, but oven bags worked very well. Meat, cut into smaller pieces, was placed in the bag with a little olive oil, herbs of choice and seasoning. This was nested at the bottom of the cooking trough and then covered with aluminium foil. Cooking times were long, generally over four or five hours, but this slow cooking process in the meat's own juice reduced the toughest cut to a tender delicious meal. Stopping the car for a short period was not a problem as there was residual heat in the manifold casting and this tended to help the process. But beyond 20 minutes, cooking would stop.

With practice, ECMs included vegetables, rice or pasta. Vegetables were added to the oven bag a little later than the meat and a separate technique was developed for rice. A measure of washed rice plus two measures of boiling water were added to a preheated glass jar and the lid fitted tightly (a tiny hole in the lid prevented problems). The jar was placed in the frame on its side for two hours and by the end, the rice was fluffy and light. The best South American ECM was Guinea Pig Al a Huaraz, but everything cooked well - goat, camel, donkey and alpaca were all cooked to tenderness, as well as the normal slabs of tough beef and lamb bought in rural markets. We likened the process to Moroccan tajine cooking.

When we returned to the UK we were curious to check the temperatures, using a meat thermometer. For those interested in the technicalities, a bag of cooking food reached between 70 and 80°C in one hour, then stayed constant at around 80°C. On the meat thermometer this was about one-quarter up the scale. In our Discovery there was sufficient space and heat to cook for two people easily during the day but larger meals for three or four people would be a problem. Good luck!

Appendix Four:
Ocean Shipping

Rabia made six ocean crossings during our two circuits. Of these, five were made when she was secured in a 20 foot container. The remaining crossing, through the Persian Gulf and over the top end of the Indian Ocean, was a colourful affair when she was deck cargo on a Dhow. Planning these crossings was an aspect of our journey that improved with each crossing and became relatively straight forward although the lessons learned were often hard. The following points summarise the key aspects.

We always researched the carriers servicing a particular route in advance. Looking for a shipper and negotiating rates after arriving at the port of departure can be time consuming and may leave you in a position of weakness if there is only one carrier available. The internet provides good contacts now, but when we first started travelling, communications were mostly by fax. The first step, to find the contact details of shipping companies in the country of departure, relied on advice from (a) the Commercial Section of the local British Embassy, (b) the country's Embassy in London, (c) contacts already formed in the shipping industry or (d) the management of the port of departure or arrival. Somewhere in these contacts there would be someone through whom we could network to other local contacts that would finally lead to the best carrier and commercial rate. The process was just like fishing.

Fitting Rabia into a 20ft container was a tight process! She passed the door frame with only a few inches to spare but knowing she had entered one container meant she would always fit – they are a standard size. Once safely inside we provided our own heavy-duty ratchet tie-downs to anchor her to the container, attaching these to the back and front axles. We found that the best process was to attach a ratchet strap to one end of an axle, just behind the wheel, take the strap to the other side of the container and hook it to a floor mounting point. Repeating that process at the other end of the axle resulted in the two tie-down straps being crossed under the front of the car. Tying the rear axle to the container the same way completely secured the vehicle. If someone else performs this work, check that they do not attach the tie-downs to any part of the steering system – that happed to us between the Middle East and Australia. The shipper will usually nail down chocks to the container floor around the vehicle wheels. We always tried to arrange that we would drive her into the container ourselves, then disconnect the batteries, and keep the keys after locking her. Customs clearance would be complete by that stage and the container could be locked and sealed whilst we were there – a reassuring security step.

The most important practical learning experience over our travels was to always plan to be at the port of arrival after an ocean crossing. There would be a three day period after docking without demurrage charges (storage) and that would be the time to clear customs and immigration. If we were not present there was scope for things to go badly wrong and this could be costly.

Shipping costs vary but, on average, we found that freight was US$1000 to cross any ocean, but only with forward planning. Often a lower rate was negotiable if we were able to utilise empty containers returning to their country of origin. The most important aspect of costing a particular route was not the shipping cost but the extra expense at each end. Typically, this might include loading the container or moving it from outside the port to the loading wharf. Wharf handling charges might sometimes be proposed, as well as document preparation costs. Often, the biggest dilemma was to decide whether to pay for a customs agent to ease the way through port bureaucracy. We tried to avoid that by using our own time to get through the formalities – people were usually helpful especially shipping staff who would know the procedure intimately. We always tried to clear up the extras costs for the port of arrival before committing to a particular route. If costs were vague or too high there might be an option to another port close by.

Shipping documentation was usually straight-forward. Our vehicle ownership document was always important and it sometimes helped to have a copy translated into the language relevant to the region. Invariably, we would fly from a country after Rabia had cleared formalities but before she was loaded onto the vessel. The original Bill of Lading, which we needed at the port of arrival, was therefore not available to us when we left and rather than have that couriered to us we usually arranged for it to be sent on to a designated contact in the office of the shipping line at the port of arrival, using their own internal mail.

Never assume that customs inspection will go smoothly – always expect the worst! In Venezuela, the constant concern of customs staff was dealing with innovative drug smugglers from South America. Typically, they would remove tyres from wheels and could cut open any sealed containers, such as gas cylinders. Before leaving, we avoided that problem but every internal cavity of Rabia was inspected by delicate optical probes. On leaving Russia, we were held up because staff had found, and confiscated, strong analgesics which formed part of our first aid supplies. Our advice is not to carry drugs without a letter confirming that they were prescribed.

Modern electronics are becoming familiar to customs staff but at the start of our travels we found sensitivity in some countries to satellite phones, GPS and occasionally to video cameras. These are still best declared and where necessary a temporary import receipt obtained from customs staff. In fact, have an inventory of everything aboard, showing its storage location.

Appendix Five:
The Journey Statistics

		AUS NORTH	AUS SOUTH	SOUTH AMERICA	N W AFRICA	EUROPE	TRIP TOTAL
*	Net Distance Driven (Km)	19036	10824	15285	7137	5603	**57885**
	Net Fuel Consumed (Litres)	3284	1694	2653	1072	892	**9595**
	Cost of Fuel Consumed ($)	1835	955	1397	1072	998	**6257**
	Weight of Fuel Consumed (kg)	2552	1316	2061	833	693	**7533**
**	Net Driving Time (Hrs)	321	166	307	160	90	**1044**
	Km per Litre achieved	5.74	6.32	5.77	6.29	6.28	**6.03**
***	Ave. Cost of Fuel ($ per Litre)	0.56	0.56	0.5	1.07	1.12	**0.65**
	Ave. speed achieved (Km/hr)	59.3	65.2	48.2	44.6	62.2	**55.4**

* Excludes 5414 km driven in New Zealand but not with the expedition vehicle

** Net driving time excludes all petrol, food, and photo stops. Border crossing time and sightseeing time is excluded. Driving time includes all periods with a driver at the wheel in control of the vehicle.

*** Local costs in South America were as follows; shown in equivalent US$

	per litre	
Chile:	$0.775	(3804 km)
Peru:	$0.720	(4132 km)
Ecuador	$0.458	(2240 km)
Colombia	$0.471	(1583 km)
Venezuela	$0.043	(3526 km)

The Authors

Peter and Eileen Crichton lived in Saudi Arabia between 1991 and 2003. During that time Peter was employed by the Olayan Group. Their long distance travelling in Rabia began in 1997, after some adventurous journeys which were mostly centred on desert travel. They now live in England.

Peter was born and educated in Scotland where he studied Mechanical Engineering and Eileen was born in Yorkshire. During their first years together they travelled extensively using mostly local transport in the countries they were in and selecting routes broadly to be of a circular plan. As time passed the circles got bigger!

Sailing had been a big interest in their early years of travel and journeys by yacht had featured for a while but evolved in favour of land, trading time at sea for what seemed to them the better payback from travel on land. But many aspects of their approach to planning and executing their circumnavigations had strong ties to earlier experiences in sailing.

Their travel philosophy is to journey quietly, leaving only footprints and taking only memories, without impacting the natural flow and balance of life in remote places they were privileged to visit.